# AT WAR ON THE GOTHIC LINE

OSPREY
PUBLISHING

# At War on the Gothic Line

# Gothic Line

## Fighting in Italy, 1944–1945

# Christian Jennings

*History with its flickering lamp stumbles along the trail of the past, trying to reconstruct its scenes, to revive its echoes, and kindle with pale gleams the passion of former days.*

Winston Churchill

*Con disavvantaggio grande si fa la guerra con chi non ha che perdere.*
*(We fight to great disadvantage when we fight with those who have nothing to lose.)*

Francesco Guicciardini, *Storia d'Italia*, 1561

First published in Great Britain in 2016 by Osprey Publishing,
PO Box 883, Oxford, OX1 9PL, UK
1385 Broadway, 5th Floor, New York, NY 10018, USA
E-mail: info@ospreypublishing.com
OSPREY PUBLISHING, PART OF BLOOMSBURY PUBLISHING PLC

Published in the United States in 2016 by Thomas Dunne Books, an imprint of St. Martin's Press.

A CIP catalogue record for this book is available from the British Library.

ISBN: 978 1 47282 164 5
PDF ISBN: 978 1 47282 167 6
ePub ISBN: 978 1 47282 165 2

Index by Fionbar Lyons
Cartography by Bounford.com
Typeset in Adobe Garamond
Originated by PDQ Media, Bungay, UK
Printed and bound in Great Britain by CPI (Group) UK Ltd, Croydon CR0 4YY

16 17 18 19 20   10 9 8 7 6 5 4 3 2 1

Front cover: The silhouette of Corporal Cecil E. Barnes of the US Army, on guard near San
Marcello, Italy. Photograph, 1944. (The Granger Collection / TopFoto)

Osprey Publishing supports the Woodland Trust, the UK's leading woodland conservation
charity. Between 2014 and 2018 our donations will be spent on their Centenary Woods project
in the UK.

www.ospreypublishing.com

**Imperial War Museum Collections**
Many of the photos in this book come from the Imperial War Museum's huge collections which
cover all aspects of conflict involving Britain and the Commonwealth since the start of the twentieth
century. These rich resources are available online to search, browse and buy at www.iwm.org.uk/
collections. In addition to Collections Online, you can visit the Visitor Rooms where you can
explore over 8 million photographs, thousands of hours of moving images, the largest sound archive
of its kind in the world, thousands of diaries and letters written by people in wartime, and a huge
reference library. Imperial War Museum www.iwm.org.uk.

# CONTENTS

# MAPS

# Author's Note

Many thanks go to my literary agent in London, Andrew Lownie, and to my editor Kate Moore at Osprey Publishing in Oxford. And to the staff at various Archives and Museums of the Liberation and Resistance across northern and central Italy, especially in Imperia, Trieste, Turin and Rimini, and at the Museum to the Liberation and Resistance at Via Tasso in Rome. I am very grateful also to Ivan Houston and the veterans of the 92nd US Infantry Division, to Ken Inouye and the Daniel K. Inouye Institute, Commodore Sanjay Chaubey, formerly Defence Attaché at the Indian Embassy in Rome, and to the Veterans of Canada Association in Vancouver, British Columbia. Many thanks to Simon and Toby Churchill, sons of Major Oliver Churchill DSO, MC, formerly of the Special Operations Executive. And to Andrea Cominini, who showed me around the partisan battle areas outside Milan, and to the last surviving Italian resistance fighters of that era. Lastly, I'm grateful as ever to the members of my family, particularly my brothers Anthony, James and Martin, and my sister Perpetua.

# Preface

## Turin, Italy, June 2015

I was six, I remember, when my father first gave me advice on the best way to attach two loaded thirty-round magazines on a .45 Thompson submachine gun. We were sitting in a railway carriage together in West Sussex, in the south of England, on the way to join my mother and my siblings for a day's outing by the sea. I remember three things very distinctly about that moment: First, my father was smoking, through his war-wounded fingers, a Player's No. 6 filterless. Second, the blue cigarette smoke in the railway carriage batted and swirled in the warm air, buffering against the dust motes raised from the hot Southern Region Railways upholstery on which we were sitting. Third, it was 1968, and I had recently been reading an article in a Sunday newsmagazine about the war in Vietnam, containing striking images of US Marines fighting in the citadel of Hue, taken by the photographer Don McCullin. What, I asked my eternally patient father, would he have taken to Hue if he had had to go that day? A tommy gun or a Sten? And why was the former so much better?

Drawing on his cigarette, my father talked me through the benefits of the Thompson. Attaching two magazines together was easy, he said, and gave you double the amount of available ammunition. You took a strong rubber band, he said, and attached the clips together with one of them upside down. It was a technique, he said, that he and his men had been taught by American paratroopers from the 101st Airborne Division, with whom his wartime British cavalry unit, the 15th/19th King's Royal Hussars, had operated in Holland in autumn 1944.[1]

My father liked the .45 Thompson that he had kept in the turret of his Cromwell tank, a heavy but reliable weapon, without the shoddy faults of the British Sten gun, which he said jammed repeatedly and was cheaply made. He also liked the American paras from the 101st, men whom he remembered as very young, very brave, and irreverent wisecrackers, smoking Lucky Strikes, carrying 'a lot of weapons' as they rode into battle on the back of his fellow Hussars' tanks. It was a reciprocal relationship, and one that years later would see light of day in film, in an episode of the television series *Band of Brothers*, a dramatization of Stephen Ambrose's account of the men of Easy Company, from the 2nd Battalion, 506th Parachute Infantry Regiment of the 101st Airborne, at war in Europe. The 15th/19th and the 101st had briefly fought together in the autumn of 1944 during and after Operation *Market-Garden* outside Eindhoven in Holland, where my father had learned his skills with rubber bands and submachine-gun magazines.

Like so many of his generation, my father didn't talk very much about the operational specifics of the war. His tank unit had arrived in Normandy in August 1944, as armoured reinforcements for British cavalry units decimated in the fighting around the town of Caen. His regiment's enemy was a mixture of panzergrenadiers and SS tank units in Tigers and Panthers, an enemy that he found brave, arrogant, ruthless, and tactically brilliant.

As children, we had heard about the physical exhaustion of the tank advance from Normandy to the Seine, and across Belgium into Holland. He told of being so exhausted after a day in combat in France that he fell asleep in the pouring rain, lying facedown in a waterlogged ploughed field, bivouacked next to his tank. He told the ubiquitous and probably apocryphal story of the young British cavalry subaltern, an Oxford graduate, who had disembarked from his tank in a Normandy orchard, exhausted after an afternoon of combat against the SS. The young officer, face stained with smoke and oil, had loosened on his battledress blouse the khaki ties that officers wore in those days, often even in battle. A wry comment had come from across the orchard from an aristocratic squadron commander, admonishing the subaltern for this atrocious display of sartorial laxity. 'Christ Church? Never a very dressy college, clearly.'

My father had told of using the horns of a Friesian cow, killed by shellfire in a Dutch orchard, as props on which to rest his binoculars during a reconnaissance mission of a German position, and of watching Typhoon fighter-bombers strafing German tanks. His tank had been the first in the regiment to knock out a German King Tiger, my father directing fire by lying on the outside of the tank, on the engine cowling. His binoculars observed the fall of the twelve shells fired at it, of which three hit the armoured giant, setting it on fire. The moments of tragedy were many. In late August, his unit engaged some three hundred Germans, dug in behind stooks of corn. Half of them turned out to be Poles, conscripted on the German side. The enemy surrendered and white flags went up, but in the dying, confused moments of the firefight, moving forward to help a wounded colleague, a close friend of my father's was mortally wounded and died that evening.

But our father never really talked about his time in combat. We all knew he'd been in the wars, as they say, from his badly burned face and head, to his disfigured hands clasped in an eternal clench where the tendons had retracted when he was burned. It made it easier, he said later, rather drily, to roll up his own cigarettes. We'd seen his Military Cross, but we never knew what exactly had happened that day in Holland in October 1944. It was something he kept to himself and a few former colleagues. A fellow Hussars officer who had fought with him in Holland said fifty years afterward that what my father had done had completely changed the course of that day's battle.

We grew up in the 1960s. Half the adults around us seemed to have fought in the Second World War. A bearded ex-Royal Navy lieutenant commander taught us mathematics at prep school; he could always be relied upon to be diverted from quadratic equations and Pythagoras by myself or a classmate asking him to recount, just once more, the events of the night his Motor Torpedo Boat had taken on a German E-boat in the English Channel. The story always ended the same way, with the description of a German Kriegsmarine bosun being riddled with British

20mm cannon fire at close range, the drum of heavy automatic fire hammered out for us on the school desk by the lieutenant commander with the blackboard eraser. Meanwhile, unbeknownst to him, one of our classmates was covertly looking up the answers to that day's mathematics test questions in a textbook hidden under a sweater on his lap.

Then there were my mother's male friends who had, in the vernacular, 'a good war'. First among these was Lewis 'Bobby' Hodges, an RAF bomber pilot who went on to fly Special Operations Executive agents in and out of occupied France in a Lysander. Hodges ended the war in one piece, as a squadron leader with a Distinguished Service Order and bar to his name, a brace of Distinguished Flying Crosses, and the French Croix de Guerre and Legion d'Honneur. The latter was awarded for his bravery and flying skill in whisking two future presidents of France, Vincent Auriol and François Mitterand, out of the country to attend a meeting with De Gaulle in London. As children, we were encouraged by our mother to eat as many carrots as possible – hadn't that made the eyesight of Group Captain John 'Cat's Eyes' Cunningham so acute? Enabling the British RAF night-fighter ace to shoot down twenty German aircraft? It was, of course, radar, but we didn't know then, so ate carrots at any given opportunity.

Then there was my paternal grandfather, who'd gone over the top on the Somme in 1916 with the Leicestershire Regiment, survived, become a staff officer, and then spent part of 1918 as a prisoner of the Germans. He wrote in his war diary that during his time as a POW he met the Kaiser. His wife's two brothers – my great-uncles – had been at Gallipoli and on the Western Front in the Royal Flying Corps respectively. The latter had been a pilot, shot down in 1918. The former a sixteen-year-old in charge of a Royal Navy landing craft, who later went on to become part of the team that developed ASDIC, the British sonar radar system used to track submarines. My mother's brother, my uncle John, had served with the Norfolk Regiment in India in 1945 and then during the partition of the country. My father's sister Elizabeth, ever mindful of the dictats of wartime secrecy, had waited until she was ninety to tell me she'd worked at the code-breaking establishment at Bletchley Park in southern England. Her husband, Peter, had served in France. And on the American side of the family – my aunt Anne had married an American – my uncle John had served as an engineer officer in Normandy with the US Army. Both world wars were therefore present in our childhood and family history.

But it was to be only a year or two before his death in 2002, age eighty-two, that my father stood in the kitchen of our house in rural Herefordshire, in the west of England, and told me what had happened that day in Holland in 1944. I think he knew that his days were coming to an end, and he'd realized by then that as a foreign correspondent who'd reported from Rwanda and Somalia and Kosovo, I'd probably seen my own share of battle and bullet, and might know what he was talking about. So that day, he leaned against my mother's ancient stove, fiddled with his regimental tie, and outlined how best to address the difficult and thorny problem of attacking German soldiers dug in to good defensive positions.

'If you can't outflank them, go straight at them,' he said. 'Move very fast, and not hang around. No shilly-shallying' (one of his favourite condemnatory phrases, meaning 'to dawdle').

'It'll cost you casualties, but it'll take half an hour, not three days, and it will save countless lives later.'

It was pretty much the first time he had spoken of that day when, as an acting captain in Holland on October 17, 1944, he had put this operational stratagem to the test. We talked for much of the afternoon, as outside the kitchen window one of my mother's cats positioned itself atop a fence post on pigeon watch. My father talked of unsung and undersung heroes, of medals given and not given, of friends who had died in Burma and Italy, of men whose bravery had changed the course of a dozen small battles in the war. He talked of a Cambridge University friend who'd disappeared at the hands of the Japanese, and he talked a lot about Italy, a lamentably forgotten war, he said, where a friend serving in the Welsh Guards had won the second two of his three Military Crosses. My father was to die himself the following year, from a heart that had never really recovered from his wartime wounds. At his funeral, six of his sons carried his coffin, as a party of veterans from the Royal British Legion marched in front of it. Two of his favourite hymns were played, 'Abide with Me' and 'The Battle Hymn of the Republic'. I remembered, standing that afternoon in the chilly British village church, that the latter was something he had once hummed, a mischievous smile on his burned face, when stoking a garden bonfire. The smell of smoke, he said, reminded him of Normandy and Holland, of going into battle with the 101st Airborne. It was to be six years later that one of my brothers recovered, from London's National Archives, the original citation of his Military Cross.

The signature scrawled across the bottom of it is easy to read, nearly seventy years after it was written in an operational headquarters somewhere in Holland. 'B. L. Montgomery', it says, with a stamp below it reading: 'Field Marshal, Commander in Chief, 21st Army Group.' The prose is the dry, clipped, and understated wording of the Second World War gallantry citation. My father had, on October 17, 1944, led four Cromwell tanks of the 15th/19th King's Royal Hussars in an attack on a heavily defended Dutch village of IJsselstein. It lay on the axis of the Allied advance towards the town of Overloon, in eastern Holland. My father's attack was just one very small part of Operation *Aintree*, the British assault to take the Venlo salient in eastern Holland. The four tanks of B Squadron were supporting two companies of 1st Battalion, the Herefordshire Regiment, which had been tasked with advancing up the road leading to the village: the boggy ground on either side of this access route was not just flooded but also mined. Steep banks made any tanks driving down the road highly visible targets. Intelligence said that German 88mm guns and mortars were covering the road. They didn't know the strength of the Germans defending it. Within minutes of the advance beginning up the road, the Herefords started taking heavy incoming mortar and artillery fire, and took cover behind a road bridge. The citation describes it crisply and with admirable understatement: 'There were a number of officer casualties and very little progress was being made. Enemy fire was extremely heavy and others were hanging back. Captain Jennings' troop was therefore ordered to advance up the road unsupported by infantry, owing to the conditions mentioned above, a most unpleasant and hazardous operation.'

'Hanging back.' Clearly shilly-shallying was going on. Within minutes of his Cromwell tanks pushing ahead of the pinned-down infantry, my father's tank was hit and immobilized. He radioed back to his squadron commander that he had driven over a mine. By this time the four tanks, exposed on the road that ran like a spine through the soggy fields, were coming under heavy and accurate machine-gun and anti-tank fire. IJsselstein and its outskirts were occupied by a German battle group of SS soldiers and regular army panzergrenadiers, supported by the 88mm anti-tank weapons, capable of busting through the armour of any known Allied tank at distances up to 1,000 yards. Along the side of the roads, in the edge of the surrounding pine forests, were dug in 75mm PaK anti-tank guns and MG-42 machine-gun nests. A German officer present that day in the village estimated there were around 400 panzergrenadiers, many of them with substantial experience fighting in Russia, dug in around and in IJsselstein. They also had tanks. Against them on the approach road? My father, with four Cromwells, one of them immobilized, and 15 men. An unpleasant and hazardous operation indeed.

Climbing out of the second tank in the line (the citation describes him as 'completely unperturbed'), my father, in a sodden overcoat and battledress, poured himself into the turret of the first tank and roared off up the road. The 7.92mm Besa machine gun in the hull was firing left and right into the fields. Within minutes, the tank was hit by an enormous jarring smash as an anti-tank round went through the engine compartment, the Cromwell crunching to a halt. My father radioed back that he was engaging the anti-tank guns dug into the tree line and was firing at the infantry supporting them. A sitting duck, he continued to fire on the Germans with the tank's 75mm gun and its machine gun. Then the tank was hit again. Twice. One of their own phosphorus shells inside their hull ignited, the German anti-tank round blasted 'metal splash' off the inside of the turret, and my father was hurled out of the turret, into the air, and onto the metalled road by what he later described as a 'Pentecostal wind'.

His gunner and signaller, both wounded, took cover on different sides of the road's embankment. The driver was stuck inside the blazing hull. Rifle, bazooka, and machine-gun fire from the German infantry whizzed and sang over their heads, into the soggy ground, or ricocheted off the tarmac. My father's greatcoat was on fire; he'd been hit in the foot and was very seriously burned, with his ears, mouth, and nostrils half scorched away. His goggles had, luckily, protected his eyes. His gunner ran across the road and stamped out the flames on his coat. My father looked down at his hands and described the skin on them 'peeling off like a pair of white gloves'. Nevertheless, he climbed back onto the blazing hull of the tank to try to get his driver out to safety. But he was dead.

Pulling himself down, he ran around to the back of the tank, pulled off the first-aid box, and dashed over to one side of the road, as rounds bounced off the tarmac around him. He did his best to help his wounded gunner lying in the ditch, then crossed the road again, under heavy fire, and gave first aid to his signaller. He then ran and stumbled back down the road to the next tank in the troop, and reported the position of the lead German anti-tank gun to its commander: the gun was immediately knocked out. With his arm then slung around the shoulder of his wounded gunner, who had joined him, he staggered back down the road to report to his squadron commander. His next memory was of waking the following morning in a hospital in Eindhoven. He'd had a tracheotomy during the night, as his scorched windpipe had closed up, and had received the last rites.

When he was eventually to stand in front of King George VI at Buckingham Palace several months later and receive the Military Cross – the gallantry citation signed by Field Marshal Montgomery recommended an immediate MC – my father was lost for words. The king, with his famous stutter, dramatized in the film *The King's Speech,* stood in front of my father, and asked 'Were you b-b-b-brewed up?'

All my father could say was, 'Yes, Your Majesty.'

•○•

Ten years after his death, and after fifteen years of reporting wars and the eternal residues of conflict across the Balkans and central Africa, I moved to Italy, to the heartland of the 'forgotten war' that my father had talked about in the Herefordshire kitchen the year before his death. And within days of arriving in Turin, a classical city of history and melancholy tucked up in the northwest near the French Alps, I discovered something very fast. Seventy years on, the Second World War in Italy was not remotely forgotten. Very far from it. On an exploratory walk one winter's day into the centre of the city, I emerged from a side street into the Baroque glory of Piazza Castello. To my left was the Palazzo Reale, former home of the dukes of Savoy. Just behind me was the entry to one of Turin's many Catholic churches. On the wall outside the church entrance was a huge stone plaque, curlicued and designed like an ancient scroll. In front of it was a small Italian man, smartly dressed, overcoated against the pre-Christmas chill. His homburg hat was clasped in front of him as he stood before the scroll. On it were listed the names of the Italian divisions whose men had fought, and mostly died, on the Russian Front, largely at Stalingrad. There were the names of some of the Alpini mountain divisions – Julia, Tridentina, and Cuneense – and the motorized division, Duca d'Aosta, all from around Turin. I said nothing. Behind me, on his plinth with rifle and bayonet, the statue of a nineteenth-century Italian soldier, sabre drawn, stood silently, his form softly flickering in the snow falling across the square.

Reminders of the last war seemed to be everywhere. Walking back from Piazza Castello, I passed the windows of an Italian antiques dealer in a cobbled side street. The shop's wares were piled dustily on little shelves: a Wehrmacht pay book, a cigarette lighter embossed with Mussolini's head, a statue of the Virgin Mary that was lit from within, and a ham-fisted nineteenth-century oil painting of a moustachioed lord and master interfering with one of his servant girls. Half hidden behind them I saw a silver teaspoon embossed with the twin lightning flashes of the SS, and a cereal bowl, made in Bavaria in 1938, with the same runic device in large black markings on the bottom. Italy had been, it must be remembered, a country very strongly occupied by the Germans. In Turin, reminders of dead Italian partisans surprised one on random buildings.

Outside a popular supermarket, a small brass square, three inches by three, was set into the pavement. It announced that this was the spot at which an Italian man had lived, before he was deported in 1944 to Mauthausen concentration camp, where he was executed in March 1945. On the wall of the main train station at Porta Nuova, an engraved carving commemorated the Italian Jews who were put onto cattle trucks there. When I went out running, the route I took led me past at least four different plaques set into the walls on street corners, where Italian partisans had breathed their last during street fighting to liberate the city in April 1945. One park I ran through was named after a partisan leader killed in Auschwitz. To get down to the towpath by the sluggish, green waters of the wide river Po, I took a curved and steep little alleyway, named for all those who died in German concentration camps.

A book on Italian partisans in the Second World War was on the country's spring bestseller lists. On a Saturday morning in April, the queue outside the Museum of Resistance was made up of ten-year-old children, its noisy line snaking around the block. A huge poster prominently displayed across the city showed one of American photographer Robert Capa's pictures from Sicily in 1943. In it an American soldier, helmeted, crouching, listens to a Sicilian peasant in clogs and waistcoat who, with a stick, is pointing out the location of nearby German positions. And all of this was before the annual celebrations for Liberation Day on 25 April. This commemorated the day in 1945 when Turin and Milan were liberated, and when the National Liberation Committee of Upper Italy announced the end of twenty years of Fascist dictatorship. This led to the liberation of northern Italy, and the death – by shooting and public hanging – of Mussolini three days later. The liberation of Bologna, Venice, and Genoa followed, and resulted, in the eyes of Italians, in the referendum of 2 June 1946, which led to the end of the monarchy and the creation of the Italian Republic.

That day, on 25 April, the news on Italian television was filled with pictures from war memorials and cemeteries across the country. Italian generals, soldiers, police officers, carabinieri, air force pilots, naval officials, customs officers – essentially everybody in the country entitled to wear any form of uniform – had put it on that day. And in Italy, where sartorial display is an art form, this was an awful lot of people. Even the staff from Turin's glistening metro system seemed to have spruced up in a full-dress version of their dark blue costume. But what struck one was the sheer number of cemeteries containing the bodies of Allied servicemen that seemed to feature in the Liberation Day proceedings. Military attachés from several foreign embassies in Rome – including India, Poland, Great Britain, Brazil, New Zealand, South Africa – seemed to be saluting on television everywhere one looked. They were in those war graves around Salerno and Anzio, of course, where the Allies had come ashore on the Italian mainland in autumn 1943 and spring 1944. They were there near the rows of crosses in the graveyards at Monte Cassino, and those near the old defensive lines on Lake Trasimene and the river Arno.

But looking at the hours of television footage, and tracking the locations across the map of northern Italy, you could see that cemetery after cemetery followed a line that stretched diagonally across the north of the country from northwest to east. It went from La Spezia in the west, on the Mediterranean coast of Tuscany, to Rimini on the Adriatic coast. And if you watched the television closely, or visited the cemeteries themselves in the days after 25 April, you'd see the piles of wreaths left for the different nationalities of soldiers who had died on or near this line of battles that stretched across the whole of Italy. There were the Americans, of course, GIs from Lieutenant General Mark Clark's 5th Army, buried at Florence and Nettuno, and the men of the British 8th Army who'd fought under Lieutenant General Oliver Leese, buried at Forli. There were the Canadians buried at Coriano Ridge cemetery outside Rimini, and the South Africans at Castiglione. From then on, the number of nationalities burgeoned, diversified, and branched out to encompass the different continents of the globe. There were Brazilians buried at the Moro River, while elsewhere were interred Jewish volunteers from Palestine, Maoris from New Zealand, Rhodesians, Poles, French, Indians, Gurkhas from Nepal, Greeks, and French colonial troops from Senegal. And, in the Pietrasanta war cemetery outside La Spezia, on the Mediterranean coast, were some of the bravest and most heavily decorated soldiers who had fought for the Allied and Commonwealth cause. These were the Nisei, the second-generation Japanese Americans who had joined the US Army rather than face internment. Fighting in Italy in the 442nd Regimental Combat Team, they were to win so many gallantry awards that they became, for their unit size and length of service, the most highly decorated unit ever in the history of the US military.

The fighting among the Allies, the Germans, and the Italians between 1943 and 1945 was to produce an extraordinary selection of unsung heroes, some decorated, some not, who, like my father in Holland, had believed in taking the initiative against Germans, of unthinkingly turning the course of battle. These were all men who had embarked on the 'hazardous and unpleasant operation' of attacking Germans dug in to good defensive positions. Many of them, the Japanese Americans, the African-American 'Buffalo Soldiers' of the US 92nd Infantry Division, the Indians, the Brazilians, were from units that didn't necessarily match the popular stereotype of the Allied soldier, which made their exploits, and the often untold stories of their units, all the more remarkable. Like my father, who with his four tanks had been the tip of 11th Armoured Division's spear, many of these men and their units' actions had helped change the course of battles. For the German defensive positions they had attacked in those last two years of the war in Italy had been part of one of the biggest, best-constructed man-made and natural defence positions of the whole Second World War. This was the string of defensive redoubts and positions that followed the Apennines across northern Italy, Generalfeldmarschall Kesselring's last line of defence designed to stop the vast multi-national Allied armies breaking through into central Europe. Its name? The Gothic Line.

# PART ONE

# INTRODUCTION – THE ROAD TO THE GOTHIC LINE

# 1

## BEWARE OF THE RABBIT

On 4 May 1944, a day of early-summer heat in Rome, a man was brought to the Gestapo's headquarters in the city. It was the ninth month of the German occupation. The HQ was located halfway up Via Tasso, a gently sloping street of cobbles and sand-coloured apartment buildings in the San Giovanni quarter of the city centre. The prisoner was Arrigo Paladini, a teacher of Latin and Greek. He was a scholarly, bespectacled man whose face wore the same look of chronic undernourishment that could be seen all over wartime Europe. On arrival at Via Tasso, SS police beat him with rubber hosepipes for eight hours. He scratched a diary – called *il libro nero,* the black book, into the blue-grey plaster of his cell wall. The only entries for the days in question, beginning on 4 May, were *botte,* beatings, over and over again. The last entry was on 4 June.

In the thirty days he was confined in the cell, the only light he saw entered through a small barred opening twelve by eighteen inches above the door. The stifling heat of the Italian summer and the ubiquitous Roman mosquitoes came in too. The German state security apparatus, headed by the Gestapo, had taken over the building in September 1943, and one of the first things they did was brick up almost all the windows in each room that had been converted into a cell. Only small openings were left for ventilation so the prisoners didn't actually suffocate. But in the dark, Paladini managed to keep his diary on the wall with the help of a small nail. He also wrote other messages – including two lines of the Italian national anthem, and a long letter to his mother, to God, and to his girlfriend.

'Those whom I love infinitely I will leave as the guardians of my spirit, the last hope has not been lost, perhaps life is safe,' he wrote to his girlfriend. As a partisan caught smuggling radio equipment to and from Allied agents in Rome, it was a given that he would be condemned to death, and Arrigo also knew that his torturers would stretch out the process to gain as much information as they could before they executed him. What they most wanted to know were the names of his fellow partisans, and where they were hiding their secret radio sets, delivered to them by American agents from the OSS, the Office of Strategic Services, the precursor of the modern CIA. Crucially, they also wanted to know where in or around Rome the Americans were hiding.[1]

Paladini also wrote, in Greek, a well-known aphorism attributed to the philosopher Heraclitus: πάντα ῥεῖ, or 'Panta Rhei', meaning 'Everything moves onward, nothing will remain still.' He was not the only one to leave messages scratched into the plaster. Another prisoner before him had written 'Facile saper vivere, grande saper morire' (It's easy to know how to live, but a fine thing to know how to die).

Next to Paladini's messages to his mother, God, and his girlfriend, there is a scratched line drawing of a rabbit, ears aloft, sitting on its hindquarters. 'Beware', says a scratched message alongside it, with an arrow pointing to one of Paladini's quotes above it. 'The Rabbit' was the code name for a double agent in Rome who had operated for both the Allies and the Germans, and Paladini suspected his true loyalties lay with the latter. He knew he had been betrayed. So, knowing that he was going to die, Paladini was leaving a message for any other partisan inmates who might follow him into the cell, or anybody who might read the messages. But was Paladini also hoping his warning would be read by his German captors, or by eventual Allied liberators? What is certain is that for a man as intelligent as

Paladini, who could recite whole passages of Dante by heart, the message was not left for nothing.

When he was arrested by the Germans on 3 May, Paladini was bringing radio equipment into Rome from the province of Abruzzo, northeast of the capital, where he was a partisan. The radio had been air-dropped by the Allies. Working as a senior partisan liaison officer with the American OSS mission in Rome, he had infiltrated his way into the capital and made contact with the underground cell. An informer had betrayed him, and he had been arrested in the Piazza delle Croce Rossa.

By early 1944, the huge Allied armies that landed in Sicily the summer before, and then on the Italian mainland at Salerno in September 1943, were bogged down south of Rome. The blood-soaked mountain bottleneck that was Monte Cassino had held up half of them, the beachhead at Anzio the other. But in German-occupied Rome, American and Italian agents from the OSS were living and operating under cover, playing an incredibly dangerous game of cat and mouse with the Gestapo and the Italian Fascist authorities. The OSS operated in Italy alongside the British Special Operations Executive, or SOE, in running agents and supplying partisan groups operating behind German lines.

Under questioning, Paladini was saying nothing. So in addition to his beatings, the Germans put him on a starvation diet. One day, a fellow prisoner managed to sneak him a cup of dirty water that had been used for washing, the only traces of food in it some flecks of meat caught in the soapy foam at the top. Later in his confinement, to prevent him actually dying, he was given a few spoonfuls of broth every two days. He was told his father would be killed unless he talked, and his misery was compounded by guilt, thinking that his silence was condemning his father to death. (In fact Paladini Senior had died in a German prison on 25 October 1943.)[2] Sitting in his cell, starving, beaten half to death, the partisan clung to a small spark of hope. Like everyone in Italy, he knew that it was only a matter of time before the Allied armies liberated Rome. So he scratched his desperate hopes on the wall of the cell: 'Perhaps I will escape with my life.'

## THE ROAD TO ROME

By late spring 1943, the Americans and British and their Commonwealth and colonial Allies had won the war in North Africa. The opening of a Second Front in northwest Europe was still a distant possibility, and the victory in Africa left the Allies in the Mediterranean with a choice of where next to fight the Germans. Italy? The Balkans? Greece and the Aegean? The war had to be fought somewhere: Allied planners estimated that a possible D-day in France was still a year away. The triumvirate of leaders – Roosevelt, Stalin, and Churchill – were at odds over where to fight next. The Russian victory at Stalingrad in February 1943, and the British triumph at El Alamein, had proved to be turning points. The preceding year in the Pacific, the Americans' aircraft carrier groups had broken the invincibility of the Japanese navy at the Battle of Midway, only six months after Pearl Harbor.

Churchill argued that control of the Mediterranean meant control of Europe, and he wanted England, its armies, and the Royal Navy to have it. In the telegrams that the three leaders exchanged daily, early summer 1943 was devoted to deciding how the war in south and southeastern Europe would be fought. Control of Italy, with its 4,750 miles of coastline commanding every shipping lane in the middle of the Mediterranean, and thus access to the Suez Canal and India, was crucial for the British. It would also decide how military operations in neighbouring countries in southern Europe, like Yugoslavia, Austria, and southern France, could be carried out. These in turn would dictate the post-war map of the northern Mediterranean.

A liberated Sicily and Italy would enable the Allies to dominate the Mediterranean sea-lanes and the air bases within striking distance of Germany and the whole of southern Europe. The Allies had three possible courses of action. First, invade Sicily and the Italian mainland, and fight from bottom to top, thus tying down hundreds of thousands of German troops who could otherwise be deployed against a forthcoming invasion of northwestern Europe, or else used in Russia. Second, they could stage seaborne landings at the very top of Italy, on the Mediterranean and Adriatic coasts, fight across the country, and cut off the whole mainland and the German and Italian forces in it. Third, they could negotiate an armistice and surrender with the Italians, move fast, and invade and occupy the country before the Germans had time to reinforce it from the north. Having occupied Italy, the Allies could then race up the spine of the country towards the Alps, outflanking and trapping German divisions by a series of leapfrogging amphibious landings on both Adriatic and Mediterranean coastlines. They chose the first option. And at first it all went according to plan.

Meeting at Casablanca in January 1943, the Americans and British argued about whether Sicily or Sardinia should be the first target. Sicily won. In Operation *Husky*, begun on the night of 9 July 1943, the British 8th Army under General Bernard Montgomery and the American 7th Army under Lieutenant General George S. Patton launched amphibious and airborne assaults across the southern and eastern coasts of Sicily. It was the largest venture of its kind in the war to date, and was successful, although many of the problems that could beset a combined amphibious, naval, and airborne operation did so. *Husky* was preceded by a series of diversions, the most imaginative of which was code-named 'Operation *Mincemeat*'. The Allies were obviously desperate to persuade the Germans and Italians the landings were planned elsewhere, for as Winston Churchill had said after the success of the North Africa campaign, 'Everyone but a bloody fool would *know* it's Sicily next.'

So the Allies devised a cunning plan. The dead body of a homeless Welshman from north London was painstakingly disguised to resemble the corpse of a British Royal Marines officer. The scheme pretended that he had drowned after an air crash while carrying secret documents destined for General Harold Alexander, commander-in-chief of the Mediterranean theatre. The body, with a fictitious identity – 'Major Martin' – was dumped overboard by a British Royal Navy submarine off the southern coast of neutral Spain. A leather briefcase was chained to it, containing papers purporting to show that the

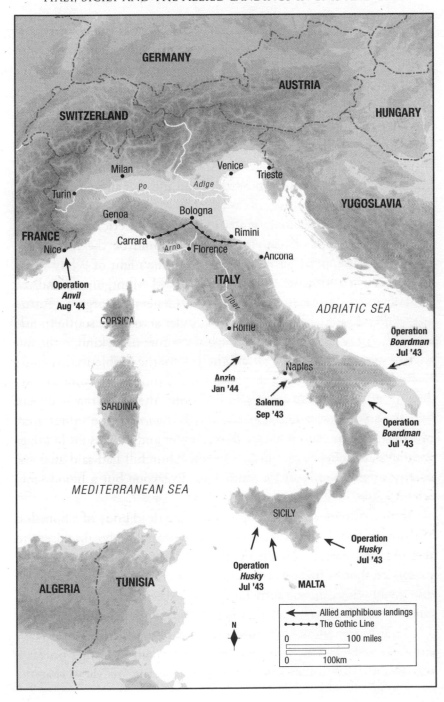

Allies intended to invade Sardinia or Greece. A local fisherman found the body after it washed ashore, and it was passed to the Spanish navy, which in turn allowed German military intelligence in Madrid to copy the documents. Hitler fell for it. Generalfeldmarschall Erwin Rommel was transferred to Greece to command German operations there against the supposed Allied invasion and, most importantly, three German tank divisions were transferred from Russia and France to Greece, just before the strategically crucial armoured battle at Kursk in southern Ukraine in 1943.

But the actual invasion of Sicily, which began on the night of 9 July, got off to a discouraging start. Because of strong winds and the inexperienced pilots of the 147 gliders carrying the first wave of British airborne assault teams, only 12 reached their correct targets and 69 crashed into the sea. American paratroopers were scattered across southeastern Sicily. The initial landings were almost unopposed, but within hours the Germans and Italians counterattacked with tanks. The Italian army fought much harder than expected, and the British, overconfident after beating them in North Africa, found themselves out-fought by them, albeit briefly, on two occasions. But then the weather swung in the Allies' favour: the Italians and Germans had assumed that nobody would attack in the bad weather that prevailed before the attack, and so they were slow to react. The enormous dominance in Allied air power hindered the German tanks' ability to move easily in the open Sicilian countryside. Using their infantry and tanks together, the Allies – who were numerically outnumbered almost two to one – swung north, west, and east across Sicily, pushing the Germans into the northeastern corner towards the Strait of Messina. The Germans fought a series of bitter rearguard actions as they withdrew towards the port of Messina, from where they could rescue their troops back onto the toe of the mainland.

For the Allies, the fighting was characterized by several factors they would encounter on the mainland. The combat was dominated by the physical terrain and the Germans' exemplary command of the fighting withdrawal. Both sides effectively deployed armour and infantry together: the Germans used lightning counterattacks to keep the Allies off guard as their main force withdrew from one defensive position to the next. It was to prove a precursor to the fighting on the mainland. There was also the heat, dust, mosquitoes, the lack of water, the beauty of the countryside, the 2,000-year history, and the rural poverty.

The fighting in Sicily introduced the Allied soldiers and their commanders to a new German opponent, which was to dominate the strategic and operational dictats of their lives for the next eighteen months. Luftwaffe Feldmarschall Albert Kesselring was in charge of the German Army Command South. He was a fifty-eight-year-old veteran of the First World War who had commanded the German air forces during the invasion of Poland and France, and during Operation *Barbarossa* in Russia. He made several decisive observations in Sicily. Without German support, the Italians would collapse, although they were around 230,000 in number. So he decided to evacuate his 60,000 Germans back to the mainland and save them for the defence of southern Italy. He did this in a series of tactically brilliant fighting withdrawals, using the geography on land and sea to his advantage. More than 50,000 Germans escaped from Sicily by August, including two elite paratroop divisions, along with nearly 4,500 vehicles. Kesselring achieved this despite the fact that the Allies had command of land, sea, and air.

The campaign lasted four weeks. The British and Americans lost around 25,000 killed, wounded, missing, or captured, and the Germans some 20,000. The Italians surrendered and lost around 140,000, the majority of whom were taken prisoner. Fighting was brutal. But after a morning spent observing combat in a peach orchard, a British war artist said that he couldn't decide which was more compelling: the physical beauty of the island or the visceral violence of infantry fighting. The combat casualties on the American side were exceeded only by the number of soldiers who caught malaria, from the *Anopheles gambiae* mosquito, breeding in the ponds, swamps, and drainage ditches that crisscrossed Sicily.

The Allies ran head-on into the world of Sicilian organized crime, and into la dolce vita too. In one key town, American troops fought alongside Italian Mafia gunmen masquerading as partisans, after their battalion commander agreed with the local capo that political and material control of the area would revert to him once the Germans had retreated. The geography was new too. Suddenly, after the throat-scorching heat and arid lack of compromise that were the sand and rocks of North Africa, here were the southern gardens of the old Roman Empire. The idiosyncratic colour of war was also far from absent.

A unit of British special forces was the first to liberate the eastern port of Augusta. They outfought and outmanoeuvred a numerically superior German unit, which withdrew towards a viaduct above the town. The British soldiers then liberated not just the bar in the local brothel but also the wardrobes of the prostitutes who worked in it. When an English company of soldiers arrived to link up with the Special Raiding Squadron, they found a small group of rugged, ragged men in special forces berets, captured German weapons slung over their shoulders, some wearing a mix of combat uniforms and women's negligees and underwear. One was playing an upright piano under the orange trees in the town square, surrounded by the others, who were drinking Campari and singing.[3]

But then the Italians made a move that very nearly caught the Germans by surprise. In secret, they had negotiated an armistice with the British and Americans: it was signed on 3 September at a military base at Cassibile outside Syracuse in southern Sicily. Italy's Fascist infrastructure, under the twenty-year dictatorship of Il Duce, Benito Mussolini, was by now on the ropes. The country, badly defeated in North Africa and at sea in the Mediterranean, was exhausted by war. Il Duce's lavish architectural designs, feckless colonial wars, and huge public spending had bankrupted Italy. His cloying, sycophantic allegiance with Hitler had motivated him to dispatch 235,000 Italian troops of the 8th Army to fight alongside the Germans, Romanians, and Hungarians around Stalingrad. They were badly equipped, with

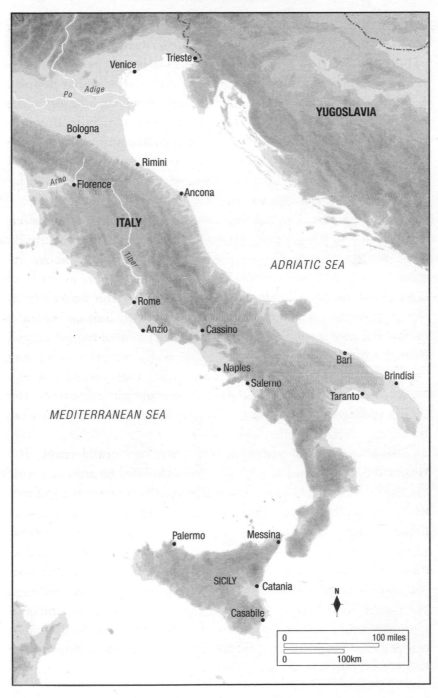

weapons that, at best, semi-functioned in the Russian winter, and they had no suitable clothing for the sub-zero temperatures. In seven months, from August 1942 to February 1943, 88,000 were killed or went missing; 34,000 were wounded, many of them with extreme frostbite. And by July 1943, the Italian mainland was already being bombed by the Allies. The country's predominantly Catholic population was at risk of reprisals if Pope Pius XII spoke out too vociferously about the Germans' treatment of Europe's Jews.

So the end, when it came, was draconian. Mussolini was told by the Grand Council of Fascism on 25 July 1943, that not only would his powers be curtailed, but control of the armed forces would be handed over to King Victor Emmanuel and Prime Minister Pietro Badoglio. The former was considered ineffectual; the latter, with a shameful record in the First World War, was thought little better than Il Duce. So the next day Mussolini was arrested at Villa Savoia in Rome. The signature of the armistice was effectively a total capitulation of the country's armed forces. For the Germans, who by chance had intercepted an Allied radio conversation from Sicily about the negotiations, it was a confirmation of what they had feared and expected all along. Their capricious and militarily lacklustre allies had done a deal behind their backs.

Fearing that with the Italian army incapacitated, the British and Americans would quickly occupy Italy, the Germans moved as fast as they could and launched Operation *Alarich*, their plan to occupy Italy. If the Allies had been prepared to cooperate in full with the anti-fascist Italian resistance before Mussolini was deposed, the British landings in mainland Italy could have taken place unopposed. But British foreign secretary Anthony Eden insisted on a full and unconditional surrender by the Italians. During the 1935 Abyssinian crisis, Mussolini had described Eden, then an undersecretary of state at the Office of Foreign and Commonwealth Affairs, as 'the best dressed fool in Europe'. Eden remembered and smarted at this, and demanded the surrender be unconditional.

Badoglio was timid and terrified of offending the Germans, so the chance to provide muscular military leadership to the many Italians who would be prepared to resist both Fascists and Germans was lost, and the Allies' opportunity to join forces with the anti-fascist partisans was squandered. The Germans' speedy reaction paid off: while the Allies were still negotiating final terms, and arguing about what should become of Italy's monarchy, Hitler dispatched nine extra divisions down through the Brenner Pass, eastward from southern France and westward from Yugoslavia. After a short-lived defence by Italians loyal to the king, Rome was occupied by the Germans on 9 September 1943. The Italian army collapsed into three pieces.

## ITALY FALLS APART

As an Italian army officer, Arrigo Paladini had volunteered for service in Russia in 1941 and fought near Stalingrad. But unlike 88,000 other Italian soldiers in Russia who were killed or taken prisoner, Paladini made it home alive, with nothing worse than a bad case of frostbite in one foot. It meant that for the rest of his life he could hardly run. When the armistice was signed at Cassibile in September 1943, Arrigo Paladini was still a twenty-six-year-old second lieutenant in an artillery unit of the Italian army, based near Padua in northern Italy.

As soon as he heard news of the armistice, broadcast from Allied-occupied Algeria by the American major general Dwight Eisenhower, and then on the BBC and Radio Italy, Paladini quickly decided which side he was on. Fellow soldiers in the Italian army faced four choices: desert and go home; follow the orders of superior officers and face detention in squalid camps to await the eventual arrival of the Allies, or possible execution by the Germans; remain loyal to the deposed Mussolini and his Fascist regime; or join a partisan group. As a confirmed anti-fascist, he felt his only choice was to move south and enlist with a group operating in the Abruzzo region, which lies between the Apennines and the country's eastern seaboard on the Adriatic.

Tens of thousands of former Italian soldiers, accompanied by civilians who hated the German occupation of their country, formed partisan groups. Loosely aligned along political lines, they were looking to the future while fighting in the present. The Germans were the immediate enemy, their defeat the immediate goal. But regional political control at the end of the war was the ultimate objective. Paladini's group was allied to the Christian Democrats: its main rivals in the Abruzzo area were Communists. It started life at a meeting in an ilex grove above a village, and at the very beginning had around twenty men, with four Carcano rifles, two submachine guns, and a few Beretta pistols, captured from the police, among them. Paladini took the code name of 'Eugene'.[4]

After being deposed, Mussolini had been put under the guard of a force of 200 *carabinieri*, Italian paramilitary police officers who had remained loyal to the king. They hid the former dictator and his mistress, Clara Petacci, on the small Mediterranean island of La Maddalena, off Sardinia. After the Germans infiltrated an Italian-speaking agent onto the island, and then flew over it in a Heinkel He 111 taking aerial photographs, Mussolini was hurriedly moved.

They took him to the Hotel Campo Imperatore, a skiing resort in the Apennine mountains, high up on the plateau of the Gran Sasso and accessible only by cable car. Here he spent his time in his bedroom, eating in the deserted restaurant surrounded by carabinieri guards, and taking walks on the bare, deserted mountainside outside the hotel. Hitler, meanwhile, had been planning.

In September 1943, he ordered an Austrian colonel in the Waffen-SS, Otto Skorzeny, to come up with a plan to rescue Mussolini, and to assemble a group of men to do it. Thus was born Operation *Eiche*, or Oak. Skorzeny was colourful, charismatic, and austere, and one of Germany's foremost practitioners of commando and anti-guerrilla warfare. As a teenager growing up in Vienna in the 1920s depression, he once complained to his father that he had never tasted butter. Best get used to going without, replied his father. Skorzeny was a skilled fencer too, and one cheek bore the scar of a dueling *schmiss,* or blow from an opponent's blade.[5] By 1943 he was an officer in the Waffen-SS with a hard-earned reputation for success in counterinsurgency operations in France, Holland, the Balkans, and Russia. He commanded the newly formed SS commando unit Sonderverband Friedenthal, and with paratroopers from the German Luftwaffe, he rescued Mussolini without firing a shot.

The 200 Italian carabinieri protecting Il Duce surrendered after Skorzeny and his assault team landed by glider on the top of the plateau next to the Imperatore. Mussolini, in a black homburg and overcoated against the autumnal Apennine chill, was flown to Rome – with a stop in Berlin to be greeted by Hitler – in a light aircraft. Then he returned to northern Italy, where he created the Italian Socialist Republic, a puppet Fascist state that the Germans drew out within the territory they occupied. It became known as the Salò Republic, from the northern Italian town in which it was headquartered. So with Mussolini now temporarily safe in his small Fascist statelet, Germany occupying Italy, and the Allies arriving on the mainland, Paladini and his small band got to work.

## THE ARGUING ALLIES

By the time the Americans landed on the beaches at Salerno, south of Rome, in September 1943, the Allies had just lost one of their more capable generals. The irascible, direct, but tactically effective battlefield commander Lieutenant General George Patton had led the US 7th Army in the invasion of Sicily. He had no time for soldiers under his command who complained of suffering from 'battle fatigue', or any form of neuropsychiatric combat-related stress. At the beginning of August 1943, visiting American military hospitals in Sicily, he assaulted and abused two soldiers who were claiming to be affected by fatigue. Army medical corpsmen had diagnosed at least one, if not both, of them to be in the early stages of malaria, alternating between high fever and shivering fits, with attendant paranoia, hallucinations, nausea, and vomiting. It is questionable that either of them knew what he was saying.[6] Patton slapped both of them, kicked one in the behind, and threatened to shoot the other. News of the incident mushroomed, and despite there being as much support for Patton as criticism over the incident, he was sidelined from combat command for several months as the 7th Army was split up.[7] His successor was a general who would influence the Allies' strategy as much as Albert Kesselring, though in different ways.

## GENERALS MARK CLARK AND HAROLD ALEXANDER

Lieutenant General Mark Clark was a brave and ambitious staff commander who had risen fast through the ranks of the American officer corps. Born in 1896, his father was a career soldier in the US Army; his mother, an army wife, was the daughter of Romanian Jews. He grew up on a series of army posts, joined the army in 1913 at age seventeen, and graduated from West Point in 1917 as a second lieutenant, 110th out of a class of 139. In the manner in which promotion often works in wartime, he was a captain five months later, before being wounded in France later that year fighting in the Vosges mountains. He remained in the military between the wars, holding a variety of staff appointments, at which he excelled, and was quickly promoted. By 1942, he was a major general and deputy commander-in-chief under Eisenhower in North Africa. He was awarded the Distinguished Service Medal by his friend and superior, General Eisenhower after the successful completion of Operation *Flagpole* in October 1942.

The Allies were determined that the French army in Tunisia and Algeria not oppose the landings code-named 'Operation *Torch*', the invasion of North Africa. A group of pro-Allied senior officers from the pro-German Vichy French government, based in Tunisia, had indicated that they would be able to persuade the French forces in that country not to resist an Allied invasion. Along with a group of senior officers and three British commandos, Clark was sent to meet them. The group flew by B-17 Flying Fortress to Gibraltar and then boarded the British Royal Navy submarine HMS *Seraph*. (This vessel would later drop the body of the fake 'Major Martin' off the coast of southern Spain during Operation *Mincemeat*.) Clark spent three days ashore in Tunisia, the mission was a success, and senior French officers announced that when Allied troops came ashore in North Africa, they, the French, would arrange a cease-fire. Eisenhower was delighted. It showed Mark Clark's diplomatic flexibility and powers of persuasion and command, and added to his staff capability. By November 1942, Clark was the youngest lieutenant general in the US military.[8]

In January 1943, he took over command of America's first field army of the Second World War – the 5th Army in Italy. Eisenhower was an admirer, and Clark was certainly brave in a mildly reckless way, but he had a reputation for being vainglorious and ambitious. Neither of these were unnatural or surprising qualities in a West Point cadet who had finished near the bottom of his class yet had risen so quickly in the military. Clark was also a classic product of the political economics of 1930s America, a country that was becoming a world superpower and where post-Depression industrial strength restored much of the people's confidence. It was a country where merit, personal drive, and ambition went hand in hand. Clark was not lacking in of any of these, and he found that war and high command provided the fuse for this volatile trio of qualities.

The commander of the 15th Army Group, which contained the British 8th and American 5th Armies, was General Harold Alexander. The son of an earl, he was educated at Harrow, one of England's leading private schools. He joined the Irish Guards in 1911, after briefly considering becoming an artist. Unlike so many of his generation, he survived the First World War, where he fought on the Somme, and was decorated for gallantry three times. Britain's leading balladeer of Empire, Rudyard Kipling, arranged for his severely nearsighted son, John, to serve in Alexander's battalion at the Battle of

Loos in 1915, where he was killed. Afterward, he wrote that 'it is undeniable that Colonel Alexander had the gift of handling the men on the lines to which they most readily responded . . . His subordinates loved him, even when he fell upon them blisteringly for their shortcomings; and his men were all his own.'[9]

Alexander served in India between the wars, and in 1937 was promoted to major general, the youngest in the British Army. After Dunkirk in 1940 and service in England, in 1942 he was dispatched to Burma to lead the army's retreat to India. Recalled to the Western Desert by Churchill, he led the Allied advance across North Africa after the battle of El Alamein, and then took command of the 15th Army Group, reporting to Eisenhower. The British diplomat David Hunt, who served as an intelligence officer in North Africa, Italy, and Greece, was, after the war, on the British Committee of Historians of the Second World War. He considered Alexander the leading Allied general of the war.[10] He quotes the American general Omar Bradley as saying that he was 'the outstanding general's general of the European war'. But despite this, he had an uneasy relationship with Mark Clark, who found him too reserved.

In September 1943, the main body of the two Allied armies landed at Salerno, south of Naples, on Operation *Avalanche*. Two other British landings took place in Calabria and at Taranto, on the toe and heel, respectively, of Italy. A deception operation code-named 'Boardman' coincided with it, in which the British Special Operations Executive leaked faked plans to invade the Balkans via the Dalmatian Adriatic coast. The plan was successful, and these fell into the hands of the Germans in Yugoslavia. Winston Churchill was, in the words of an American staff officer, 'obsessed with invading the Balkans', part of his master plan to pre-empt a post-war Russian occupation of territory in southern Europe that Churchill saw as rightfully European, not Soviet.

Salerno was as far north as the Allies could land in Italy while still retaining fighter cover from Sicily. The advance bogged down. American troops that managed to break out of the Salerno bridgehead headed eastward instead of north; they tried to link up with American, British, Polish, Canadian, and Indian troops that were advancing northwest towards Rome from their landing grounds at the bottom of Italy. The linkup failed. The mountainous geography of the southern Apennines dictated that an advance to seize the main access routes into the outskirts Rome would have to cross three key rivers, then force its way up the valley of a fourth, the Liri, flowing from the mountains that lay to the south of the capital. Kesselring had anticipated this. The high ground that dominated these river crossings and the main roads were controlled by German artillery, anti-tank weapons, and infantry. Looming over the entrance to the Liri valley itself was a huge mountain, which had a large ancient Benedictine monastery on top of it. It was called Monte Cassino.

Trying to push northward and break the gridlock at Salerno, the Allies made a crucial strategic decision that turned into a tactical error. They carried out a huge amphibious landing north of Salerno, on the Mediterranean coast, at a small fishing port called Anzio. It was only thirty miles south of Rome. When 35,000 British and American troops landed there on 10 January 1944, they found themselves completely unopposed, and they took the Germans by surprise. They could have marched on the capital. But the querulous, disagreeing Allied generalship – 'the Arguing Allies', as they were known – came to the Germans' rescue. Mark Clark placed the operation ashore under the command of an over-hesitant American general. The British and Americans were then trapped for five months in an area where German gunners on the surrounding Alban Hills had every square mile mapped onto their fire plans. The fighting for both sides resembled the trench warfare of the Western Front, and one German officer described it as being worse than Stalingrad.

British General Harold Alexander's 15th Army Group comprised Mark Clark's 5th Army, with English General Oliver Leese commanding the 8th Army. The Allies' command structure then took another blow: Montgomery had left for England in December

1943 to help lead the Allied invasion of Normandy. He left behind him what he saw as a situation of strategic and tactical disorganization, particularly by the Americans, that he was subsequently to describe as a 'dog's breakfast'.

Clark's dislike of Alexander was compounded by his frustration at being the US general who had to implement Alexander's decision to bomb the monastery of Cassino – although Clark personally furiously disagreed with the order. The British in turn blamed Clark for the near failure of the landings at Salerno. Into this goulash of mutual dissatisfaction, they also stirred another ingredient. Clark had personally assigned the over-cautious American major general John Lucas to command the Anzio bridgehead, and the British, who took enormous casualties there, blamed Lucas for not breaking out of the isolated enclave.

The landing at Anzio had been designed to solve Salerno and the Cassino quagmire. It did neither. What it did do was give Generalfeldmarschall Albert Kesselring plenty of time to prepare successive defensive lines north of Rome, to which he could fall back one by one in a series of tactical withdrawals. It allowed him to reinforce the north of the country and establish a major defensive line that led diagonally across north-central Italy exactly where the Apeninne mountains and the Po river valley perfectly suited defensive warfare. It allowed him months to focus his capabilities and to build a string of mutually supporting positions all along this line, which led from the Adriatic coast on the east to the Mediterranean on the west. It was the strongest German defensive position in southern Europe. Kesselring called it *Gotenstellung,* the Gothic Line.

Italy was now a land of several opposing and cooperating forces. There were the Americans and British, with their multi-national corps and divisions from India, Canada, and countries such as South Africa; there were the Germans; there were the Italian partisan groups, with their myriad political allegiances; and there were Italian Fascists loyal to Hitler and Mussolini. The list of protagonists in the fight for one of Western civilization's oldest lands was as complex and tricky as the terrain and the history of Italy itself.

# 2

## THE TORTURERS OF VIA TASSO

Arrigo Paladini's partisan group in the Abruzzo had gotten bigger and better equipped over the winter of 1943 and the early spring of 1944. They had weapons taken from the Germans and Italian Fascist troops, and from an airdrop from the British. Numbering some two hundred men, their arsenal now included .303 Bren light machine guns, British Sten submachine guns, Schmeisser MP-40 submachine guns, and Beretta machine pistols, and most of them now had shoes or boots captured from a raid on a German barracks.[1] As the Allies advanced slowly on Rome, the group had three operational priorities. The first was attacking roads and railway lines used by German troops advancing or withdrawing northward into pre-prepared defensive positions farther up the Apennines. Second, they were helping escaped Allied prisoners of war avoid the Germans. In one operation, POWs made for a rendezvous on the Adriatic coast where they could be picked up by fast motorboats and taken back to Allied-captured territory. Last, the partisans were preparing to help liberate their province, particularly the flat coastal stretch around the port of Pescara.

Abruzzo has one of the largest expanses of wild forest in Italy, and the roads and railway lines the German troops were using to withdraw were all on the coast. Attacking them required the partisans to leave the forests and operate in the open, and that meant cooperating with rival groups of partisans from the towns on the Adriatic. Then in December 1943, Paladini crossed the Apennines and linked up with the OSS and partisans in Rome. He became a partisan liaison officer with the OSS cell in Rome. Then he moved south again, across the front lines to liaise with the Allies north of Salerno. They gave him training and radio equipment, and at the beginning of 1944 he was landed by submarine near Pesaro, on the Adriatic coast near his partisan group's area of operations in the Abruzzo region.

At the beginning of May 1944, Paladini was one part of a team that was taking a radio transmitter from Abruzzo to another team of partisan couriers outside Rome, and then into the capital itself. Paladini was one of the latest links in the human chain. The Allies were by now south of Rome. Since March, when another OSS–partisan liaison officer had been captured and executed, Paladini was now the main link officer with Peter Tompkins' OSS cell.[2] Its agents in Rome were reporting back to Allied HQ as often as five times per day: their information on troop movements in Rome, on the highways, and in the countryside surrounding it was crucial. Although the Ultra decryption programme based at Bletchley Park in southern England could intercept and decode almost everything the Germans sent on their Enigma encryption machines, the decoding took time, and there was always a priority queue for which signal got decoded first. Italy in May 1944, a month before the launch of Operation *Overlord* in northwestern Europe, was not always at the top of the list. Sometimes it took as long as three days for a Wehrmacht or Luftwaffe or SS signal from Berlin to Rome to be intercepted, decoded at Bletchley, and then transmitted to the Allies in Naples or Bari or Algiers. The OSS head of station in Rome, an American journalist named Peter Tompkins, could receive information by telephone or in person from a courier or partisan or friendly Italian minutes after it had happened. The movement of a half battalion of

## German defensive lines in Italy 1943–45

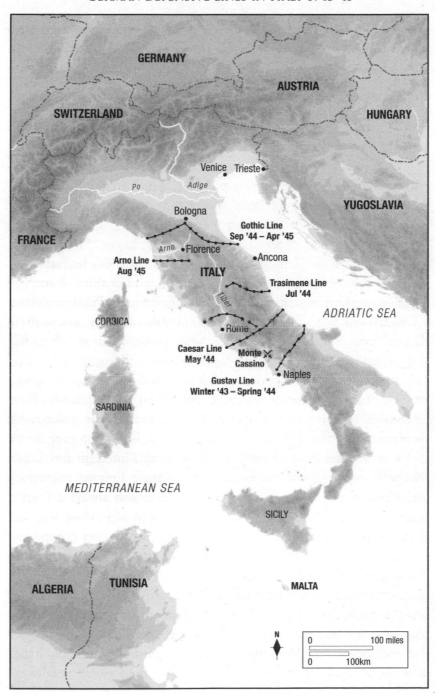

German tanks onto railway low loaders at the marshalling yards outside Tiburtina station in eastern Rome could be the subject of a priority Morse transmission from Tompkins or one of his radio operators an hour later. Radios were thus vital.

What the headquarters of Generals Clark and Leese most needed to know was what Kesselring was going to do. Would he fight for Rome? Leave it and retreat northward, keeping his 10th and 14th Armies intact? Leave a diversionary force to fight the partisans and advance parties of Allied tanks and infantry in the capital's suburbs? The Allies had, by the beginning of June, finally broken through Kesselring's defences on the Gustav Line, south of Rome, and pushed out of the Anzio beachhead. The OSS agents in Rome had clear instructions from their missions in Switzerland and Naples: find out what the Germans' operational intentions *really* were. Would they even burn down the capital and massacre sections of the inhabitants? Churchill received a telegram on 23 June from the South African prime minister, Field Marshal Jan Smuts, who served in the Imperial War Cabinet under him. Smuts said that Harold Alexander felt, optimistically, that if Kesselring's 10th Army could be cut off outside Rome as the capital fell, then the British and Americans could be in the Po valley, north of the Apennines, and through the Gothic Line by summer. And in Trieste by September.[3] The Italians had declared Rome an 'open city', hoping to save it from violently destructive urban combat. This could have made occupying it even less of a priority for the Allies. But it was the seat of governmental and national power, and so the Allies ignored the status the Italians had bestowed on it, bombing it some fifty times. After all, they argued, their entire military energies from Sicily onward had been directed towards the capture of Italy's capital city.

For his part, Luftwaffe Feldmarschall Albert Kesselring was pulling his forces back from around the capital, having decided to leave what he saw as a strategically valueless city to its inhabitants. He was determined to head to one of the prepared defensive lines outside Rome. The next one, immediately north of the capital, was called the Trasimene Line, after the huge lake of the same name north of the medieval walled city of Perugia. Kesselring knew that if he could prevent his 10th and 14th Armies from being encircled by the Allies north or east of Rome, he'd live to fight another day. Crucially, another day would mean the next defensive battle after Trasimene would be fought to his tactical and strategic advantage, and would unfold north of Florence on the Gothic Line. And the Allies would have no choice but to fight it on his terms, on the geographical terrain of his choosing. The war in Italy would thus continue until the end of 1944, at least. Hundreds of thousands of Allied troops, as well as hundreds of tanks and aircraft, would be kept from reinforcing the Second Front in northwestern Europe. But if, however, the British and Americans outflanked Rome, ignored it, and blocked Kesselring's defensive withdrawal north of the capital, they would have the opportunity to fight the last major battle of the Italian campaign in the summer of 1944. Which would they do? The SS, Luftwaffe, and German Army hierarchy were desperate to find out, and the urgency of this task was communicated daily to the Gestapo men in Rome from the Oberkommando der Wehrmacht, the German High Command in Berlin.

On the afternoon of 3 May 1944, on his way to a liaison mission in the capital, Arrigo Paladini waited with two other men in a car in Rome's Piazza della Croce Rossa, several hundred yards south-east of the gardens of the Villa Borghese, half a mile from the centre of classical Rome. They were in the shade of one of the huge, dark green umbrella pines that line the main roads. The day was hot. The car was then stopped by Italian Fascist troops, accompanied by ten soldiers from the Wehrmacht *Heer*, the German regular army. With a set of radio crystals in a parcel in his jacket pocket, and a radio in the boot of the car, it was obvious who he was. German soldiers rushed him to Via Tasso immediately.[4]

## THE GERMAN HUNT FOR INTELLIGENCE

By May 1944, Herbert Kappler, a former electrician from Stuttgart, was an obersturmbannführer, lieutenant colonel, in the SS. He served as head of the secret state police, the Geheime Staatspolizei, Gestapo, for the whole of Rome. He ran the Via Tasso prison as his *hausgefängnis,* or private prison, as one Italian partisan called it. He had joined the SS in 1933, and on becoming a full-time member, he volunteered to join the Sicherheitspolizei, the SS Security Police, in 1935. He rose through the ranks and was commissioned as a lieutenant in 1938, working for the Gestapo in Stuttgart. He never joined the military wing, the Waffen-SS, and all of his uniformed experience was in police and anti-partisan work, never seeing front-line active duty. He served in Poland on *einsatzgruppen* (paramilitary death squads) duties in 1939, disposing of Jews and Polish Communists with firing squads. Gestapo duty followed in Belgium, and then he was transferred to Italy as a liaison officer to Mussolini: he spoke fluent Italian and was well connected in the SS. He was on personal terms with Reinhard Heydrich, then the head of the Reich Main Security Office and second only to Heinrich Himmler in the SS hierarchy.[5] Kappler was a dutiful member of the Nazi party, a willing accomplice to the Final Solution, and a sharp and ruthless police officer and intelligence operative determined to please and impress his superiors. As the war on the Eastern Front progressed, and the former electrician continued to avoid a posting there, this determination only increased. One of his thornier tasks in Rome was to liaise with the Vatican, and to spy on it. The Germans knew that both fugitive Jews and escaped Allied prisoners of war were being harboured by the Vatican, and Kappler was in charge of finding out where, and how. The relationship between Nazi Germany and the papacy of Pius XII is a contested one. On the one hand, the Vatican sheltered Jews and Allied POWs, denounced racial murders, condemned the invasion of Poland, and helped both Allied intelligence and the German resistance. On the other, it failed to condemn outright the Nazis' campaign of mass murder, for fear that it would lead to categorical persecution of Catholics across the Third Reich. The pope was also determined to preserve Vatican City, its architecture and vast wealth intact. He had a separate agenda towards the partisans: the Catholic Church was averse to a post-war takeover by political parties that sprung out of partisan groups aligned with the Communist Party.

The Germans knew that if they had simply occupied Rome, declared open war on the Italian soldiers and partisans who opposed them, and publicly condemned the Vatican and Catholics, Italy could have erupted in open civil war within days of their occupation in September 1943. But they were cleverer than that. They didn't need another front to fight on; Western Europe and Russia were quite enough. They knew that if the Italian population under their control was carefully separated through bureaucracy into different hierarchies of good or bad, a numbing cloak of bureaucratic, semi-legitimate normality could prevail. So partisans and their collaborators were evil, Jews were to be deported, civilians who collaborated with the partisans were the enemy, but those who worked for the Germans were rewarded. Italian Fascist soldiers were considered as a B-list ally. An avalanche of irrelevant paperwork and process and orders and permissions would lay a sheen of officialdom over what could otherwise be civil war.

On 11 September 1943, Luftwaffe Generalfeldmarschall Albert Kesselring declared martial law in areas of Italy occupied by German forces. This included new measures for *bandenbekämpfung*, anti-partisan activity. Kesselring had full authority from Hitler, and Italians in German-held areas were held responsible to him for law and order and preventing sabotage. Partisans and *franc-tireurs* (guerrilla fighters) were to be shot. He recommended that his men use 'measures of the utmost severity' when dealing with partisans, and Kesselring threw in the proviso for his men that he would 'protect any commander who exceeds our usual restraint in the choice of the severity of the methods he adopts against the partisans'.[6]

These orders were Kappler's operational raison d'être. And so the daily routine on Via Tasso reflected these imperatives, this Teutonic bureaucracy. An example of this took place on 17 May 1944. A Roman widow arrived at the Gestapo prison in the San Giovanni quarter with a letter, written in pencil in an educated hand. Her husband had been imprisoned at Via Tasso, and then had been taken to the main Regina Coeli 'Queen of Heaven' civilian prison. The prison was the largest in Rome, and was built in a former Catholic convent in Trastevere, a district set in a bend in the Tiber River. At that time, it served as a detention centre for political prisoners of the Fascist regime. Her husband had been taken to the prison and the Germans had executed him either there or at a remote villa that lay behind wire fences, in a garden of palm trees and umbrella pines, on a curve on one of the roads leading north from Rome. This villa, known as La Storta, The Bend, was where the Germans shot many of the condemned prisoners from Via Tasso who couldn't be tortured anymore.

The widow's request was simple: when her husband was arrested and taken to Via Tasso, he had been wearing a full set of clothing, including a hat, coat, and watch.[7] He was also carrying a spare woollen undershirt, two blankets, a towel, seven handkerchiefs, three lunch boxes, and a thermos. His wallet contained more than 2,000 lire. When the prison authorities told her that he was dead, she went to Regina Coeli to pick up his possessions, but she received only his shoelaces and a belt, no hat, no coat, no shoes, and the wallet was 1,500 lire light. What, she wanted to know from the SS men at Via Tasso, had happened? SS-Oberscharführer Ruhlmann was on duty on 17 and 18 May, but if he knew or cared, he wasn't saying anything. He had his bureaucracy to take care of. That day's prison roster told him that there were 324 prisoners at Via Tasso, 36 new arrivals, 5 transfers from other regional sectors, while 25 had left. Nobody had died overnight. All was in order.[8]

Herbert Kappler, meanwhile, was a favourite of Hitler and Mussolini – it was he whose interrogation methods at Via Tasso, along with use of wiretaps, had yielded the information about where Mussolini was being held in the Apennines. Operation *Eiche* had been physically carried out by German paratroopers from the Luftwaffe and SS special forces, but the hard work required to track Mussolini was handled by the Gestapo, questioning Italian prisoners under torture in Rome at Via Tasso. Kappler had pleased Reinhard Heydrich as well. When the Germans occupied Rome, Kappler had made short shrift of the job of deporting more than 1,000 Roman Jews in railway wagons, northward from Tiburtina station, across the Reich to Auschwitz; sixteen of them survived. And as the Allies approached Rome, what Kappler needed to do fast was find out where the leading OSS cell there was based: he knew it was headed by an American called Peter Tompkins.

As the Allies advanced up Italy and as partisan groups formed direct links with SOE and OSS cells, guerrilla activity in the country increased. And so at the same pace did reprisals. In March 1944, a partisan cell in Rome supplied by the OSS detonated a bomb made from forty pounds of TNT, killing a squad of German soldiers. The bomb had been hidden in a street sweeper's cart parked on Via Rasella, a steeply sloping street of apartment buildings that ran down from the palm trees and Baroque glory of the Palazzo Barberini in the middle of Rome. On a pre-arranged march through the city centre on 3 March, designed to intimidate its citizens, a company of SS police came striding up the street in formation, singing.

The bomb, hidden under litter and ash in the bottom of the steel cart, blew thirty-three of them into pieces on the cobblestones. Hitler ordered a reprisal massacre and decided that ten Italians would be killed for every German who died – the exact number of Italians to be killed for each dead German had gone back and forth between ten and fifty. One German commander in Rome had wanted to burn down whole districts of the city centre, as the SS had done in Warsaw.

In the end, SS-Obersturmbannführer Kappler made a list of 335 men who could be used as execution fodder – these included inmates at Via Tasso already condemned to death, Italian political prisoners from the Regina Coeli, and Jews. They were taken by truck to a quiet suburb of southern Rome, down the black cobbles of Via Appia, shiny from 2,000 years of use, that line the old 350-mile Roman highway from Rome to Brindisi. In a small wood of umbrella pines less than a mile from this road are the Ardeatine Caves. These had been used for hundreds of years for mining pozzolana, a kind of volcanic ash used as a binding agent in cement, and the caves were filled with large and long tunnels. Some of the German SS officers had never killed anybody before, so Kappler ordered that several cases of cognac and grappa, Italian brandy, be distributed to the execution party. In groups of five, the Germans made the prisoners kneel and shot them in the base of the skull with pistols. As the executions progressed, and more brandy drunk, the killings became far less precise. Bullets missed craniums; sides were blown off skulls. Prisoners, badly wounded, crawled off into corners of the caves to die. One SS officer drunkenly refused to shoot his allotted prisoners until forced to do so by a senior officer. Once the 335 victims were dead, German Army engineers detonated explosives inside the caves that caused the rock ceilings to collapse, burying the corpses under tons of rubble. The caves' entrances were then blocked shut with more explosions to further hide the evidence.

## THE QUESTIONING OF ARRIGO PALADINI

For the inmates at Via Tasso like Arrigo Paladini who refused to talk, there were different forms of torture. During one session, Kappler pushed a small piece of metal, heated until red hot and glowing, into the side of Paladini's leg. In the cell next to his, another Italian anti-fascist army officer, loyal to the Allies, had his teeth and fingernails pulled out with pliers. The Germans were desperate to find out about partisan and American groups operating in Rome, keenly aware that as they did so, huge Allied armies of Americans, British, Canadians, Poles, South Africans, Indians, and a dozen other nationalities were closing in on the city. But in cell number two, Arrigo Paladini was still keeping silent. Unknown to him, he had been betrayed by a colleague, but only when the Gestapo threatened to kill the man's two-year-old son in front of him by fracturing his skull with a table lamp.[9] And Paladini's supplication about 'The Rabbit', *Il Coniglio,* was to prove especially urgent, as the alleged double agent had been either a partisan or a German informer at Via Tasso itself.

War produces twists of irony peacetime sometimes fails to match. Kappler had, without knowing it, met Peter Tompkins from the OSS. The Gestapo chief had been invited to a social evening gathering in Rome in the spring of 1944. Present were Italian businessmen sympathetic to the German cause, Italian Fascist officers, and their wives and girlfriends. And Tompkins, pretending to be an Italian-

American expatriate. Kappler was concentrating his efforts on an attempted seduction of two Italian women, but he broke off at one point to persuade the American spy to cook him an omelette, washed down with grappa. He left the party none the wiser.[10]

On 4 June Arrigo Paladini's time was up. His Gestapo torturers could get nothing out of him. The Allies were moving through the outskirts of Rome. Kesselring's 10th and 14th Armies were in retreat northward, and the Allies had an opportunity to exploit a gap that had formed in the German line and try to outflank them. Paladini knew nothing of this, only that on that morning he was taken outside to Via Tasso itself and loaded onto a German Army truck along with other condemned prisoners. Their destination? La Storta. The Bend. And a firing squad.

⎯⎯ · ○ · ⎯⎯

As they drove away, the American general Mark Clark was being driven in a Willys Jeep through the southwesterly suburbs of the capital. His behaviour that day couldn't have suited Albert Kesselring's strategic plans better. In late May, General Alexander, Clark's direct superior and commanding officer, had ordered that the American VI Corps, consisting of three combat divisions, head northwest from the Anzio beachhead towards Rome. They would cut the main highway that led southeast out of Rome, and then forge due north, cutting the main highway which, in turn, led due east from Rome. This would effectively outflank and trap much of Kesselring's 10th Army, including a key corps of paratroopers. The American divisions could then wheel around the capital and head straight up the main axis that led northwest past Rome, towards Tuscany and Florence. But Clark didn't do this. Instead, he altered the orders given to Major General Lucian Truscott Jr.'s VI Corps. Clark's main personal and strategic aim was getting to Rome first: it was a prize that he felt very strongly belonged to him and the US 5th Army, and was a due return for the murderous combat they had endured since Salerno. He was determined not to let the British enter the city first. He knew that the invasion of Europe was imminent, and that he had only a matter of days to liberate Rome before the world's attention swung towards Normandy. He intended to present the American people with an American victory achieved by American troops. So he and VI Corps didn't swing northwest of Rome: they turned left and drove straight into the capital. Kesselring's 10th Army escaped.

Before Anzio, the bitter fighting on the Gothic Line was only a possibility. After Salerno, it became a probability. When Kesselring's troops escaped northward from Rome, at the same time as American and British paratroopers were leaping out of their Dakotas over their drop zones in Normandy, it became a certainty. And if there was one factor that was going to affect the strategy and tactics of both Allies and Germans in the coming months, it was the physical terrain of Italy itself.

So in the last moments before Rome fell, Arrigo Paladini waited in Via Tasso prison for a Spa 38 truck to take him off for his execution. There were fourteen prisoners, including him, all with their hands tied behind their backs. The party of twelve Italians, a Pole and an unknown Allied agent, was guarded by four SS men and two Italians. Then the SS soldiers bolted – the Allies were inside Rome, and gunfire and shelling was audible in the streets close by. Paladini and the thirteen others waited with some new Austrian guards, who seemed less vicious and slightly more humane than the German SS men. Among their group of prisoners was a hunchback, and the condemned men took turns stroking his hump, thinking it might bring them good luck in their final moments. It did. The Spa 38 truck broke down. Until it was repaired, they could not be taken off for execution. The prisoners were now on borrowed time. Then their guards made a run for it. So in the blazing midsummer heat, exhausted, dehydrated, starving, beaten half-to-death and still convinced he was going to die, Arrigo Paladini lay down in a corner of the large cell he now shared with the thirteen other prisoners. He fell asleep. And suddenly woke to find somebody shaking him. He stumbled to his feet, and his fellow prisoners took him outside into the sunshine. Their guards had disappeared. A cheering crowd waited for him and the other inmates outside in the blazing light. The Allies had liberated Rome. Arrigo Paladini promptly fainted.

# PART TWO

## BEFORE THE LINE

# 3

## ITALY

### *A Country Made for Defensive Warfare*

The vast Apennines mountain range stretches for 750 miles straight down the spine of much of the country, from the port of Genoa in the northwest down to Taranto, which lies on the heel, sticking out into the southern Mediterranean. This enormous geographical feature makes the country much easier to defend than to attack. The distance from the very northwest of Italy, on the French Alps, down to the far south is around 800 miles. At its widest, in the north, the country is about 400 miles wide. There is an island – Sicily – at the bottom and a very large agricultural plain at the top near the French and Swiss Alps. The country is shaped like a leg lying diagonally, with its heel and toe at the southeast extremity, and the thigh lying crossways at the top. Another description could be of a reclining capital letter T. In 1944, the country bordered France, Switzerland, Austria, and Yugoslavia, the frontiers marked by the long semi-circular curve of the Alps. At the foot of these mountains lay the main cities of the industrial north, Genoa, Turin, Milan, and Bologna, which stretch from west to east, along a flat fertile plain bordering the dark grey-green waters of

the slow river Po. These flatlands extend as far as the Adriatic coast, Italy's eastern seaboard; on it lie the ports of Trieste, Venice, Rimini, and Ancona. The northern agricultural and industrial plain, and the Adriatic ports, are separated from the rest of the country by the enormous Apennines, which can rise as high as 9,000 feet on razor-sharp, snowy crests. Steep slopes lead down from the mountains on both the eastern and western elevations, and along both the Adriatic and Mediterranean littorals there are fertile coastal plains.

Generalfeldmarschall Albert Kesselring knew how to wage a successful campaign of defensive warfare in Italy. First, he was aware that in any assault on land, the offensive movements of his Allied enemy were going to be at least partially dictated by the terrain and the weather. Kesselring also knew that despite the Allies' superiority in tanks, aircraft and artillery, their tanks were badly suited to offensive mountain warfare: narrow roads overlooked by high ground, defended by dug-in artillery and anti-tank weapons made columns of slow-moving armour easy targets. He also knew the Allies would have to capture key towns and access routes that lay on both slopes of the central mountains and take and hold the high ground that ran down the middle of the country. The Italian climate and terrain had become huge, dominant features in the lives of the soldiers on both sides; geographical and natural absolutes dictated much of the progress of the fighting during the whole Italian campaign. They governed how tanks and artillery could or couldn't be used, and how defensive positions could be sited, and they enabled the German defenders to place their positions in such a way as to be able to dictate how any attacking forces would approach them.

The weather in the summer of 1944 was typical of Italy: hot, dry, and very dusty. But the autumns and winters like the one of 1943, through which the Allies had just fought, were very different. 'Muddy awful', was one Allied soldier's description of it. The cheery, clipped tones of a Pathé newsreel shown to troops summed it up: 'The snow and mud of sunny Italy – something had gone wrong with the weather. It wasn't up to guidebook standards!' American and British soldiers had christened the glutinous brown autumn and spring mud that swallowed vehicles up to the axles 'Italian soup'. In autumn and winter, slit trenches were dug, but then filled with muddy, silty water a foot deep. The annual rainfall in Italy is about 34 inches a year, compared to 37 in the American midwestern state of Wisconsin, and 46 in Great Britain. Whereas the rain in the United States and in Britain is spread across ten months of the year, with a perpetual drizzle in northern Europe, Italy's rainfall is concentrated in massive downpours of torrential rain in spring and autumn: 34 inches fall every year in only 75 days. Rivers and streams flood, roads are washed out, low-lying areas become impromptu lakes, landslides are common, the earth becomes marshy, vehicles bog down, mud and rain are everywhere. It makes the movement and logistical supply of troops a nightmare.

A second factor helped decide the outcome of defensive warfare. Kesselring knew that a successful general was in a stronger position if he had time to prepare his positions. And 'Smiling Albert' had weeks to pull his armies back from their positions north of Rome, towards the two carefully prepared defensive lines in the centre and north of Italy. As his 10th and 14th Armies withdrew up the spine of the country, they first made a stand in late summer 1944 along the river Arno, which stretches from Florence, in Tuscany, down to the Mediterranean Sea. The Germans knew that General Alexander's armies had to march up both sides of the spine of the Apennines, capturing ports on both the Adriatic and Mediterranean coasts. They had learned from the fighting around Monte Cassino and the Liri river valley in the appalling weather of the spring of 1944, where their defensive strategies and the terrain had dictated the Allies' tactical and operational movements.

The Gothic Line was about 200 miles long. It stretched all the way across the top of Italy from the seaside town of Pesaro, south of Rimini on the Adriatic coast, where Arrigo Paladini had been landed by submarine in December 1943, to Massa Carrara on the Mediterranean, where Michelangelo had bought his marble in the late Middle Ages.

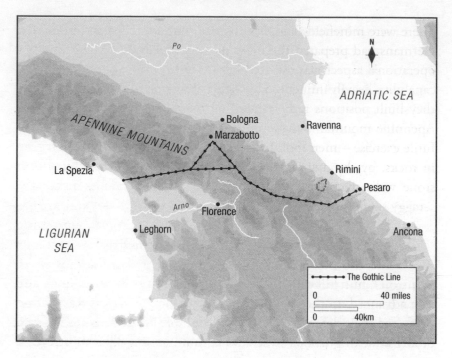

It was a series of carefully constructed defensive positions that made the most of the terrain on which they were situated – the crests, slopes and ravines of the Apennine mountains. They were sited on the tactical and strategic premise that any attacking forces would have to advance along a limited number of main access roads, across a limited number of bridges or bridgeable rivers, and through a limited number of key towns that lay in the shadow of easily dominated mountainous high ground.

On the Gothic Line, positions were dug onto mountaintops, the sides of hills, reverse slopes, wooded and rocky ridges, flat plateaus, at key crossroads, and in farmland and vineyards. A favoured technique was to dig a Panther tank into the ground so only the top of the turret and the 75mm gun itself were showing.[1] In addition, 81mm mortar positions were sited with carefully planned fields of fire, and some 2,370 machine-gun posts positioned to dominate lines of possible advance. About 470 anti-tank guns were waiting for the Allied armour.

There were minefields laid, and barbed wire stretched for miles. The Germans had prepared the ultimate defensive position, where every operational aspect was dictated by their own tactical knowledge and capability, heavily influenced by their experiences in Russia. Sometimes they built positions rather than dug them: the rocky terrain in the Apennine mountains made trench digging an exhausting and often futile exercise – men took cover and formed positions in the crevices in rocks, by the dug-out roots of trees, and behind the ubiquitous stone walls that marched like stacked grey sugar cubes across the scraggy small fields.

## GERMAN DEFENSIVE WARFARE

Winston Churchill called it 'the red-hot rake of the battle-line', and as it advanced up the spine of the country, the Germans refined and perfected their defensive tactics. The first obstacles they put in front of any attacking troops were anti-tank mines and land mines. One type of anti-personnel device they used was the Schu-mine 42, a simple construction of half a pound of TNT in a small wooden box, about six inches by four. When the lid was stepped on, the pressure caused the mine to detonate. The wooden casing made it difficult to detect with a minesweeping device, and the Germans also wrapped it in plastic or cardboard, making it even harder to find. These small mines were then sown and spread in the thousands on approach paths, tracks, and roads, and on verges, in fields, and around centres of habitation. A big, muddy puddle in the middle of a track would make an advancing American or British or Indian patrol step off the path onto the verge to avoid it; at precisely the point where an incautious infantryman would place his foot, skipping sideways to avoid the mud, a Schu-mine would be buried. The smashed doorway to a semi-destroyed house was a commonly mined area; Allied troops would learn to avoid them and enter through downstairs windows, so Schu-mines would be buried on the floors inside the windows, exactly where the foot of a soldier climbing in would fall.

The mine would blow the foot off a man, and apart from the shock of the blast, the loss of blood, and the intense pain, earth, mud, gravel, pieces of wood from the mine's casing, and brick fragments would be blown into the wound, increasing the likelihood of compound infection.

German artillery forward observation officers would map out the precise ranges to specific targets so that artillery and 81mm mortar fire could be directed onto pre-assigned fire grids. These officers would be positioned with the forward squads of infantry, in radio contact with the guns and mortars behind them. The mainstays of German heavy weapons were their PaK anti-tank guns, which ranged from 30mm up to 128mm, as well as 105mm and sFH-18 150mm howitzers. The FlaK range of anti-aircraft weapons were often used in the artillery and anti-tank role too, with the 88mm FlaK 41 being one of the most common and effective.

When it came to the infantrymen on both sides, the firepower composition of the American and British infantry squads differed enormously from the Germans', and individual unit firefights and 'contacts' with the enemy were hugely affected by it. The Germans based their squad or section defensive tactics around their automatic weapons. Their Maschinengewehr-42, or MG-42, known to the British as a 'Spandau', from the town of its manufacture, stamped on the weapon's casing, was a much-feared weapon, which time and again in the fighting across Italy pinned down Allied infantry troops. It was made for defensive warfare. The successor to the MG-34, it was introduced in 1942, and it could fire up to 1,200 rounds per minute, one of the highest rates of fire of any automatic weapon of the war. The rate of fire, between five to ten bullets per second, made it impossible for those on the receiving end to differentiate among individual shots. American soldiers watched training films to prepare themselves for being shot at by one or more MG-42s, where hundreds of 7.95mm bullets could be hitting the earth, rocks, trees, and mud around them in a matter of a minute. One British officer said its report sounded like 'the scream of an enormous bedsheet being torn in half'.[2]

Weighing only twenty-five pounds, the MG-42 was highly portable, could be fired from the shoulder, and with a bipod and tripod be used as an anti-aircraft weapon, or in the sustained fire role. It could be fed with 200-round belts (most German infantrymen carried at least one of these), or with 50-round drums. It was highly reliable, didn't jam, and in the most arduous of conditions, in the winter fighting at Stalingrad, it had proved its worth. Its only shortcoming was that its rate of fire was so high that the barrels tended to overheat quickly and had to be changed every 250–350 rounds.

The Germans also issued the MP-38 and MP-40 machine pistols to several members of a squad, so their automatic fire rate was higher than that of the Americans or British. In combat, this often meant that the unit that won the firefight was the one that got its automatic weapons sited and operational first and most advantageously. And in the fighting on the Gothic Line, often uphill, almost always against Germans in defensive positions, the infantry fight was frequently dominated by the effort to knock out their machine-gun positions. This tactical ethos extended upward in an inverted triangle as the calibre of the dug-in weapon increased. An entrenched Spandau needed an American section, with its light machine guns and automatic rifles and grenades, to dislodge it. Or one exceptionally brave man to crawl up to it unnoticed, or attack it head-on. A German PaK 75mm anti-tank gun or 81mm mortar carefully sited on a mountain slope overlooking all available routes of approach would require bazookas, tanks, or often artillery to knock it out. A dug-in Panther tank turret with its 75mm gun would need multiple tanks or sustained artillery to destroy it.

The American infantry squad, often with only one or two Browning Automatic Rifles (BAR), was much more dependent on fire-and-manoeuvre than the Germans. It centred on its riflemen, with the semi-automatic Garand rifles and the automatic BAR supporting each other. Almost every weapon in an American squad was a high-calibre automatic one. In defensive fighting, the German squad focused on protecting its MG-42 position, with soldiers armed with low-calibre 9mm Schmeisser submachine guns or bolt-action Mauser K98 rifles with a low rate of fire. Thus the side that was on the defensive, commanded the high ground, and had time to prepare carefully sited machine-gun positions could very frequently dictate the course of battle. And this side in central and northern Italy in 1944 was very often the Germans.

The Germans' positions on the Gothic Line were constructed across some of the most naturally defensible country in southern Europe. And if the Allies were going to be able to push north from Florence, through the mountains, into the plains of the river Po in northern Italy, then taking the central Italian city of Bologna was vital. It controlled access from the Apennines down onto the coastal plain. Generalfeldmarschall Kesselring and his generals would have known that if one draws a rough square with Florence at bottom right, Bologna top right, Parma top left, and La Spezia at the bottom left, the square contains some 5,000 square miles of mountainous, wooded terrain that dominates all of the possible approach routes into north and northwestern Italy. All the Germans needed to do was hold it. The Allies needed to take this land, the key towns surrounding it, and the three main roads going through it. To keep this vast square of land secure for themselves, the Germans needed to remove from it the area's natural inhabitants: partisans, and the American agents from the Office of Strategic Services and the British from the Special Operations Executive, who were supplying and guiding them.

Only when the Allies broke through the defences on the Arno, captured Bologna, Florence, and the mountains surrounding it, could they attack the Gothic Line itself. And only once they had pushed the Germans out of Ancona and Rimini, and won the day over the massive defensive positions on the line, could they exploit through into the flat valley of the Po. The Gothic Line barred them from northern Italy. Kesselring had deployed each of his wide variety of units precisely to try to prevent the Allies achieving these objectives before spring 1945. So Field Marshal Alexander must have been in a very optimistic frame of mind at the end of June 1944 when he met the South African Field Marshal Jan Smuts, who was in Italy at the time. Smuts sent a telegram to Churchill: 'As regards plans for Alexander's advance, he and [Lieutenant General Henry Maitland] Wilson agree that there will be no difficulty in his breakthrough to the Po, and thereafter swinging east towards Istria [on the Yugoslav coast], Ljubliana, and so on to Austria.'[3]

Alexander told Churchill shortly afterward that he estimated he could win through the Gothic Line and cross the river Po in seven weeks, by the end of August 1944. But in fact it was to take him nearly a year. The fighting over the following twelve months would help decide the fate of southern Europe and all of post-war Italy, and could rightly be called the one of the most important battles of the war in Europe.

Echoes of the Roman Empire were strong in Italy in 1944: Kesselring had reversed the classical nomenclature, whereby the Romans had built defensive positions to keep the Goths, Huns, and attendant barbarians out of the dying empire in the years after AD 420. This modern Gothic Line was designed to keep the Allies out of southern Europe, and to prevent them from exploiting westward into southern France, northward across the Alps, and eastward through the 'Ljubljana Gap' into Yugoslavia and Austria. Attacking it was going to be one very hazardous and unpleasant operation.

# 4

## Nisei Soldiers and the Battle for Belvedere

### June 1944

After the fall of Rome on 5 June, the Germans pulled their 10th and 14th Armies northward. First they withdrew them to an ad hoc defensive line around Lake Trasimene, and once the Allies had fought through this, the next stop was a line of positions on the Arno River near Florence. These were their last defences before the Apennine mountains and the Gothic Line itself. By 6 June, the day after the fall of Rome, the war in Italy was suddenly no longer top of the headlines. The Allied armies had parachuted into the night over Normandy and poured out of landing craft onto five beaches in France. Operation *Overlord*, the invasion of northwestern Europe, was under way. It was the largest amphibious military operation in history. At the same time, in the Pacific, a huge American Marine, Navy, and military task force left Pearl Harbor bound for the island of Saipan in the Mariana Islands, a key target in the US island-hopping campaign. The Americans hoped to lure the Japanese Pacific fleet into a maritime ambush, and destroy or cripple their aircraft carrier capability. Marshal Joseph Stalin had just launched an offensive against Finland, wanting to knock it out of the war before he moved against the German heartland. With fighting in the Pacific, northwest Europe, and Italy, the Allies needed every single soldier, sailor, and airman they could possibly find. And so nowhere more than in Italy was there such a variety of different nationalities fighting on the Allied side. One of these was a new and idiosyncratic unit made up of Japanese Americans, which had arrived in Italy before the fall of Rome. And one of their number was a young sergeant named Daniel Inouye.

Daniel Inouye was a seventeen-year-old high school senior in Honolulu on Sunday, 7 December 1941. He was listening to a show on the radio when the disc jockey interrupted the music to say that Pearl Harbor was under attack from the air. Inouye had no idea what he talking about and thought it was just part of the broadcast. Then he went outside, and flying overhead, coming in to attack, were three grey Japanese aircraft, with the emblem of the red circle of the sun on their wings. At that moment, he knew his life had changed.

He rushed down towards the huge harbour area to help as a Red Cross volunteer. The line of battleships that included the *Arizona* and the *Oklahoma* had just been hit; the airfield, with its rows of neatly parked fighter aircraft, was a pall of smoking destruction. Inouye headed towards the main hospital. One of the first things he saw was a body with no head, so he found a box and started to put the body parts into it, when a man ran up, shouting, demanding to see his wife. A nearby doctor told Inouye to show him the contents of the box. So he did. The man started screaming, and went on and on. As Inouye walked away and left him with the doctor, he didn't stop.[1]

Daniel Inouye knew that day that he wanted to join the US Army, and that he wanted to fight. He was the son of first-generation Japanese immigrants, a mother and father whose parents had moved to America to find work. The concept of the debt of honour to their adoptive country ran incredibly strong in the family; it was one core of their values. In Japanese the words for one, two, and three are *ichi, ni,* and *san.* So Inouye's parents, as first-generation immigrants, were called Issei, while Inouye was Nisei, or second generation. He had been brought up in Honolulu by a strict Methodist mother, with a sense of honour and duty stressed from childhood. There was a strong theme not just of honour but also of gratitude to America, the land that had welcomed the Inouye family to its shores. Inouye senior had left Japan after an accidental fire in his home village had burned down a neighbour's property. A village council meeting had adjudicated against the Inouye family and declared that they must reimburse the neighbours for their torched house. So Inouye's father had taken the family to Hawaii to seek work to repay the debt. Forty years later, Daniel Inouye, desperate to enlist in the ranks of the military, tried to join up, but he found it wasn't as easy as he had imagined.

Immediately post-Pearl Harbor, anti-Japanese sentiment in America skyrocketed. The 'Japs' were suddenly the enemy. A comic strip appeared in a US War Department guide to China, intended for American soldiers serving there. The comic strip was titled *How to Spot a Jap*.[2] The Japanese national is portrayed as a bucktoothed, evasive, dishonest victim, who can't look white men in the face and expects to be taken off and shot at any moment. And so like all Japanese Americans, the Inouye family was immediately declared Category 4C, 'enemy alien, unfit for military service'. Daniel Inouye graduated from high school and began his medical training at the University of Hawaii in the autumn of 1942. He still dreamed of joining the military, but it was next to impossible. In February, President Franklin Roosevelt had signed Executive Order 9066, which paved the way in early 1942 for the internment of more than110,000 Japanese Americans in detention camps. The Japanese-American students who were cadets in the university training programmes were discharged, but Inouye and his colleagues in Hawaii managed to persuade the military authorities that they could be used as a pool of useful labour for the war effort. So the army created the Varsity Victory Volunteers, who dug roads, built barracks, and laid out military training areas. For Inouye and his friends, it was a start.

Two existing Japanese-American battalions in the Hawaii National Guard now became the problem. The American military commanders on the island were concerned that, in the event of a

Japanese invasion of Hawaii, these Nisei might side with the enemy. So the two battalions were merged into one and sent as far away as possible from Hawaii for training. They went to Wisconsin, where on arrival they were renamed the 100th Infantry Battalion. And there the worm turned.

They proved so successful in training, so dedicated to the cause of the American military, and so keen to prove themselves good American soldiers, that at the beginning of 1943 the army reversed its ruling and decided that a Japanese-American combat unit could actually be formed. There was a call for volunteers. As most Japanese Americans on the mainland were interned, the response was less enthusiastic than it was on Hawaii, so a unit was formed that contained 3,000 men from the islands and only 800 from the mainland. When Roosevelt formally announced that the 442nd Regimental Combat Team was now in existence, he summed up an ethos, a spirit, a mentality that every single member of the 442nd was going to spend his entire military career affirming. The president said, 'Americanism is not, and never was, a matter of race or ancestry. Every loyal American citizen should be given the opportunity to serve this country wherever his skills will make the greatest contribution'[3] The motto of the 442nd was 'Go for Broke'. While the 100th Battalion trained in the freezing woods of Wisconsin, the rest of the 442nd, including Daniel Inouye, were sent to the deepest part of the Deep South, Hattiesburg, Mississippi. Inouye and his colleagues expected to encounter fierce racism and prejudice in this part of the country, but the welcome proved to be completely the opposite. The main enemy in the humid pine forests east of the rolling Mississippi River were the mosquitoes. Then, training complete, they shipped out.

The 100th Infantry Battalion was sent to Italy first, arriving via North Africa in 1943. The 442nd, minus its 1st Battalion, which stayed behind in Hattiesburg to train new Nisei recruits, arrived at Anzio in May 1944. There were three battalions of some 800 men each in the 442nd Regimental Combat Team, a unit designation in the American army that was the equivalent of a brigade. Along with engineers, medical support, artillery, and signals, the 442 RCT thus comprised some 2,400 infantrymen and another 800 support personnel. Both the American and British armies sub-divided their units in roughly the same way. Eight or ten infantrymen would make up a section or a squad, and three of these would comprise a platoon of some thirty men. Three or four infantry platoons, along with some headquarters men, made up a company. Depending on availability of men, the number wounded or sick, the paper strength of a company was around 130 men. Four companies of riflemen, with two additional companies of heavy-weapons specialists and headquarters troops, made a battalion, which could number anywhere from 700 to 900 men. Three battalions made a brigade; three or four brigades, a corps; and two or three corps made an army. Two or more armies made an army group, like the 15th, commanded by General Alexander, which contained both the British 8th and American 5th Armies.

The 442nd RCT was a unique outfit, a pure product of the human, economic, and geopolitical circumstances of the war in which it was fighting. World War II was to throw up several similar units, one-time creations of time and place and necessity, and Italy seemed to have drawn many of them together. There were the American 92nd Infantry Division, made up entirely of African Americans, and there were the Tuskegee Airmen, African-American pilots who flew Kittyhawks and P-51 Mustangs, escorting Allied bombers. There were Gurkhas, from Nepal, and the thousands of soldiers from the Indian Army with their British officers, as well as a unit of Jewish soldiers from the British-mandated territory in Palestine. The fighting in Italy seemed to have drawn together the warrior castes of a dozen different ethnic and national sub-groups, such as the Moroccan Goums, fighters from the Atlas mountains. Along with the British and Americans, there were Canadians, Poles, Brazilians, Rhodesians, Greeks, and New Zealanders in the Allied 5th and 8th Armies. But the men from Hawaii, the Japanese-American Nisei, were a unit apart, even among this vast coalition of ethnic and national difference fighting with one common cause.

After landing at Anzio in May 1944, Easy Company of the 2nd Battalion of the 442nd RCT transited to the front via the port of Naples. Never had Inouye seen such poverty or destruction, with children begging for food in the streets and girls selling themselves to passing Allied soldiers. As the honourable son of the Methodist mother from Hawaii, who himself had walked to school barefoot as a child, he was appalled. By late spring he had been promoted to sergeant, and his unit saw its first fighting south of the capital. Easy Company arrived outside Rome on 10 June. It was five days since Lieutenant General Mark Clark had 'liberated' the city – in the face of zero opposition – and four days since the invasion of Normandy had begun. The German armies outside Rome had now escaped north. Inouye and his men were stopped at one of the gates of the capital by MPs, as a unit of American soldiers wearing neckties, polished boots, and ironed uniforms were directed down the road towards the centre of the city. Too scruffy, said the military police detachment, when Inouye requested that his unit be allowed to proceed after them. So the sergeant and his men shouldered their arms and headed north.

While the 100th Battalion served at Anzio and Monte Cassino, the rest of the 442nd saw only sporadic contacts with the enemy in Italy until the end of June, when they linked up with the 100th at the port of Civitavecchia north of Rome. On 25 June, the Japanese Americans prepared to attack the town of Belvedere, in Tuscany. To Inouye's professional pride, he had just been granted the honour of becoming his squad's sniper. There were eleven other men in his squad, and as the best shot of them all, he now carried the Springfield M1903 with its sniper scope. When the 2nd Battalion had been training in the humid pine forests outside Hattiesburg, Mississippi, before deploying to Italy, Inouye had proved the best shot of his entire company. Personally, he found it ironic, because when he was a child back in Hawaii, his Japanese-American mother, a strict Methodist, had refused to let him own even a slingshot. The benefits of being the squad sniper in Italy were mixed: as the best scout in his group, Inouye would go out ahead of his men to reconnoitre the ground before an attack. Not long after arriving in Italy, he had taken part in one such action. Ahead of his men, he had crawled over the top of a drystone wall into a sunken road and crept up a track that led the other side of it. The last section of men that had set off up the road had not returned: there had been several fast, long bursts of German machine-gun fire, a few rifle shots, then silence. The Japanese-American non-commissioned officer had been told to go find out what had happened. So he crawled up the dried dirt of the sunken road, which was little more than a mud cart track. Oak scrub and ilex trees provided shade and some small cover over the top of him, the Springfield rifle cradled under his body as he leopard-crawled. He rounded a corner in the track, as he slid and crawled, the webbing equipment on his belt and chest gathering a coating of the mud of the road, dried grey-brown by the Italian summer. There in front of him was the unit that had gone up the path before him. A tumbled pile of deadness, of jumbled arms and legs and heads and chests, the American soldiers' limbs thrown around in the sprawling way corpses mysteriously adopt. The soldiers' weapons lay scattered on the track. There were flies already. They were all unmistakeably dead.

'We're not going up that road,' Inouye said simply to his platoon lieutenant. 'There's stacks of bodies. We don't need the men to see them.'

With its 24-inch barrel, weighty .30-06 calibre and sights configured up to 2,700 yards, the Springfield M1903 was very accurate, especially with the sniper scope. At only 8½ pounds, it was comparatively light. It had been the US Army's standard issue rifle since 1903, but by the time Inouye and his squad stood in the dust and heat of the Italian summer of 1944, it had been superseded by the M1 Garand. Until the Germans introduced their Sturmgewehr assault rifles in 1944, the Garand, with its 8-round clips, was to prove the fastest-firing semi-automatic rifle of the war on any side; General Patton called it 'the greatest battle implement ever devised'. Inouye, however, was happy with his Springfield, and it hadn't taken long for him to prove his ability to use it. He had been on a patrol shortly after arrival in Italy, moving up the slope of a mountain. With his good eyesight, and his sniper scope, he spotted a German crouching on the top of the neighbouring hill. So he told the patrol to wait, set his sights very carefully, and fired.

'Not only was he my first,' said Inouye, 'I think back with horror because I was proud. We saw propaganda films in training, we were trained to hate the Germans. That's war.'

## THE BATTLE FOR BELVEDERE

As the Germans withdrew up the spine of Italy towards the Gothic Line in June and July 1944, they left behind them a string of temporary defences stretching across the country from east to west. These emplacements were designed to buy them time to get back to their main positions farther north. In the west of Italy, the province of Tuscany borders the Mediterranean, and here these defences followed the river Arno, which runs through Florence. But before the Allied advance could even get to this key city, they had to deal with German positions in the hills and towns of Tuscany that lay to the south. In late June, the American 34th Infantry Division, which included the 442nd RCT, was ordered to take some of these. One of them was the road that led between the small towns of Suvereto and Sassetta, and a key road junction north of it. It lies on an open plain, about fifty-five miles southwest of Florence and fifteen miles from the Mediterranean. It lay on the route the 34th Division was taking north, and it and the high ground surrounding it were the first of a series of objectives for the American unit. The 442nd was given the job of taking the town of Suvereto and the string of hills around it, which the local inhabitants called Belvedere.

The town is set on a low hill, with sand-coloured stone houses, the ubiquitous Italian Catholic church with its steeple and bell tower, and a series of vaulted colonnades from the Middle Ages. From the high ground on Belvedere, the German defenders – some of whom were from an SS battalion – could see the town of Suvereto, the plain in front of it, and the gentle slope of olive groves in clear detail. It was perfect country to defend. And the 442nd Regimental Combat Team had to attack it. It was June, so pink and white oleander were growing and flowering over the walls of the houses and in the patches of land between them. There were grapes and olives growing in the fields and on the slopes of the surrounding hills, and the temperature in the midday sun was about eighty degrees. In the plain that lay between the town and the high ground of Belvedere were fields of maize and wheat, peach and lemon trees, vineyards and olive groves. There was an interlinking series of irrigation ditches, set in trenches four feet deep dug across the small fields, and little cover. The high ground dominating this plain was typical of that which the Allies attacked, and the Germans defended, in that long summer and autumn of 1944. Drystone walls made of chunks of grey rock divided small pieces of land from each other and marched waist-high up the lower slopes of the hills. The earth was red-black, and on the patches of land that had not been cultivated with olives or vines or fruit, the rocks had been gathered by hand by the Italian *contadini,* smallholders, and used for the walls or else piled in heaps in the corners of the fields so the ground could be cultivated. As the gradient rose, the olives and vines gave way to scrubby slopes, covered in more rocks, with stands of pine and oak trees.

On the evening of 25 June three battalions of the 442nd arrived south of the town in lorries and on foot. At their O Groups, or orders briefings, the commanding officer gave the battalion and company commanders their instructions. They in turn went off to brief their platoon commanders and sergeants. The unit prepared for the coming fight. It was the eve of battle. As the sun set over the Tuscan countryside, for the Nisei soldiers it was a moment almost unchanged for 2,000 years, since the Roman legions of Scipio Africanus had sharpened their swords and lances the night before the Battle of Zama in 202 BC, when Hannibal was finally defeated outside Carthage in North Africa.

By the evening of the attack on Belvedere, Daniel Inouye had, in his own words, 'learned to be a good sergeant'. He made the rounds of the eleven other men in his squad, encouraging them, listening to fears and worries, sharing a joke, and keeping an eye on battle preparations. Weapons were cleaned and dried of excess oil. In the fierce summer dust of Italy, too much oil attracted dust and grit, which stuck to the moving parts of weapons, causing them to jam.

Among the twelve infantrymen, they had a good selection of firepower. Their weapons were those of a typical American Army squad in that fourth year of the war. They had a mixture of Garand M1 semi-automatic rifles, and the .30-06 Springfield sniper rifle, now operated by a friend of Inouye's. Then there was one .45 Thompson submachine gun carried by Sergeant Inouye himself, a .30-06 Browning Automatic Rifle, or BAR, and the smaller and lighter .30 calibre M1 carbine. The main supporting firepower of American infantry platoons was the .30 Browning belt-fed machine gun and two-inch mortars and bazookas used for knocking out tanks. These heavier weapons were operated at platoon and company level. The infantry squad was still centred around the firepower of the eight or nine Garands, with the BAR used as a light machine gun. At seventeen pounds, this was heavy, had a powerful recoil, a barrel that overheated quickly, and a small magazine capacity of twenty rounds. But it had excellent stopping power, long range, and in the hands of a well-trained operator was accurate. The M1 carbine was a smaller, semi-automatic weapon issued to junior non-commissioned officers and radio operators.

The German defences around Belvedere, Sassetta, and Suvereto were typical of those that the Allies had encountered time after time all the way from the toe of Italy upward. The morning of 26 June dawned hot and clear. Inouye's squad went into battle just after the sun came up, one of the men so nervous he had kept cleaning and re-cleaning his weapon throughout the night. Inouye tried to keep focused, to keep the bigger tactical picture in his head, while thinking about the men he was leading, the positions he was attacking, the units on his left and right, the gun in his hands, and the sudden hailstorm of incoming German fire. His squad advanced, crouched down, running, stopping, kneeling, lying flat under olive trees, suddenly bogged down in an irrigation ditch, then opening fire, then flat on their faces in cornfields, unable to see anything beyond the ends of their own rifles. They were covered in mud, dust, earth, sweat, and grass. German machine-gun fire whipped through the air in unendingly fast *brrrppps*. Semi-ripe lemons on the trees above the Nisei exploded as bullets stormed through the foliage, bright green leaves and small branches pattering down onto the soldiers taking cover beneath.

And then there was the artillery. The air whistled with the incoming shriek of a shell, then it impacted and exploded, displacing the air around it with a massive percussive *whump* that for several seconds took possession of everything in its immediate vicinity. Inouye discovered what soldiers have known for centuries: battle is terrifyingly, devastatingly noisy. Men were hoarse after less than an hour from shouting at each other. The tearing rips of the German machine guns were interrupted only by the blasting roar of artillery shells, and the sicklier, more contained explosive cracks of mortar rounds. The summer heat made throats parched. The sun was a constant, like the German fire. The plodding wallop of the Browning Automatic Rifles harmonized with the swifter buzzing clack of the Thompsons. Through the middle of the squad, the battle-trained ear could hear the noise of metallic, springy pinging, as the Garand rifles automatically ejected their empty metal magazine clips into the air after each eight shots. And wounded and dying men screamed in agony for their friends, and swore murderously at themselves for being so stupid as to be wounded.

In the chaos, men wondered how on earth it could be possible to keep to any sort of attack plan. Yet somehow Inouye and his men did. When an exploding shell blew parts of his platoon leader into pieces, Inouye found himself without an officer, and he knew that only a cool head, fast movement, and single-minded aggressive forward movement could take the day. His Thompson .45 submachine gun was chewing through the cartridges in the twenty-round magazines as fast as he could depress the trigger. The heavy round had formidable stopping power: the Nisei sergeant shot one German in the ankle, and his whole foot was blown off. Then the squad closed in on the German dug-in positions. The small stone houses of the town and on the slopes of Belvedere provided perfect defences. MG-42s would be in upper windows, often sited farther back inside a room so the muzzles could not be seen protruding. Once a squad reached the walls of a house, it was time for hand grenades. Weighing around a pound each, resembling a small oval pineapple, the Mk 2 fragmentation grenade had a five-second fuse and was activated by pulling out a pin with a ring-pull attached. The spring-loaded fusing lever leaped off, the grenade was armed, and it was hurled. One or two lobbed into a small room of a village house, where the hard stone walls contained the blast and produced hundreds of tiny, flying chips of rock, would silence German defenders. Then the door was breached, a blast of BAR or Thompson fire would go up the stairs and into the entrance, then more grenades, and then the American troopers would storm in. And instantly come face to violent face with screaming, adrenaline-fueled, sweating, camouflaged, battle-eyed men whom they had waited for since the days of training back in the pine forests outside Hattiesburg. The Germans.

The official overview of that day's battle put the fighting into the wider strategic perspective of the fighting in Italy. The 442nd, and the US 34th Infantry Division, were at the far western end of a line of battles just south of the river Arno, itself the gateway to the Gothic Line positions. On the far right of the Allied line, towards the Adriatic, the Polish 2nd Corps was fighting for the port of Ancona: its capture would give the Allies a vitally needed port closer to their front lines. Then, moving from east to west, came the Canadians, New Zealanders, Indians, British, and South Africans who were fighting up the centre towards Florence, which lay on the Arno. A tiny speck in these hundreds of thousands of troops, Inouye and his eleven men were in the far west. Their next mission? To make a fighting advance up the Mediterranean coast and take the seaside town of Livorno. This was as vital to the Allies as Ancona, as it would give them control of a major port on their western flank, 200 miles farther north than Anzio, from where their supplies were currently flowing.

At Belvedere, all three battalions of the 442nd Regimental Combat Team were in action. The essence of their victory was simple: they outflanked the Germans, blocked their exit from the town and the high ground around it, and pushed the German defenders into blocking positions formed by each company. The 100th Infantry Battalion fought so well that it received a Presidential Unit Citation, first proof that the Nisei, who'd started their military life as second-rate citizens, had proved their worth. 'All three companies went into action, boldly facing murderous fire from all types of weapons and tanks and at times fighting without artillery support . . . The stubborn desire of the men to close with a numerically superior enemy and the rapidity with which they fought enabled the 100th Infantry Battalion to destroy completely the right flank positions of a German Army . . . The fortitude and intrepidity displayed by the officers and men of the 100th Infantry Battalion reflect the finest traditions of the Army of the United States.'

As night fell over Belvedere on 26 June, and he gulped down some hot food, drank water, and cleaned his Thompson, Sergeant Daniel Inouye didn't know that the unit had achieved such a strategic success. All he knew was that he was still alive.

# 5

## INDIANS ON THE ROAD TO FLORENCE

### July and August 1944

By July 1944, the Germans and the Japanese were putting up dogged and stubborn resistance in Europe, in the Pacific, on the Russian Front, and in Italy, but they were losing. In the Pacific, the Americans had taken the key island of Saipan, and off the Mariana Islands they had won a naval victory over the Japanese, dubbed the 'Great Marianas Turkey Shoot'. Two hundred Japanese aircraft were shot down, compared to 29 American ones. In Burma, British and Commonwealth forces had defeated the Japanese at Kohima. But the most decisive victory was won by the Red Army in Belorussia, north of the Ukraine, on Operation *Bagration*. An entire German Army group was destroyed in late June, the largest single successful operation against the German Wehrmacht Heer of the war. And in Normandy, the British and Americans had finally broken out of their beachhead after they captured the town of Caen. A boa constrictor of massively superior air power, economic might, and troop numbers was laying its coils around Nazi Germany and Japan and starting to tighten them.

Four weeks after Sergeant Daniel Inouye and the men of the 442nd had fought the battle of Belvedere in central Italy, the Allied front line

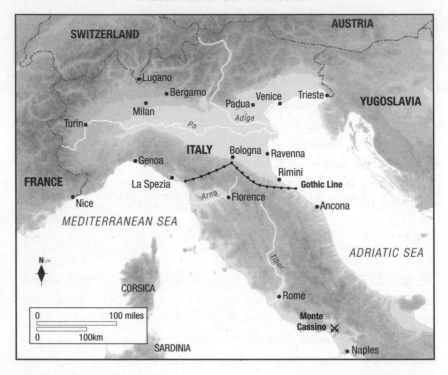

had crept steadily northward towards the next German defensive position. By late July 1944, this was loosely strung along the river Arno, which leads from the old Tuscan city of Florence westward to the Mediterranean. It was the last set of German defences before the Gothic Line itself.

Of the many Allied units advancing up western Italy that summer, one of them came from in and around Bombay, on the western coast of India, on the Arabian Sea. And in the days before the battle for the liberation for Florence began, this particular unit found itself suddenly billeted in a beautiful old Tuscan castle. There, many of the Indian soldiers saw a naked woman for the first time.

This unit advancing towards Florence was a battalion of the Maratha Light Infantry, which had arrived in Italy in September 1943. One of their junior officers was an acting captain named Eustace D'Souza, of Indian and Portuguese descent. As the battalion approached Florence, in August, a task arrived out of the blue. C Company of the 1st Battalion, the Maratha Light Infantry had paused by the side of a road in the hot sun. They had been marching from their last bivouac position, walking along a road lined with cypress trees and occasional small chapels, then through vineyards where the vivid green of the leaves had not yet been flattened by the scorching heat. Runners, grasping signals forms in their dusty, mud-stained hands, dashed to deliver them to the company's officers. They had received an urgent assignment: to occupy and protect a palazzo southwest of Florence, the Castello di Montegufoni.[1]

The Indian soldiers were sitting at the side of a road, trying to find some shade, sipping from their water bottles, listening carefully for the incoming whistle of German mortar rounds attracted by their dust. When the orders arrived, they pulled themselves to their feet and changed their course of march. 'Nearing the river [Arno] the Mahrattas turned southeast on a non-military mission to secure the castle of the Chesterfield Sitwells at Montegufoni. Here the priceless art treasures of the Florentine galleries were stored, including Botticelli's *Primavera* and other of the world's most famous paintings.'[2]

The castle that awaited them was like nothing they had ever seen before. Amid ordered stands of cypress trees, its walls of golden stone surrounded a central courtyard where pomegranate trees were growing. It belonged to an aristocratic British family, the Sitwells, and dated from before 1500. It was as old as the Renaissance, and in 1909 Sir George Sitwell had bought it for his son Osbert. German detachments were now dug in within a mile of the castle. The Marathas suspected that the dust being raised the other side of a vineyard came from their most feared enemy: a German Tiger tank. So the Indians were quick to make the Montegufoni palace their own. Tin helmets were hung on top of medieval suits of armour in a hall of weapons that had once heard Cosimo de' Medici's footfall. In a long row of pikes and halberds, one

Maratha leaned his Bren gun, modern blued gunmetal lying next to medieval steel. Guards were posted, positions prepared in front of the castle. Artillery bombardments thumped against the night sky as the Italian summer dusk closed in, lighting the undersides of the clouds in vast orange flashes. The world was at war.

Some of the men under D'Souza's command that night were no older than sixteen. One young Maratha, when standing at attention, was barely taller than his Lee–Enfield .303 rifle with its attached eighteen-inch bayonet.

Now they were billeted in and around the sumptuous Castello di Montegufoni, their job to keep Italian and German looters at bay, as well as SS tanks. The Germans had occupied the castle before them. They had stored some 260 works of art, which they had removed from the Uffizi and Pitti galleries in Florence, in the cellars. These included Sandro Botticelli's 1482 masterpiece *Primavera,* the Allegory of Spring. If the Indians could prevent the Germans and Italian Fascists from stealing any more of the world's finest art, their deployment away from the battle line would be worth it. And the dark, dusty corridors of the palace, with its vast cellars and basements, were full of strange and new surprises.

After posting his guard, acting captain D'Souza was making his rounds in the gardens full of mandarin trees. He had a sergeant with him, and the two of them were approaching the palace, walking down a path, their booted feet crunching through deep cream-coloured gravel, when they heard an Indian soldier giggling. D'Souza went up to him and asked him what was the matter. The soldier told him. They followed him down dusty stairs into one of the cavernous cellars, and the first thing they heard was a lot of Indian men giggling shyly. A young soldier approached them: the other Marathas, he said, had found 'naked women'. D'Souza was immediately concerned and alarmed: there were two things that in Italy could lead to a total breakdown of any relations between the Allies and the Italians, who since 1943 were fighting predominantly on their side. One was artillery or aerial attacks on consecrated ground – which led to the Germans often using churches and cemeteries as defensive positions – and the other was any inappropriate treatment of Italian women. But the Indians had developed a good reputation for politeness and kindness to Italian civilians, so D'Souza didn't immediately worry that his men might be raping captured Italians. He walked forward, into the musty darkness, and heard one of his men say in Marathi that he'd 'never seen a woman without her clothes'. In front of him was a circle of Indian soldiers looking at Botticelli's *The Birth of Venus* and other pictures by some of the most famous painters of the Renaissance, tittering as they studied the perfectly painted breasts and behinds of naked fifteenth-century women.

The Marathas made a report about their discovery, and the next day two Indian Army regimental historians arrived, along with some Maratha officers and two British journalists, Eric Linklater and Wynford Vaughan-Thomas. D'Souza says that Linklater, who had been based in Bombay in the 1920s, wrote an inscription in the castle's visitors' book thanking the Marathas. One of D'Souza's fellow officers was to say later that signatures of Karl Marx, D. H. Lawrence, and Stalin were also in the book.[5] In later accounts, the two journalists claimed they had arrived at the castle the day before the Indians and tipped them off. The American writer Robert Edsel, author of *The Monuments Men*, credits an American, Frederick Hartt, with discovering the artwork after the Indian soldiers had left.

## THE MARATHAS AND THEIR FIGHT UP ITALY

The Marathas had travelled 4,000 miles to go to war in Italy. For most of them, it was the first time they had left their home state. They are from a long line of Indian warriors, their heritage 500 years old. They come predominantly from the western Indian states of Maharashtra, Madhya Pradesh, Gujarat, and Goa, which stretch around the mountains surrounding Mumbai, then Bombay, on the Arabian Sea. Maharashtra is tiger country: fierce, wooded mountains; sharp ravines with plunging rock faces; sweeping forests of ilex trees; hot and bright in the dry season, muddy and dark in the thunderous rains of the monsoon. It was like the Apennines of central Italy. They were just one of a huge variety of Allied units from some twenty-eight different countries, including Daniel Inouye and the Nisei, Scottish Highlanders and Nepalese Gurkhas, closing in on the River Arno. By this stage in the war, both sides were putting uniforms on everybody and anybody they could: the Germans had Turkomans, Russians, and captured Poles fighting with them. The British even had Poles who had fought for Poland in 1939, been captured, fought for the Germans, been recaptured by the Allies, and then sent to Italy.

D'Souza had arrived with his exhausted men from the 1st Battalion of the Marathas ten miles outside Florence on 29 July, in the operation to liberate the town on the Arno River. The soldiers were so covered in dust that one Indian officer said he couldn't remember what colour his skin was anymore. Exhaustion seemed to be in their bones. The only thing about the soldiers that was clean were their .303 Lee–Enfield rifles, Bren guns, and .45 Thompson submachine guns. Captain D'Souza's men were just one unit in the three Indian Army divisions – the 4th, 8th, and 10th – that were fighting in the British 8th Army, the Desert Rats, in Italy.

D'Souza himself was twenty-three that burning summer; he had been born in 1921 in Bombay, the capital of Maharashtra state. The grandson of Portuguese immigrants, he'd been educated and brought up by Spanish Jesuits from the Philippines who ran a high school on Hill Road in Bandra, a suburb of Bombay on the edge of the Arabian Sea. The school's motto was 'Born for Greater Things', something he remembered during an audience with Pope Pius XII in St Peter's after the liberation of Rome. Waiting to walk through into the audience chamber in the Vatican, D'Souza glanced at a visitors' book. The pope had received a Gestapo delegation only a month before.

The Jesuit high school imbued D'Souza with the values of self-sacrifice, determination, and service to others and to the community. The British Empire and the Indian Army did the rest. His sense of aggression, fair play, and tactics was focused on the hockey field. D'Souza joined the Indian Army as soon as he could after the outbreak of war, originally imagining 'without really thinking about it, that we'd go off and defend the British Empire in India against the Japanese'. But after being commissioned in 1943, he spent four months with his regiment as a young officer, and then three months of jungle training in central India saw him earmarked for a unit that was to fight in Burma. But as he remembers, 'We got the shock of our lives when we were told we had to proceed to Italy to join the First Battalion that had suffered very heavy casualties. Four of us officers were shipped to Italy.'

They left Bombay on a troop ship in March 1944, and on arrival in Port Suez, the four officers were packed onto a steaming hot train that chugged across the desert to Cairo. They spent a month in the Egyptian capital waiting. By the beginning of that year, the city was considerably less crowded with soldiers than it had been in 1942 and '43, at the height of the desert fighting with the Germans and Italians. There was little to do except to wait for news of transport, which turned out to be a Polish cruise liner that had been converted into a troop ship. D'Souza sailed across the Mediterranean, landing at the port of Taranto. Keen to move out of the transit camp, where he was posted to serve as the assistant adjutant, D'Souza asked to speak to the second in command of the battalion, an Anglo-Indian colonel named Henderson Brooks. More than fifty years later, D'Souza hadn't forgotten that meeting. 'Brooks told me, "So you are D'Souza who will be going to join the First Battalion." I said, "Sir, I am fed up of waiting." He said, 'My dear boy, you don't know what war is.'"

Shortly afterward, he learned. He travelled north on a troop train in time to take part in the third battle of Monte Cassino. They were given the job of launching a bridge across the fast-flowing River Gari. D'Souza ordered two of his sepoys to swim across it, under direct observation from the German defensive positions. The Poles, Free French, and Canadians were able to cross the bridge that the engineers then built, in time for the third main attack on the slopes of Cassino. After the battle, those soldiers who had survived were simply glad to be alive. They had slogged through the gluey mud of the slopes around the destroyed abbey. The shredded corpses of pack mules hung in the trees. Advancing uphill, they had looked into the blank, staring faces of their comrades coming out of the line.

D'Souza moved again, this time up to Perugia, arriving in mid-July. That had been the worst time. He was allocated to the battalion's C Company, as second in command to a British tea planter from the hills of Assam, Major Jimmy Winter. The company then advanced northeast up the spine of Italy as the Germans fought what D'Souza described as 'a beautiful rearguard action'.

This type of warfare suited Indian troops. It reminded the men of the fighting on the North-West Frontier. The Marathas' ancestors had been soldiers and tribal fighters for 500 years. But if naked women were something new to the men of the Maratha Light Infantry, the climate and terrain in Italy were not. These were mountain men, used to the extremities of the weather. Their unit, one of the oldest and most prestigious in the Indian Army, had been formed in 1768; it had fought both with and against the British in India. Thirty battalions of the MLI were formed in World War II. Service to the crown, to Empire, and to their long-dead Emperor Shivaji were their guiding principles. They charged into battle with the cry *'Bol Shri Chhatrapati Shivaji Maharaj ki Jai!'* (Cry Victory to Emperor Shivaji). They, and the Gurkhas in particular, terrified the Germans. They came out of the dark, they said, you couldn't see them, and they were completely unafraid.

The fighting against German defensive positions in Italy was little different from warfare in Roman times: it consisted, at its most basic, of climbing up rocky mountains, getting close to the enemy, and killing him, often in hand-to-hand fighting. The wiry and resilient Indian and Nepalese soldiers like the Marathas and Gurkhas were adept at this. D'Souza was by no means the first army officer to recognize this tactical aptitude. The British soldier and author Lieutenant Colonel John Masters won the DSO in the war on a Chindit operation. Born in India, he had first served as a subaltern with the Gurkhas in 1938 in Waziristan (now part of Pakistan, whose mountainous redoubts on the Afghan border are the Taliban's operational hideaway). Masters described the Indian and northern Indian tribes like the Waziris as 'physically the hardest people on earth'.[4]

The Marathas, too, had had moments when extreme gallantry had turned the course of battle, and had been rewarded. Again, in the clipped and understated words of an official citation, one soldier from the Marathas' 5th Battalion had taken matters into his own hands: 'On 10th July 1944 in the Upper Tiber Valley, Italy, a rifle section commanded by Naik Yeshwant Ghadge came under heavy machine-gun fire at close range, which killed or wounded all members of the section except the commander. Without hesitation Naik Yeshwant Ghadge rushed the machine-gun position, first throwing a grenade which knocked out the machine-gun and firer and then he shot one of the gun crew. Finally, having no time to change his magazine, he clubbed to death the two remaining members of the crew. He fell mortally wounded, shot by an enemy sniper.'

Ghadge was awarded a posthumous Victoria Cross, one of several members of the Maratha Light Infantry to win Great Britain and the Commonwealth's highest award in the fighting in Italy. In another heroic action, a nineteen-year-old trooper, his unit pinned down by an MG-42 machine-gun position barricaded behind a line of rocks, ran forward towards the German gun. He crouched under the lee of the rocks as the gun fired over his head, then jumped up, pulling the barrel of the Spandau out of the firer's hands, severely burning his own palms in the process. He turned the weapon on the two men behind it, machine-gunning both of the Germans instantly, and then shot a German officer in the chest. When the ammunition belt ran out, he reversed the weapon and clubbed another man to death, taking a bullet himself in the chest. Before dying, the Marathi waved the rest of his section forward, indicating that the route was clear. He didn't receive an award, says D'Souza, although the feeling in the company was that a VC, or at least a Distinguished Conduct Medal, would have been in order. After his death, said D'Souza, 'We all just sort of got on with things.'

Along with the Sikhs and Gurkhas serving in the Indian divisions, the Marathas knew how to turn the hostile terrain to their advantage. They were accustomed to climbing and scrambling over such terrain at night, chasing goats, running from tigers, outwitting British redcoats in the early days of the Raj, or just living their lives in the Ghat mountains that rise sharp and severe 100 miles east of Bombay.

The weather was an obstacle: autumn and winter rain and mud meant that boots and clothing were constantly filthy, feet rarely completely dry. The leather 'ammunition' boots with hobnailed soles that the British and Indian soldiers wore dried very slowly. The 37 Webbing equipment the men wore was the same: it was made of cotton webbing, waterproofed and dyed before being woven. It was tough and durable, but when wet it became hard and unpliable. The summer brought different challenges – heat and dust, exhausting humidity and, in the low-lying areas, the ubiquitous mosquitoes. The Marathas, like all the Indians, were no strangers to hot weather in mountainous terrain, and summer in Italy was certainly no hotter than the scorching plains of India. Their resilience and habituation to the climate and terrain was one reason why their tactical and operational performance on the Italian battlefield proved so exceptional.

So in their Renaissance billet, D'Souza's men dug in and waited for orders. Bren guns were mounted in the windows of the castle, and on the edges of the vineyards, slit trenches were dug in the Tuscan loam. Similar to hundreds of thousands of Allied soldiers around them, the Indian positions were a mix of Lee–Enfield rifles, .303 ammunition, knapsacks, water bottles, shovels, and army blankets. Most Indian and British soldiers, who used the same basic equipment, modified it, particularly in the field. In the hot summer, water and access to it was paramount, so soldiers carried one water bottle on their belts, another one or two in their backpacks, and sometimes an additional one in a musette bag slung around the neck. Frequent stops by streams and rivers enabled them to refill their bottles.

In the backpack, extra ammunition was also carried – .303 calibre rounds for the Brens and Lee–Enfields, .45 cartridges for the Thompsons. Two hundred rounds of .303 ammunition weighed around twelve pounds, and most of the men in an Indian or British infantry section also carried at least another 100 rounds, normally in three full magazines for the Bren gun. Additional rifle ammunition was slung around the neck in a pre-packed bandolier containing 50 or 100 rounds. They carried food, signal flares, cigarettes, socks, small religious icons from home, and medical kits. D'Souza had one breast pocket with his ID card and Bible in it, and the pockets of his shorts were filled with cartridges for his pistol.

Other equipment carried by the Indians – and most Allied units – included entrenching tools, picks and shovels, that sat on the small of the back and jogged and bumped as the men ran. Officers carried pistols, normally .38 or .45 Webley revolvers, though as everywhere, captured Lugers and Walthers from German officers were prized. Although seized Schmeisser machine pistols were a trophy, men were careful not to use them in any action where their signature muzzle report could lead to the firer being mistaken by his own side for a German. They were mostly used behind the lines where no other Allied troops were present. Many British and Commonwealth sergeants and officers carried Thompson submachine guns, the soldiers the ever-trusted .303 Lee–Enfield rifle, heavy, reliable, and extremely accurate. And when it came to attacking German positions at close range, an eighteen-inch bayonet was fixed. The .303 rifle was prized for its accuracy. In northern Burma in 1944, a bridge had to be blown as the Japanese were crossing it. A British engineer officer had to hit a fuse of gun cotton, or nitrocellulose, at 900 yards to blow the bridge. So accurate was the Lee–Enfield, he did it with his first shot. This was the most accurate and reliable personal weapon, and with its magazine capacity of ten rounds, it proved a superior weapon to the German Mauser K98. It was faster and easier to use because of its bolt design, more accurate, had greater range, didn't jam, and could fire a lot of bullets, twenty to thirty in one minute.

## THE ROAD TO THE GOTHIC LINE

The route that D'Souza's men of the Maratha Light Infantry had marched and fought from the mountains and plains of southern Italy, from Monte Cassino to Florence, mirrored the actions of the Allied forces since they had invaded the mainland on 3 September 1943. The battles south and north of Rome – Monte Cassino, Lake Trasimene – had followed. They had shouldered their loads, fought their battles, and slogged up the mountainous spine of Italy and through the rivers and plains that surrounded it. The combat was unforgiving. In December 1943, on the Osento River, Indians and English infantrymen went head-to-head against German paratroopers in a typical engagement:

> From house to house, from cellar to loft, from one rubble pile to the next, the [infantry] and the [German] paratroopers hunted each other to the death. Quick, deadly encounters marked every yard of progress. A British section races for the shelter of a blind wall. Bren gunners edge cautiously round the corner to the door. A kick shoots it open; Tommy guns spray the hall and stairs; the remainder of the section spring to the windows, and roll grenades over the sills. On the blast of the bombs the Tommy gunners charge inside to the close. In the cellar, on the stairs, under the eaves, Germans are dead and dying. With all speed the British section mans observation posts from which to rake the next house, and to cover their own approaches. Often they are too late. German paratroopers emerge from a near-by hide-out, and crawl stealthily into the shelter of the blind wall. Once again the battered door bursts in. Bullets hose the hall and stairway, and the house rocks with the shock of grenades. Over the sprawled bodies of British and Germans, the paratroopers feverishly mount their weapons to meet the next assault, which may be only minutes away. The Indians entered the village to find a shambles, with dead Germans sprawled on the rubble heaps, in the entrances to dug-outs, or floating in water-filled slit trenches. Villa Grande, as one correspondent put it, looked 'as though a giant had trodden on a child's box of blocks.' Out of this desolation emerged men, women and children – the villagers who had cowered in cellars and crypts while the battle raged above them. They stared unbelievingly at the insane tangle of wreckage which was all that remained of their homes. A simple community had been threshed under the flail of war.[5]

So by 30 July 1944, the 1st Battalion of the Marathas found itself outside Florence, just one among dozens of Allied units that had advanced as far as they could that month. Telegrams among Churchill, Roosevelt, and Stalin ricocheted back and forth that summer like strategic pinballs. In Normandy, the Allies had broken the armoured gridlock around the town of Caen and were about to break out of their bridgehead, streaming across northeastern France towards Belgium. A group of German Army officers had tried – and failed – to assassinate Hitler on 20 July. The Russians had advanced into Poland.

So Roosevelt and Eisenhower wanted to open a second front somewhere to help the advance in Normandy. They suggested two possible landing sites – in the south of France outside Nice on the Mediterranean, and on the western Atlantic coast on the Bay of Biscay. Roosevelt favoured the second; he said it would be easier to deploy American reinforcements directly from the eastern seaboard of the continental United States. Eisenhower opted for the French Riviera, diverting Allied units straight from Italy. Churchill – and the Vatican – disagreed with both and wanted to invade the Balkans, from where Allied troops could advance around the east of the Alps into Austria, occupying Yugoslavia and keeping southeastern Europe out of Soviet hands. The Vatican was particularly keen on the latter and used its diplomatic influence with the Allies to press this point. The Soviets' massive summer offensive was meanwhile in full swing, stretching from the Baltic in the north to Romania in the south. Stalin was desperate to occupy the latter: he could seize its large oil fields and cut off Hitler's main source of fuel oil at a crucial point in the war. The Germans were fighting desperately in the west and the east. They had forty-three divisions in Italy and Yugoslavia – roughly 500,000 men – whom they vitally needed to reinforce both these western and eastern fronts. If the Allies could tie down these men fighting in southeastern Europe and northern Italy, Hitler would be overstretched and overexposed on three major fronts simultaneously. This was a major reason why Churchill advocated an attack into Yugoslavia. If, however, the Allies diverted troops to invade southern or western France, it would take the pressure off Hitler in Italy, no landings could take place in Yugoslavia, and all the Germans would have to do was blockade northern Italy at the Gothic Line, and then draw the Allies inexorably towards a naturally designed battlefield of their own making.

The Allies had the chance, in late July 1944, to profoundly affect the political and strategic layout of southeastern Europe for better or worse, and to halt the spread of the Soviet Union. Unable to reach a consensus, the Americans and British made the weaker call. On 10 August, having diverted seven experienced divisions from Italy, the Allies launched Operation *Anvil*. They made amphibious and paratroop landings on the French Riviera outside Nice. The pressure on Hitler eased. Stalin was given a free hand. And the bloody, lengthy battle of the Gothic Line, and the struggle for northern Italy, became a certainty.

The US 5th Army's commander, General Mark Clark, bitterly disagreed with Roosevelt and Eisenhower, and despite his antipathy towards Harold Alexander, he for once sided strongly with the British. In Rome in July, he wrote in his diary:

> The Boche is defeated and demoralised. Now is the time to exploit our success. Yet, in the middle of this success, I lose two corps headquarters and seven divisions. It just doesn't make sense . . . A campaign that might have changed the whole history of relations between the Western world and the Soviet Union was permitted to fade away, not into nothing, but into much less than it could have been. Not alone in my opinion, but in the opinion of a number of experts who were close to the problem, the weakening of the campaign in Italy in order to invade southern France, instead of pushing on into the Balkans, was one of the outstanding political mistakes of the war.[6]

With nearly 100,000 experienced troops pulled out of Italy, units like the Marathas and the 442nd RCT near Florence found themselves overstretched, just part of the Allied line now facing two German armies and several German divisions dug into extremely well-prepared defensive positions. So what strategic choices did this leave the Allies? Outflanking the Gothic Line by seaborne landings was one option; breaking through it and spreading out into the flatlands of the Po valley and the province of Emilia-Romagna was another. A third option was to do both, to simultaneously coordinate attacks on the German rear by thousands of Italian partisans directed by the American OSS and the British SOE. Little did the Germans know, but by August, with Operation *Dragoon* well under way in France, the Allies were not going to be doing any outflanking into the Balkans. They also had too few landing craft to stage amphibious landings into northern Italy. So their only choice was to go head-on at the Gothic Line and use the partisans to maximum effect in the rear. The stage was set.

## THE LIBERATION OF FLORENCE

The liberation of Florence, when it came, was fast, messy, and chaotic. There was an armoured dash by Allied Sherman tanks for one of the last bridges over the Arno that the Germans hadn't blown. Then street fighting. Film footage shows a squad of Allied infantry dashing across a road, covered by a Bren gunner behind a tree. Italian partisans in civilian clothes, red bandannas around their necks, edge cautiously through the suburbs, Mauser K98 rifles and captured Schmeisser machine pistols in hand. They lie on the ground at street corners to look for snipers. Then flurries of shots. The whiplash stutter of a German MG-42, then silence as a bleeding partisan, arm lolling over the side, is carried to cover, a broken door pressed into service as a makeshift stretcher. A German paratrooper sprawls dead on the street, legs splayed, face down, a thick coagulation of blood draining from a head wound. And then the explosion of Italian civilians jumping up and down and cheering as Allied troops, the Indian Marathas among them, wind through the streets, tank hatches open, the cautious light infantrymen with their eyes on the roofs around them and their Lee–Enfields at the shoulder. Gurkhas advance warily, scanning the windows and roofs for snipers, treading carefully where mines are suspected. They dart from corner to corner: ahead is heard the clatter of machine guns. Italian partisans turn up, warning of booby traps, furious at the damage to their beloved city. The Florentines begin to appear at windows, cheering the Gurkhas. People throng the streets, picking their way through miles of rubble, to queue up for water or to gaze angrily at the destruction. The Marathas and the Gurkhas had come into Florence alongside the armoured cars of the King's Dragoon Guards, a predominantly Welsh cavalry unit, supporting the 8th Indian Infantry Brigade and the Italian partisans.

The Germans had blown all the bridges over the Arno with the exception of the Ponte Vecchio, where they had blown down the houses on each side of the streets approaching the bridge. Allied tanks crossed over via a weir, helped by Royal Engineers, as German 80mm mortars rained down on them. (This weapon was estimated to have caused more Allied casualties in Italy than any other.)[7] A Dragoon squadron commander set up his headquarters over a bar in Piazza Vittorio Emanuele, where he was to support the Indians and partisans who were clearing the city. When the Engineers building a Bailey bridge across the Arno at the Ponte Santa Trìnita were being harassed by sniper fire from Italian Fascist troops, a Dragoon sniper killed the sniper with a single shot into his position at an upstairs window. The liberated city was full of civilians, out in the streets during the day, but at night German paratroopers and Italian Fascist troops came out. The fighting outside and into the city was intense – by 20 August, when the King's Dragoon Guards went back into reserve near Lake Trasimene, one of its units received its fifth squadron commander in five months. Each major was lasting an average of four weeks in combat before being killed, wounded, or replaced.

During the next few days, a number of Germans and even German tanks came out onto the cobbled streets of Florence. Eight Italian policemen, from the carabinieri loyal to Mussolini, were shot dead. On Piazza Vasari, German infantrymen and two Panther tanks drove towards houses where the Maratha Light Infantry was in position – they opened fire, then retreated. A group of German *fallschirmjäger* (paratroopers) confronted some British infantrymen from the Royal West Kents: both sides opened fire, without casualties. But by 16 August, the British brigade that had liberated the city was relieved. Florence was in the hands of the Allies. Now there was nothing between them and the enormous German defences of the Gothic Line.

# 6

## BLOOD AND HONOUR

### *Partisans and the SS on*
### *the Road North*

### August 1944

Arrigo Paladini and the partisans had been busy. It was seven weeks since the scholarly resistance leader had cheated death by jumping from the truck full of condemned men. He had put on weight in liberated Rome, thanks in part to eating as much as he could of an ad hoc wartime version of spaghetti carbonara. This was made from mixing pasta with the tinned chopped ham and eggs that American soldiers gave him from their K-ration packs. He had seen the summer sunshine and woken up each morning at least halfway sure that he might live to see the following one. Other partisans from the Radio Victoria network that the OSS ran in Rome had not been so lucky. At least eighteen had been executed, either at the Ardeatine Caves in March or as the Germans pulled out of Rome. Paladini was now working with the OSS as it recruited, trained, and dispatched parties of agents northward behind German lines. For the partisans, insurrection and sabotage north of the Arno was the order of the day.

The Office of Strategic Services was working in loosely coordinated tandem and occasional competition with the British SOE. The Special Operations Executive handled British covert intelligence work in Italy along with the British Foreign Office's spy network, the Secret Intelligence Service. The British were based at a training centre at Monopoli, north of Brindisi on the Adriatic coast; the OSS, in Rome, Naples, and Corsica. Like the British, Paladini and the Americans had three priorities. First, to recruit potential political and partisan leaders from the mass of anti-fascist Italians who could now live and operate in Allied-controlled areas, and to train them for covert operations. These men and women were then inserted ahead of the ever-advancing Allied lines, north of the river Arno, by parachute, submarine, on foot, or by fast patrol boat. Second, they were gathering information from Italian partisans prepared to cross the German lines into British or American territory. Third, by August 1944, it was clear that the Russians, British, Americans, and their League of Nations allies were going to win the war. What became of Italy after the war was now a pressing concern. If the Germans could destroy any significant part of the economic powerhouse that was northern Italy – Turin, Milan, Genoa, Bologna – the country, bereft of its hydroelectric, banking, and manufacturing infrastructure, could emerge bankrupt from the conflict and easily fragment in a regional civil war. With a full frontal attack on the Gothic Line now inevitable, and any outflanking invasion of the Balkans out of the question, the Allies were effectively opening a second front in Italy, behind the lines of the Germans and Mussolini's Fascists.

## THE GERMAN STRATEGY

Whereas the Allies had been divided among themselves over their strategic objectives, the Germans in contrast enjoyed a political and military unity of focus. By July 1944, the Germans in Italy knew they weren't going to be reinforced. Russia, Poland, the fighting in eastern Europe and in France had made sure of that. A rugged and drawn-out defence, followed by a gradual fighting withdrawal to Austria and the

Alps, was thus their basic strategic plan, helped by their strong defensive positions and the high ground. Their tanks were better, their anti-tank weapons were better, and in their individual troop units, as in those of the Allies, morale was variable. But it was their command of the defensive that gave them the advantage in the battle for the Gothic Line. Two key factors, however, had the power to undermine this: partisan attacks from the rear and in rear areas, and the superiority in artillery, air power, and men that the Allies possessed.

Kesselring's men were effectively fighting a three-front war. First, having to respond to the increasingly erratic strategic edicts of Berlin, from Hitler, Himmler, and the OKW (Oberkommando der Wehrmacht, the Supreme Command of the Armed Forces), led by Wilhelm Keitel. Second, having to confront the Allies in head-on infantry and tank assaults, supported by enormous aerial and artillery firepower. And third, having to deal with the thousands of Italian partisans in their rear areas. Since Kesselring had issued his anti-bandit orders in September 1943, the partisans knew they were dead if captured, so they had little to lose.

The paratroopers, SS soldiers, and Wehrmacht men needed to hold the Gothic Line positions for as long as possible, to pin down as many Allied troops in Italy as they could, and prevent their advancing into Austria, and thence Bavaria, eastward into Yugoslavia and Hungary, and north into eastern France. With a group of loyal Italian Fascist units fighting with them, they had five principal strategic and operational aims. To block the Allies at Rimini, Bologna, and La Spezia, on the Mediterranean, and bog them down until spring 1945 in the mud and mountains of the Apennines. Second, to fight anti-partisan operations, committing atrocities as deemed necessary to subdue the civilian population and intimidate the resistance fighters, in territory they controlled on and behind the Gothic Line, keeping the areas under German and Mussolini's Italian Fascist control. Third, to deport to concentration camps as many of Italy's Jews and Communists as possible, and loot as much art and economic materiel as they could; by the summer of 1944, this had largely been achieved. Fourth, there was already a circle of officers within the SS who wanted to cement postwar escape routes out of Italy towards South America for senior SS and Nazi party members. Last, unknown to Hitler and the loyal circle at the OKW, some senior officers knew they had to make preparations for the post-war intelligence and political cooperation they saw coming, with the Allies against the Russians.

## THE ITALIAN PARTISANS AND THE SAN POLO MASSACRE

Eugenio Calò, a Sephardic Jew from Pisa, was second in command of the Pio Borri Brigade that operated in the Tuscan mountains east of Florence. His wife, Carolina, and three children were detained by the Germans at Fossoli detention centre in May 1944, and then put on a train to Auschwitz.[1] Carolina gave birth to their fourth child in a railway wagon. She and the family were gassed immediately on arrival in Poland. At the beginning of July 1944, Calò and his men captured some thirty German prisoners, and, despite the demands of his men that they be given a summary trial and then be executed – Italian partisans were, after all, shot immediately by the Germans – Calò refused. He insisted on taking the prisoners across the German front line and handing them over to the Allies at Cortona, southwest of Arezzo. This was a suicidal undertaking: if stopped by German troops, Calò and his men would be shot on the spot. They passed radio messages to the OSS in Rome, via Arrigo Paladini's network. They informed the Americans that they were bringing the prisoners over for identification, crossed the two front lines, and delivered them.[2]

General Mark Clark had meanwhile asked for two partisan volunteers to cross back over the front lines and coordinate the arrival of the Allies into Arezzo on 14 July. The Allies were increasingly taking this tactical approach: the stronger they could make the partisans in each area, they reckoned, the easier it would be to coordinate the takeover of each Italian town. Calò volunteered. This mission was successful, but on the night of 14 July, he, a group of Italian civilians, some partisans, and another group of German prisoners were captured by German Wehrmacht soldiers near the village of San Polo. Despite orders, by no means did all German units execute their partisan prisoners, or terrorize civilians supporting them, but this particular army unit did. The partisans, along with some forty-eight of the village men, were taken to two villas that had been requisitioned by the Germans. Tortured almost to death, in the late afternoon the partisans and village men were taken into a field behind one of the houses. The civilians were made to dig three pits in the dry earth, baked hard by the sun. They were forced to lie in them alive: the partisans were placed in the pits, heads above ground, explosive charges were attached to their bodies, and then they were blown apart.

The following day, Sherman tanks of a British armoured unit, the 1st Derbyshire Yeomanry, pulled back into San Polo after coming under heavy shellfire on the road north: they immediately discovered what had happened the previous day, and alerted the British Intelligence Corps. A Field Security Section was dispatched a mile northwest of Arezzo to the cornfields and olive groves of San Polo, which lay at the foot of the wooded hills overlooking the town. The men from the intelligence unit had been billeted on mattresses on the marble floor of a hotel lobby in Arezzo. On arrival in San Polo, they met several partisans, who showed them the mass graves.

'There was no disguising the horror that had taken place,' said one member of the section afterward. 'Scraps of cloth hung on trees and there was the indescribable stench of death in the air. The partisans led us through the deserted village to a house that had been used by the German troops. We searched in the litter and debris but failed to find anything that could identify the unit responsible for these dreadful murders. However, with Teutonic thoroughness, all evidence had been destroyed or removed. Deeply saddened, we took leave of the partisans to rejoin our section, frustrated to the extreme that our efforts had been in vain, and no-one would be brought to justice for this horrific deed.'[3]

In the version given by the parish priest, he told the British tankmen that the day before the Germans withdrew, they had taken all the men of the village, except himself, to a nearby olive grove behind the house they had requisitioned, made them dig three large graves, and then bayoneted the men into the graves and placed a number of explosive charges among the dead and dying.

With their new weapons, Allied liaison officers, and aggressive agenda, the partisans now carried out more and more attacks. The Germans responded in kind, translating Kesselring's orders into a ruthless scorched-earth policy with appalling human consequences. This in turn encouraged the partisans and accelerated their operations. They had nothing to lose. The cogwheels of war often spin with a violent entropy: each event turns the wheels around it faster and harder. So it was with the partisans and the Germans. As the war moved north, inexorably, towards the Gothic Line, everything moved as one, each seemingly separate incident intermeshed as part of a greater whole.

## THE REICHSFÜHRER-SS AND SS-STURMBANNFÜHRER WALTER REDER

Sitting behind Florence was one of the best-equipped and most experienced German units, the 16th SS-Panzergrenadier Division of the Waffen-SS, whose divisional title was the Reichsführer-SS. Its commander was SS-Gruppenführer Max Simon. They were directly opposite both Daniel Inouye and Eustace D'Souza on the line. This German unit had arrived in Italy in May and had taken part in the fighting retreat defending the sector in Tuscany from Grosseto up to Cecina, roughly opposite the line of advance of the Japanese-American 442nd RCT. By July, the SS men had arrived across the Arno, holding the line from Pisa down to the Mediterranean where the river pulled sluggishly into the sea.

In mid-August, Max Simon decided to detach one of his battalion commanders to move to the north of Florence, towards a mountain complex called Monte Sole, which overlooked and dominated the main highway northwestward to Bologna. This, SS-Gruppenführer

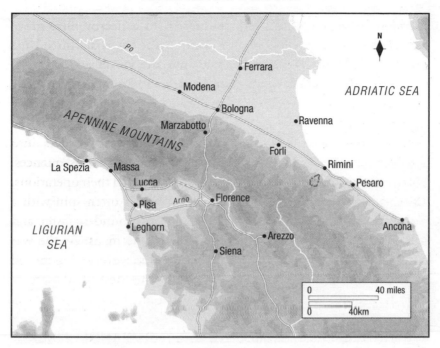

Simon had guessed correctly, would be the central focus of the American 5th Army's attack on the central sector of the Gothic Line. Like every other German officer, Simon knew the Allied assault on the Gothic Line was imminent. But where would it come? In the east, around the town of Rimini? In the centre, near Bologna? Or on the Mediterranean? Simon thought it would be around Bologna, which made it vital to occupy and defend the high ground that controlled the access roads to the city. Monte Sole was a huge mountain that lay southeast of the town of Marzabotto, and was occupied by an Italian partisan unit, the Brigata Partigiana Stella Rossa, the Red Star Brigade. The battalion commander Simon chose for the mission to take this mountain was given a clear set of instructions: destroy the partisans and their support structure at Monte Sole.[4] The officer chosen was SS-Sturmbannführer, or Major, Walter Reder. He needed no further orders. He prepared to move north to complete the task. His understanding of Max Simon's orders was simple: he had said simply that there were partisans to be 'deleted'.

Walter Reder was born in 1915 at Freiwaldau in Silesia (Austria–Hungary). Reder's father had been an industrialist who had lost his job, his company, and the family's wealth in the economic depression of the 1920s. Reder was determined from his early teens to recoup some of the family's lost financial power and the social status that had disappeared with it. After the family moved to Austria, he went to high school in Salzburg and then to business school in Vienna. Then he joined the Hitler Jugend (Hitler Youth), where he was influenced by reading *völkisch* national racial literature. In 1934, at age nineteen, he ceased to be Austro-Hungarian and was granted German citizenship. He enlisted as a private in the Allgemeine-SS, its general administration body, which differed from the two other main branches of the SS: the Waffen-SS, its combat soldiers, and the Totenkopfverbände, in charge of the concentration camps. He attended SS officer candidate school at Brunswick, graduated sixtieth in his class, close to the bottom, and emerged as a young SS lieutenant desperate to prove himself.

He was then transferred to the SS-Totenkopfstandarte, Death's Head Unit, and sent to Dachau concentration camp outside Munich in 1936 to lead the men guarding the political prisoners and Jews. Hoping to transfer to the Waffen-SS, he underwent a series of military training courses. But by the time of the invasion of Poland in September 1939, he was still in the Death's Head guard units. His duties in Poland, behind the main line of the German advance, were described as 'processing and dealing with Polish stragglers, Jews, and Communists'. Then came a stroke of administrative luck.

In October 1939, the Totenkopfstandarte were incorporated into a new SS infantry division, and Walter Reder was given his own platoon. Finally, he thought, the time had come for him to shine. But it was not to be. His first job was again an administrative one, as a divisional liaison officer between his unit and SS headquarters in Berlin. As the German blitzkrieg swept across Europe, the frustrated twenty-year-old of three different nationalities – Austrian, Czech, German – still hadn't fired a single shot at one of the Reich's enemies. But by the time he'd served as a divisional staff officer during the invasion of France in 1940, he was awarded the Iron Cross Second Class. He also got married.

In 1931, Heinrich Himmler, as head of the SS, had established the Rasse- und Siedlungshauptamt (Race and Settlement Office). This was in charge of approving the applications of SS men to marry. Both Reder and his fiancée, Beate, were deemed of ethnically and racially pure stock. They were married in October 1940. Life was suddenly moving forward for the ambitious lieutenant. And then came Operation *Barbarossa*, the invasion of Russia, which allowed him to show his true mettle. Promoted to the rank of hauptsturmführer, captain, he led his company of the Totenkopf in combat across western and northern Russia. On 28 July, a month into *Barbarossa*, he was awarded the Iron Cross First Class. He led from the front. And on 1 September, outside Leningrad, he paid the price. He was shot in the neck.

But in a typical irony of war, the young officer who had finished close to the bottom of his class at officer school was driven – by his belief in the National Socialist ideals of racial purity, ethnic superiority, and the need for German dominance over lesser *untermensch,* and also because he actually was an excellent combat soldier. His men revered him. So after convalescing, he returned to the Russian Front at the end of February 1942 for a year of almost continuous combat. First as a company commander, then at battalion level, Reder fought with the 1st and then 5th SS-Panzergrenadier Regiments of the division. In October of that year, he was awarded the Deutsches Kreuz (the German Cross) in Gold – the highest class – and he took command of his own SS battalion the following February. Then, in February 1943, came the Third Battle of Kharkov.

Reder and the SS-Totenkopf Panzer Division were part of the German Army Groups Centre and South, which in a two-month battle destroyed an estimated fifty-two Soviet divisions in the southern Ukraine. The Russians had encircled and defeated the German 6th Army at Stalingrad and, emboldened, launched a huge offensive westward at the beginning of 1943. They overstretched themselves, however, were outflanked and surrounded by the panzer armies and Wehrmacht divisions of Generalfeldmarschall Erich von Manstein, and forced to give up the key city of Kharkov. It was fighting on an epic scale, across the vast, frozen winter plains of the Donetsk region. The Soviet Red Army deployed 345,000 soldiers, of whom 86,500 were killed. The Germans, weakened by Stalingrad, could put only 70,000 men into battle, of whom they lost 4,500. It was also fighting in which very few prisoners were taken – on 5 and 6 December 1943, for instance, the SS division Liebstandarte Adolf Hitler went into action in the Ukraine. In one battle, 2,280 Red Army soldiers were killed, and only 3 prisoners taken. A German tank commander remembered the noise like a frozen, crunching mulch as his armoured vehicle drove over Red Army soldiers lying in their path.

(To put these casualty and prisoner figures into perspective, those incurred during the Allied invasion of Sicily in the same year were comparatively modest. The Germans called the fighting in Europe 'polite'. The Americans, British, and Canadians landed or parachuted 160,000 men into Sicily – the Americans lost 8,781 killed, wounded, and taken prisoner. As mentioned, the number of men afflicted by malaria hugely exceeded the battlefield killed and wounded.)

The Germans at Kharkov triumphed through their use of tank tactics, in perfect tank country. The fighting established as German household names panzer and SS commanders including Joachim Pieper and Kurt Meyer, both holders of the coveted Ritterkreuz, the Knight's Cross of the Iron Cross. And it was in the fighting for the northern Kharkov suburb of Ila Jeremejewka that Walter Reder joined their ranks. The Totenkopf division, along with two others, the Liebstandarte Adolf Hitler and Das Reich, had been deployed into the shattered, frozen muddy streets of northern Kharkov after they had outflanked the Red Army and recaptured the city's suburbs. On

9 March 1943, Reder and his company were patrolling along a semi-destroyed street in armoured patrol vehicles, backed up by tanks. Soviet troops had occupied the buildings in front of them, with dug-in machine guns and anti-tank cannons covered by snipers. It had taken the SS men four days to move from the outskirts of the city towards Dzerzhinsky Square. The fighting was street by street, house by house, room by room. One half of a squad would provide covering fire with their MG-42s, the other half would run forward with hand grenades and Schmeisser machine pistols, while armoured vehicles provided heavier fire. Once the Germans closed with the Red Army, it was time for pistols, bayonets, submachine guns, and knives, and even the *schanzzeug*, the stamped steel German entrenching tool, whose edges the men would sharpen. It was while leading and directing one such attack that Reder suddenly saw a bright red and yellow flash coming straight at him from a window, then a huge explosive thump on his lower left arm. He came to in a field hospital, the limb amputated.

By the time he was evacuated and sent to Poland, he had been decorated for gallantry six times and was SS to the tips of his remaining four fingers and one thumb. Following the wounds and his leadership at Kharkov, he was awarded the Knight's Cross of the Iron Cross. He was then sent to Poland with another SS-Panzergrenadier battalion, this time tasked with the destruction of the Warsaw ghetto. The fighting was tough. Himmler was to say, self-congratulatingly, that the battle for Warsaw was the hardest the SS had fought, 'comparable with the house to house fighting in Stalingrad.' Reder then moved south to Italy.[5] The Polish survivors of Warsaw went to Treblinka.

Following successful completion of the Warsaw mission, Reder was transferred to the newly formed 16th SS-Panzergrenadier Division, with the rank of Sturmbannführer-SS. He arrived in Italy in May 1944, his main responsibility being anti-partisan operations, a job he took to extremely quickly, combining his experience of combat in western Europe and Russia, and his eradication of the

Warsaw ghetto. For SS officers like Reder, raised and trained in the decade before the war on an unrelenting diet of National Socialism, Aryan superiority, and racial eugenics, the enormous variety of nationalities fighting for the Allied forces in Italy came as a surprise. They had regarded the Red Army as borderline sub-human, and taking prisoners in Russia had at best been academic. The racial stereotypes Reder learned at Junker officer school and from his *völkisch* reading – that Jews, Slavs, Negroes, non-Germans, Communists are inferior – would have been challenged by the fighting skills and determination of the vast variety of units deployed by the Allies. Poles, Moroccans, Indians, African Americans, Japanese Americans, and Gurkhas had consistently gone toe-to-toe with the SS and elite paratroopers across Italy and proved an even match.

## THE MASSACRE AT SANT'ANNA DI STAZZEMA

As an SS officer, Reder had three superiors to whom he was answerable, First was his immediate commanding officer, Max Simon. His ultimate superior was SS-Obergruppenführer Karl Wolff in Rome, head of the SS in Italy. But as a ground infantry commander, he was also under the command of the highest-ranking German officer in Italy, Kesselring himself. By July 1944, Kesselring's staff officers estimated that the partisans had killed up to 5,000 Germans and wounded as many as 20,000. The more the number of German casualties rose, the more the Luftwaffe field marshal was determined to bring their guerrilla war to a halt. Chaos in his rear areas meant his troops in Italy risked becoming isolated from their lines of supply northward. It was of little use being able to beat the Allies or hold them at arm's length if he faced a civil war behind the lines. So he decided to do something about it, using the most brutal tactics, stepping up the pace of anti-*bandenbekämpfung*[6] – actions against partisans, or bandits, one of Himmler's priorities – in a small mountainous area of western Tuscany that lay southwest of Florence,

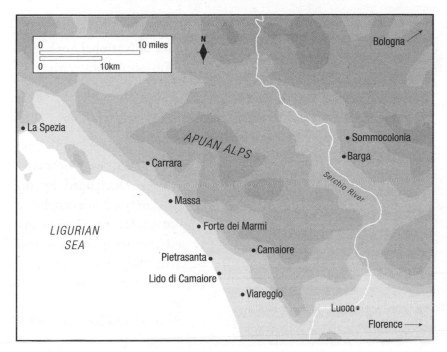

overlooking the Mediterranean coast. He intended to teach the partisans a lesson. In August, the Italian civilians in the mountain villages of San Terenzo Monti and nearby Sant'Anna di Stazzema experienced these tactics.

On the night of 14/15 July, a partisan group that called itself Olive Tree had broken into a barracks in the coastal town of Carrara. It was one of a series of seaside towns that lay directly in the path of the Allies as they advanced northwest up the coast towards the key ports of La Spezia and Livorno. This strip of littoral is overshadowed by the Apulian Alps and, further to the east, the Apennine mountains. Carrara in particular sits beneath steep slopes 6,500 feet high, where the mountains contain huge quantities of white marble. Hundreds of years of excavation had removed vast amounts of the stone to make centuries' worth of famous Italian statuary; Michelangelo's preferred marble came from Carrara. The shining white faces of the quarries sit surrounded by trees and scrub. Fine white dust spreads across nearby slopes. American soldiers such as the 442nd Regimental Combat Team were, by now, less than a week to the south, and the partisans decided it was time to liberate Carrara and surrounding villages.

So in early August, armed with the Beretta model 38 submachine guns and Carcano rifles they had stolen from the barracks, the guerrillas made for the hills above this strip of the Tuscan coast. In a confused night-time firefight in the hillside village of San Terenzo Monti, they killed everyone stationed at the small German garrison, except one soldier who fled. Responsibility for the German response was passed to the 16th SS-Panzergrenadier Division.

On the morning of 12 August, one of Reder's fellow officers, SS-Hauptsturmführer Anton Galler, led the men of the 2nd Battalion of Panzergrenadier Regiment 35 into the mountains above Lucca. This old walled citadel sits at the base of the foothills of the Apulian Alps, which run parallel to the Mediterranean coast of Tuscany. The German troops drove up to Sant'Anna di Stazzema, which lies several miles above Lucca. German Army and SS troops, as well as Italian Fascist soldiers, moved towards the village from four directions of attack. En route, in the hamlet of Vaccareccia, seventy people were locked in a stable and murdered by soldiers with hand grenades and submachine guns, and then finished off with a flamethrower. They repeated this in the nearby hamlets of Franchi and Pero.

They surrounded Sant'Anna, which consists of a small church in the centre of a grove of trees, farm buildings, and old stone houses. The SS men started to round up all the villagers in an open space in front of the church. One of Anton Galler's subordinate officers who was commanding a unit that day was SS-Untersturmführer, or lieutenant, Gerhard Sommer. He was a veteran of the invasion of France and had recently been posted to Italy. He and his men undertook the task assigned to them with ruthless efficiency. They gathered the men, women, children, and babies in the square, as well as in a number of barns, stables, and basements. Once the population of Sant'Anna was centralized, the executions began.[7]

The SS herded the largest group of villagers in front of the church, which was enclosed by a wall. There was only one entrance, so this tiny piazza became a trap. The village priest, Don Fiore Menguzzo, stood in front of the villagers trying to protect them. An SS man shot him dead. The Germans then used machine pistols and MG-42 machine guns, set on tripods at the entrance to the space in front of the church, to kill everyone in it. Between 107 and 132 people died in front of the church, and the SS reportedly then set some of their bodies on fire with flamethrowers. Then they threw hand grenades into the buildings where other people were hiding. The victims that day reportedly included Anna Pardini, three weeks old, and eight pregnant women. Surviving witnesses say that one of these expectant mothers, Evelina Berretti, had her womb cut open with a bayonet, and then her unborn baby was pulled out by the legs and executed. Inside the church, the soldiers used the pews to make a bonfire to dispose of the bodies. This all took three hours. The soldiers then sat down in the shade outside the burning village of Sant'Anna and ate lunch rations that their headquarters had issued to them the night before.

On the way back down the mountain, the SS killed another twenty people in two other clusters of houses, bringing the day's death toll in the area to an estimated 560 people, of whom seventy-five were under ten and the oldest eighty-six. It was the second-largest individual killing of civilians in Europe by German troops to date, that was not part of either *Einsatzkommando* actions or the mass killings of the Final Solution. It was surpassed only by the massacre at Oradour-sur-Glane in southwestern France in June of the same year. There, SS men of the Das Reich Division, en route to Normandy, executed 642 civilians in a small town near Limoges as a reprisal for attacks by the French Resistance.

The Reichsführer-SS, however, didn't stop at Sant'Anna di Stazzema. A week later, on 19 August 1944, a convoy from Walter Reder's reconnaissance battalion wound up the mountain road to San Terenzo Monti. This was the hamlet where the partisans had killed the small German garrison in late July. Stopping in the village, many of whose inhabitants had fled two days previously during the fighting between Germans and partisans, Reder's men dropped the tailgates of their trucks. They took out fifty-three Italian men, prisoners from the prison in Pietrasanta, one in the string of towns that lay on the Mediterranean coast before La Spezia.[8] The men were taken into the neighbouring vineyards, where they were suspended in a half-sitting, half-kneeling position, tied around the neck by wire nooses from the concrete bollards and heavy wooden posts that supported the trellises of the vines. Over the course of the afternoon, German soldiers shot or beat them to death.[9] The message to the partisans from Walter Reder and Anton Galler was clear: if we don't find you or kill you, we'll just find the civilian population instead.

# 7

---

# BEST-LAID PLANS

## *The SOE and OSS in Northern Italy*

### August 1944

The partisans on the Monte Sole plateau above Bologna had no idea that SS-Hauptsturmführer Walter Reder and his SS panzergrenadiers were on their way. Their colleagues who operated in the mountains above Milan, however, had ample warning that a four-man party from the SOE was due to arrive. The team was going to bring three things with it. First, a well-known Italian figure who could potentially unite the different political factions among the partisans in the north. Second, a promise of regular airdrops of weapons to fight the Germans. And third, stowed in bandoliers and in linen wrappings under their flying suits and jackets and in an equipment container, 2 million lire in cash. On the night of 12 August, the SOE team stood by the tarmac airstrip outside Brindisi at the bottom of the Adriatic sea coast. It was a typically hot summer's night, and the men were soon sweating heavily as they struggled with their parachute harnesses and flying suits, stowed personal weapons and possessions, and prepared for an uneven, bumpy flight 500 miles over the Adriatic and then due west into northern Italy. They were just one of four teams that would fly north that night and parachute into enemy-occupied territory.

By August 1944, the SOE was running operations in the country from two locations: directly behind the western front line in the Tuscan town of Siena, and from the far south in the heel of Italy, from a castle headquarters at Monopoli outside Brindisi. A British Royal Navy commander was in charge of Number 1 Special Force, as the Monopoli detachment was known. Before the invasion of Sicily and Italy, the SOE and the American OSS had been headquartered together at a beachfront training camp outside Algiers. As the Allies had advanced up the Italian mainland, SOE chose the castle at Monopoli because it was close to Brindisi's port and airfield, it had instant access to the Adriatic for maritime operations, and it was in aircraft range of the whole of northern Italy, the Adriatic, and Yugoslavia.

The SOE team had had to wait several days in a safe house before an RAF Halifax bomber became available. The Warsaw Uprising was now at its height: as the Red Army stood just miles outside, the Germans were destroying the Polish resistance in the capital. The Russians had halted because Stalin wanted the Germans to crush the non-communist Poles leading the rebellion. The RAF was desperately trying to supply the Poles with arms, medical supplies, food, and ammunition, but Stalin consistently refused to allow the British aircraft permission to land, refuel, or overnight in territory held by his men. The allegiances among the Americans, the British, and the Russians were starting to show large fracture lines as the Soviet Army advanced into Europe. Those lines would soon stretch and widen and reach Italy. One side effect was that the RAF couldn't supply transport aircraft for both Poland and Italy simultaneously, so the SOE team had to wait. It was not until eleven o'clock on the night of 12 August that the four men stood in the hot Adriatic night, stuffing bundles of hundreds of thousands of lire into their Sidcot flying suits, then strapping on their cumbersome and uncomfortable X-Type parachutes.

## GENERAL RAFFAELE CADORNA AND THE CLNAI

There were three Italians and one British officer in the group. The eldest was a fifty-five-year-old former general in the Italian army named Raffaele Cadorna Jr. The name Cadorna was familiar to all Italians, especially those who were now resisting Mussolini, his residual Fascist troops, and the Germans. Cadorna's grandfather had led Garibaldi's troops into Rome in 1870 during the Risorgimento, the resurgence, or political, social, and military unification movement that resulted in the Kingdom of Italy. His father, Luigi, had been a field marshal and commander-in-chief of Italian forces in the First World War: like so many commanders on all sides, he was unpopular for sending thousands of men to unnecessary deaths. Cadorna Jr. had commanded the Ariete armoured division, which had been among the only Italian anti-fascist army units to put up any effective resistance to the Germans in September 1943 when they occupied Rome.

The former general had been chosen by the Allies to drop into northern Italy to oversee the military training and supply of partisan groups there. He was also to try to cement workable allegiances among the different political factions, each with its own armed group. Cadorna was a national figurehead of the old Italy that had existed pre-Mussolini. The Christian Democrats, the Communists, the Liberals, and the Action Party – the main political groupings on the left, right, and centre – preferred him to anybody else, and he was the best the Allies had. He had been personally requested by the leaders of the Comitato di Liberazione Nazionale Alta Italia (CLNAI), the National Liberation Committee for Upper Italy, in Milan, the umbrella group that loosely bound the partisan groups and their political objectives together into one cohesive whole with one self-explanatory priority: the liberation of Italy from the Germans and Mussolini's Fascists. All sides – the Allies, the Fascists, the CLNAI, and each individual partisan leader – knew the unspoken sub-text. Once Italy was liberated, the political landscape was almost certain to be dominated by the partisan grouping that controlled the most territory, had the most arms and the most money, and controlled the labour unions that ran northern Italy's economy – and also enjoyed the temporary support of the post-war Allied authorities. So there was intense jockeying for political and military power among all the partisan groups, each of them wanting priority when it came to supplies of Allied arms, food, supplies, and money, and the OSS and SOE agents who delivered them.

The Royal Navy commander in charge of Number 1 Special Force made the Allies' operational, strategic, and political priorities clear to the CLNAI. They would support all partisan groups that contributed directly to the main war effort, but anytime political infighting interfered with this, materiel help would be suspended. The Allies defined the goal of the partisan resistance groups: 'to harass German lines of communication by sabotage and guerrilla warfare and eventually to impede the withdrawal of German forces from Italy in order that the Allied armies may be able to get at them and destroy them.'

As a central piece in the jigsaw of Allied and partisan aims and objectives, the Allies thought Cadorna fit better than anybody else. He was well connected to the partisan networks in Rome as well, particularly to the group that had carried out, and then suffered the reprisals for, the bomb attack in Via Rasella in March of that year. He was linked to Arrigo Paladini, now a political coordinator between the partisans and the Allies in Rome, as well as to the network that had been run by a former military colleague of Cadorna's, Colonel Giuseppe Montezemolo. This officer had been among those whom the SS shot at the Ardeatine Caves in March. He had occupied the cell at Via Tasso next to Arrigo Paladini after the Germans arrested him in January 1944. Although Herbert Kappler's Gestapo men had pulled his teeth and fingernails out with pliers, Montezemolo never talked. General Harold Alexander wrote a letter of thanks and congratulation to his widow, all she had to remember her husband's work by.[1]

## MAJOR OLIVER CHURCHILL AND THE SOE

Number 1 Special Force outside Brindisi answered to SOE headquarters in London as well as to its European office in Berne, Switzerland. In London, the SOE briefed the British Foreign Office about Cadorna's mission, which had been given the code name 'Operation *Fairway*'. They hoped that the arrival of the former general in Milan would keep the partisan effort 'on the right lines'. It was just one of some forty missions that the SOE was to run across northern Italy as the Allies advanced, from the far western border with France on the Alps to the frontier with Yugoslavia in the east. But *Fairway* was vitally important because Cadorna was the Allies' senior liaison with all of the CLNAI. He had two Italian agents who would parachute with him. One was a lieutenant named Augusto de Laurentiis, code-named 'Ferreo'. He would act as the link between Cadorna and the CLNAI; there was also an Italian radio operator, Sergeant Nicola Delle Monache, code-named 'Alfieri', while Cadorna himself was to be called 'Valenti'. The fourth member of the team, and the only non-Italian, was given the code name 'Peters'.

The night drop over northern Italy would not be the first operational parachute descent of the war for Peters, whose full and real name was Major Oliver Churchill of SOE. On the left chest of his military battledress, when he wore his uniform, was the inch-wide purple-and-white silk medal ribbon of the British Military Cross. The tall, black-haired, thirty-one-year-old officer had won it on the Greek island of Corfu the previous year, helping support the Italian garrison after their army switched allegiances to the Allies. Churchill came from a British diplomatic family and already had one brother working for the SOE in neighbouring France. He'd been born in Stockholm in 1914, the son of William Algernon Churchill, a consul at the British embassy in Sweden. His father's diplomatic postings had variously included Mozambique, Brazil, Holland, Italy, and Algeria. Churchill senior was also an art connoisseur and the author of the standard reference book on early European paper and watermarks. Oliver studied modern languages and architecture at King's College, Cambridge. He had joined the British Territorial Army in the late 1930s, and when war broke out in 1939, he got a reserve commission in the Worcestershire Regiment, an English county unit. His two brothers joined as well. Walter, the eldest, had been a Royal Auxiliary Air Force pilot since 1936 and won the Distinguished Flying Cross piloting Hurricanes in combat during the Battle of Britain in 1940. Then posted to the besieged Mediterranean island of Malta in 1941, he was responsible for seven destroyed German aircraft and received the Distinguished Service Order. The Germans shot down his Spitfire during a raid on the airfield of Gela in southern Sicily in 1942. Oliver's second brother, Peter, had also been selected to join the Special Operations Executive, and by 1942 was working undercover in southern France.

Oliver's ability to speak Italian and French and his international upbringing attracted him to SOE recruiters, as did a recommendation by his brother. He was detached from his infantry regiment to the fledgling secret army, and in early 1941 he underwent commando training at and around the bleak outpost of Arisaig House in the Scottish Highlands. Here recruits to the Special Operations Executive lived in canvas tents on the grounds of shooting lodges, swam in bitterly cold lochs in battledress, learned rope climbing and an early form of jujitsu and knife fighting taught by two former police officers from the Shanghai Municipal Police, called Sergeants Fairbairn and Sykes. The two invented the Fairbairn–Sykes commando knife, a fighting dagger with a seven-inch tapered blade, issued to commandos and special forces. Fairbairn had spent some twenty years with the Shanghai Police, being involved in hundreds of street-fights involving knives. The SOE recruits ran up Scottish mountains, they learned about explosives, and every morning began with a cup of tea, some powdered egg, and white bread – sometimes thinly spread with margarine – and a run. Ironically, the cerebral Churchill, who hated destruction and killing, took to it. The whole programme was a complete contrast to anything he had ever done before in his life, and the physicality of it made a refreshing break from the intellectual atmosphere at Cambridge. And it wasn't that different from his public school in Buckinghamshire, except the food was often better. He liked to use his ingenious, flexible brain to try to out-think the instructors, and they spotted it. He and his brothers' upbringing in South America, Scandinavia, Africa, and Italy had exposed them from an early age to a vast variety of human experience and human nature. Further training in tradecraft and parachuting followed, and then Churchill was passed ready for operations.

The SOE posted him to Malta and then to Cairo. Churchill's first mission was Operation *Acheron*, a code word derived from the name of a Napoleonic-era French man-o'-war. When the Italians surrendered under the 1943 armistice, General Eisenhower and Allied planners decided that some of the islands in the Aegean and Adriatic Seas, east and west, respectively, of the Greek mainland, had strategic priority. The beautiful island of Corfu, lying only nine miles off the coast of Albania, was a potential jumping-off point for any future invasion of the Adriatic seaboard of Yugoslavia. It was manned by an Italian garrison. The SOE decided that Major Oliver Churchill and a radio operator, Signalman Harrison, should be inserted by parachute to contact the Italian commander and assure him that Allied help was on the way. And in the meantime to urge him to resist any German attempts to occupy the island. Churchill's briefing from the SOE, as noted in his war record, gave some idea of the ad hoc nature of their mission. It was remarkably similar to the 'suck-it-and-see' tactical approach the Allies were often obliged to take at that stage of the war in the Mediterranean, when reliable intelligence on the ground was sparse or non-existent. Combined operations, amphibious landing techniques, multi-national command and control among nationalities as disparate as the Americans, French, British, Greeks, and Brazilians were all being honed and tried out, often for the first time, in action. Each operation was a rehearsal for the next one. The American landings in North Africa, Operation *Torch*, had been preparations for the invasion of Sicily, with all of its attendant successes and failures. The British tended to bring flair, flexibility, imagination, and derring-do to operational planning; the Americans, economic and military muscle, and a lot of perseverance and common sense. Like nitroglycerine, it was a volatile mix. If the British and American commanders got on, it worked well.

The briefing for Operation *Acheron* was simple. Churchill noted, 'Little was known of the situation in Corfu. Fighting was to be expected anywhere. We might be fired on by either or both sides.'

Germany promptly invaded Corfu in mid-September 1943. Churchill and Harrison parachuted in a week afterward, but their landing on the hard, rocky ground damaged their radio equipment. This made contact with headquarters in Cairo at first difficult, and then impossible. The two men contacted the Italian commander of the island, who was defending a shrinking perimeter centred on Corfu's capital. Four days after the arrival of the SOE team, the Italians surrendered to the Germans, who shot the Italian commander and his senior officers. Churchill and Harrison had to run for their lives. Their only way out? To buy, borrow, steal, or build some form of boat that they could use to cross the whole of the Adriatic Sea, diagonally from Corfu in the northeast to Allied-controlled territory at the bottom of the eastern coast of Italy. It was a distance of some 300 nautical miles.

One of the numerous exercises that SOE recruits at the Scottish training centres in Scotland had practiced was E&E, escape and evasion. Pursued by their instructors, the trainees had to trek across the Scottish Highlands. They would have little or no food or water, be living off the land, dressed in shabby military clothing, boots laced with old wire, with no compass, maps, weapons, money, or equipment. On Corfu, Churchill and Harrison had to do it for real. They borrowed some Greek peasants' clothing, hid in outhouses, rocky gulleys, and caves, and made their way to the island's coast. They finally found a motorboat. The captain was seventy, and Churchill described the three crew members as 'one dotard, one drunkard, and the father of a thief'.

Eleven Italian soldiers and sailors joined them, fleeing the Germans. The shoddy, incompetent crew rowed the boat to three offshore islets and then raised sail. The following day, after a chaotic night at sea, one of the Italian sailors – luckily for all aboard – recognized the Gulf of

Taranto. The drunk captain couldn't read the compass, and his bosun couldn't handle the sails. The captain thought they'd sailed in a circle and were off the coast of Albania, but the Italian seaman saw that they had sailed into Italian coastal waters. Sunburned, hungry, and very thirsty, they finally landed at Otranto, in far southern Italy. Churchill was taken by ship to Brindisi, debriefed, and then returned to Cairo.

As an operation, it was a disaster. Force majeure and bigger events had simply gotten the better of the two men. But *Acheron* demonstrated the boundless initiative and flexibility, the ability to think on their feet deep within enemy-occupied territory, that SOE recruitment and training first selected and then nurtured among its agents. Churchill was awarded the Military Cross for leading the mission.

### OPERATION *FAIRWAY*

Parachute jumps are very hard work at the best of times. In the Second World War, parachuting was still in its infancy, and everything about it, from the equipment to the modified aircraft, was being constantly developed on the move. Churchill, Cadorna, and the two Italian team members of the Fairway mission pulled on British X-Type parachutes, one-piece flying suits, and rudimentary helmets. These had large circular rubber rims so that when the men exited the Halifax bomber through a hole in the floor of the fuselage, they didn't crack their skulls on the facing rim of the hatch. Churchill had a large and heavy Webley .45 revolver, which he put down the front of his Sidcot suit, where it sat trapped by the straps of the parachute. Their Halifax took off just before midnight. The flight took three hours. Then the RAF crew chief pulled back the hatch in the floor, the aircraft slowed to just above stalling speed, and the first team member sat with his feet dangling out. He could see the dark mountainous terrain of far northern Italy speed past 600 feet below. Then the jump lights on the inside of the fuselage flicked from red to green as the pilot cut over the start of the drop zone, and the men half fell, half slid through the exit hatch. Operation *Fairway* was under way.

The drop zone, or DZ, was on the side of a mountain above Lake Endine, which sits north of the town of Bergamo, above Milan. Waiting for the SOE men on the ground were partisans from the Fiamme Verdi (Green Flame) brigade, a well-organized group of some 300 men led by former soldiers from the Alpini mountain troops. But the team landed in the wrong place. A rival group had almost certainly supplied incorrect details of their landing zone. Churchill twisted his ankle as he hit the ground, hardly surprising given the drop zone was on the steep slope of a mountain. Parachute drop zones are ideally sited on long, wide stretches of flat, dry land with no trees, boulders, houses, rivers, or obstacles of any kind. But in mountainous northern Italy, such terrain is found only in valleys, where roads and centres of habitation are located. And in 1944 in the occupied north, those areas contained Germans or Fascist Italian troops. So the SOE agents would be landed high up on hill- and mountainsides, with grid coordinates supplied by radio from partisans whose map-reading skills ranged from the workable and reliable to the non-existent.

The first major obstacle faced by any incoming SOE or OSS team was for the RAF or American pilot to find the right drop zone. There was also a perpetual risk that the teams would be guided onto a false DZ by fires lit by rival groups – or Germans – although a system of recognition lights had been devised to prevent this. Then the men had to be dropped *onto* the actual DZ, not onto a neighbouring mountain. An idea of the hazards faced by SOE agents parachuting is illustrated by a typical – and comparatively successful – operation at the end of August 1944.

Two SOE missions, code-named 'Simia' and 'Gela', consisting of nine men between them, were dropped into mountainous areas of northern Italy. Their aircraft took off from Brindisi and flew to the drop zone and back to Brindisi three times before they found it. One team jumped on the first pass over the DZ, then cloud cover forced the pilot to circle nine times before the second SOE team could parachute. From the first team, one man landed in a forest half a mile from the landing zone, another in a clump of rocks, another a mile beyond it, and the remaining men nowhere near the recognition lights. From the second team, all four men missed the DZ, two were injured, and another landed in a tree. The RAF pilot of the Dakota DC-3 circled the area again three times because of bad visibility before aborting the drop of the team's personal equipment, which included their guns and radios. The next drop took place four months later. Luckily, another team on the ground had a spare radio set. Sometimes it seemed a miracle that any of the covert missions were inserted successfully.[2]

For agents stuck isolated in the wilds of northern Italy, the broader picture could seem a distant one. The only reality was the immediacy of inhospitable and unsuitable DZs, halfway up mountains, at night, marked and illuminated by mostly amateurish partisans, all competing with each other, with the ever-present threat of betrayal to the Germans or Fascists. Compounding the risks, there was bad weather, cloud cover – a constant worry at high altitudes – aircraft engine trouble, enemy activity in the drop area, and high wind. All these factors combined to make dropping SOE and OSS agents often impossible and always dangerous.

Another constant complication was that Allied planners at their castle at Monopoli, hundreds of miles south of the areas of operations, often had little or no information about the drop zones. They were entirely dependent on information from partisans transmitted by radio, or from first-hand descriptions from Italian agents, sympathizers, or POWs who had lived in the area. The suck-it-and-see factor ran very high. One British SOE officer, Captain John Ross, described his pre-mission briefing at Monopoli castle in August: 'We went down to our headquarters in Monopoli to be briefed, which was really pathetic . . . The staff there knew virtually nothing about the area we were going to work in . . . and they had very little knowledge of what the resistance movement was doing there and they had very little idea of the geography. They had dreadful maps and sort of pre-war picture postcards of the attractive areas, but nothing much else. So as a briefing it was hopeless.'[3]

Unforgiving terrain, unreliable partisan groups, bad weather, ever-present German troops, and an inability to carry out aerial reconnaissance made it inevitable that some agents wouldn't arrive in the right place at the right time in one piece. Getting parachutists onto a flat, well-marked drop zone in broad daylight with no enemy activity is hard enough. No surprise, therefore, that the mountains of northern Italy proved such elusive night-time targets.

By August 1944, the Allies were also under the impression that the war in Italy could be over in a matter of weeks. Lieutenant General Oliver Leese had telegrammed in late July suggesting that the 8th Army could be through the Gothic Line defences in seven weeks. The chief of the Imperial General Staff, Sir Alan Brooke, wondered if the Nazis could last the winter. Brussels had fallen to the British, and American units were close to the German border. SOE and OSS planners had an optimistic vision of taking over a large, open swathe of land in northern Italy – one of the main valleys, perhaps – where they could parachute large amounts of supplies and establish forward operating bases. The truth, as Oliver Churchill and other agents were discovering, was rather different.

Once on the ground, there were two things that SOE agents feared the most. One was a rival partisan group stealing their supplies, leaving them stuck 'blind' in enemy territory without weapons or an ability to talk to base. The second was Germans and Italian Fascists carrying out a *rastrellamento,* a 'raking' operation. Enemy troops would surround huge areas of ground and physically walk and drive across it to flush agents and partisans from their hiding places. By late summer 1944, *rastrellamento* meant only one thing to most Italian civilians: death at the hands of the Germans.

So when Oliver Churchill with his sprained ankle discovered that it was not the Green Flames who were waiting for him, but another partisan group, the first fear was realized. He lost all of his personal equipment – apart from the two radio transmitters and his pistol – when the second fear, an SS unit on a search-and-destroy operation, also materialized. The SOE men's equipment was hurriedly loaded onto a number of mules, which the rival partisans drove into a field of head-high yellow corn. The Allied agents had to hide from the SS before making their way to a safe house – only to discover on arrival that the Germans had burned it down. Returning to the cornfield the following day to track down the mules, they could find nothing. The rival partisans had stolen their supplies. They also had to cover their tracks. So, with each of the four men carrying a forty-pound unravelled parachute, flapping like a vast sailcloth, they marched eight hours across the mountains to meet their hosts from the Fiamme Verdi. En route, Churchill had to take refuge for several days in a mountain hut to rest his ankle. Up in the mountains, a long way from Milan and General Cadorna, he felt lost and ineffectual.

The best-laid plans often go awry. But whether the individual SOE and OSS missions were tactical and intelligence successes or failures – and they were mostly a bit of both – they were part of a larger, more successful strategic whole. German atrocities like the killings by the SS at Sant'Anna di Stazzema were fast pushing the Italian civilian population over to the Allied side, with males from fifteen to sixty joining the partisans in ever-increasing numbers. Second, an edict that Mussolini's puppet government of the Socialist Republic of Italy issued in July 1944 increased the guerrilla strength. It said that any men of military age within the area of Italy controlled by the Salò Republic had to join Fascist units or face imprisonment. Tens of thousands of men headed for the mountains, and to the partisans. By August, very rough estimates of their strength numbered 100,000. Often unarmed, sometimes with no shoes, or holding political affiliations and aims that conflicted with the Allies', they had one overarching aim: to beat the Germans. This boom in partisan recruiting coincided with the Allies' wave of optimism about a fast end to the war in Italy, and the increase in numbers of SOE and OSS missions launched during the fine summer flying weather of 1944. Regardless of whether their agents and arms found the right recipients, the British and Americans started dropping increasing numbers of guns and advisers to increasing numbers of partisans in increasingly large areas of northern Italy, just when the German defenders needed all of their tight-stretched resources to defend the Gothic Line against a massive Allied assault. The bigger plan was working, as seemingly unrelated events pushed each other forward: the cogwheels of war were spinning faster.

Cadorna headed for Milan, as did his liaison officer. The team radio officer was terrified of operational life on the ground and frightened that the Germans would use radio-tracking equipment to find them. For the first thirty days behind the lines, he failed to make contact with base at Monopoli. The SOE's most important liaison mission with the CLNAI was 'blind'. Once his ankle was less painful, Churchill spent a month living with the Green Flames, building up his strength, marching on observation and reconnaissance treks, improving his Italian, and listening to the Alpini officers as they described the other partisan groups in neighbouring areas. The food consisted of roast goat and lamb, polenta, milk, water, and blueberries. After a month, Churchill decided to head down into the dangers of Italy's second-largest city, swarming with Fascist spies, German soldiers, SS officers, and the Gestapo. General Cadorna advised him not to attempt to infiltrate his way into the city. He warned that, at best, he would last a few hours. Another senior partisan leader in Milan, however, told him to come at once. The letter had come by mail from Milan to Bergamo and then was hand-carried up to his mountain hideout with the partisans. As late August arrived, Oliver Churchill, still limping slightly, decided to head for Milan. Unbeknownst to him, the Germans in the city were on the highest level of alert.[4]

# Part Three

ON THE LINE

# 8

## DUG-IN DEFENCE
### *The German Plan*

### August–September 1944

In the middle of August, the Allies landed on the southern coast of France, outside Nice, in the amphibious invasion Operation *Dragoon*. They faced little resistance and headed north through the valley of the Rhone River. The Red Army crossed from Poland onto the boundary of East Prussia itself, and the Americans prepared to invade the Philippines. While the war was being fought on its three other main fronts in a fluid manner, with one side advancing, the other retreating, this was not now the case in Italy. By 15 August the Allied armies had arrived up against the defences of the Gothic Line and were preparing to attack them. The Germans were largely dug in to static positions, trying to work out where the Allies would attack first. The latter were characteristically disagreeing among themselves where their assault should begin. And then they had a stroke of luck.

In northern Italy in the fifth year of the war, command responsibility often landed on young shoulders. Mino Farneti, a young Italian, had been eighteen and just out of high school when the war began, and he had luckily managed to avoid being drafted into the Italian Army. He was from Ravenna, north of Rimini, a 2,000-year-old classical city that had once been the capital of the Western Roman Empire. It was the site of eight famous early Christian churches, and in 1318 the poet Dante Alighieri, in exile from Florence, took up residence there. (He eventually died from malaria contracted from the ubiquitous mosquitoes that bred in the marshes and canals surrounding the city, and linking it to the sea.) Ravenna was old, rich, and beautiful.

By the time Farneti was nineteen, he was already evading both the Germans and Italian Fascists and was running messages on his bicycle for the local resistance group emerging around Ravenna. When the Italian Army collapsed after the Cassibile Armistice with the Allies in 1943, Farneti, brave and resourceful, couldn't wait to join the partisans and fight. Three partisan groups had sprung up in Ravenna, each with a different political allegiance and agenda. By the summer of 1944, Farneti had established his radio set in a farmhouse on the San Fortunato Ridge, one of two that overlooked from the north the pastures outside Rimini. He had organized three different drop zones onto which the Allied Dakota transports could parachute men and arms. If his first radio set was compromised by the Germans' never-ending sweeps with their radio-tracking equipment, one of his colleagues had a second hidden on the slope behind a farmhouse. Another partisan outwitted the Germans by keeping a radio inside a very busy, very active beehive. Even when German search parties had been inside the farmhouse itself, headsets attached to radio-tracking equipment mounted on a truck outside, they had been unable to locate the radio set in its honey enclave, even when it was switched on and therefore emitting a low signal.

Along with an estimated 1,200 colleagues from the partisans' Garibaldi Brigade, the operational remit of Farneti and his colleagues was simple: to make life as difficult as possible for the German defenders behind the lines, and to cooperate as much as possible with British and American SOE and OSS missions in order to be able do this effectively. The Americans, based in Corsica and Naples, and the British at their SOE headquarters and training centre at

Monopoli outside Bari, were making regular airdrops to the partisans. Farneti's group had already received three radio sets, as well as large amounts of arms: their orders were to concentrate on attacking the Germans along the length of the Gothic Line, and it was for this purpose that he had moved south from his hometown in Ravenna. Kesselring was aware of the partisans' successes and the threat they posed. One high-ranking German general stopped travelling with any flags, insignia, or identifying marks on his car. Another, Brigadier General Wilhelm Crisolli, commanding a brigade on the Ligurian coast outside Genoa, died when his staff car was riddled with machine-gun fire in an ambush.

One day in August, a group of Italian partisans were waiting behind some bushes on the side of a road near Rimini, when they saw a German motorbike and its sidecar coming towards them along the highway. The partisans were cautious. In their experience, the soldier sitting in the sidecar often had an MG-42 mounted in front of him, and it wouldn't be the first time the combination of the motorcycle's speed and manoeuvrability and the machine gun's firepower had proved a lethal offensive mix. So, with Sten guns and Carcano rifles cocked, the partisans let the Germans come close. Then they opened fire. The driver and the officer in the sidecar never saw the Italians who ambushed them, and were both dead before the BMW Zündapp motorbike came to a crashing halt. Mino Farneti, who led the small group of four partisans, was only twenty-three that summer.[1]

As the wheels of the motorbike combination still turned in the ditch, Farneti and the men with him searched the major's pouches and briefcase. They pocketed his Luger pistol, watch, and spare 9mm ammunition, and they took the bread, sausage, and cigarettes that the driver, like many other German soldiers, possibly stored in his gas-mask case. They would also have taken his MP-40 machine pistol, his six magazines of ammunition, and the precious canvas carrying pouches they came in, attached to the German's leather belt in sets of three. But it was only as they rifled hurriedly through the officer's briefcase and knapsack that Farneti realized that on the dusty road

Captain Daniel Inouye's official army photograph from 1947. (The Daniel K. Inouye Institute)

Daniel Inouye at a Second World War monument, wearing the ribbon of the Distinguished Service Cross won on Colle Musatello in April 1945. (The Daniel K. Inouye Institute)

Indian infantry advance across the aerodrome at Aquino in May 1944, among the smoking shells of destroyed German aircraft. (Photo by Mondadori Portfolio via Getty Images)

Indian soldiers from the British 8th Army studying a map in the hills of the Emilia-Romagna region, December 1944. (Photo by Mondadori Portfolio via Getty Images)

German SS-Sturmbannführer Walter Reder (left) talking to a woman during an on-the-spot investigation in Marzabotto in autumn 1944. Printed following the war crimes trial of Walter Reder in 1947. (Photo by Keystone/Hulton Archive/Getty Images)

Remains of some of the victims of the Marzabotto massacre, photographed in 1945. (Photo by Keystone-France/Gamma-Keystone via Getty Images)

German soldier during an anti-partisan operation in northern Italy. (Photo by: SeM/ UIG via Getty Images)

Oliver Churchill of the Special Operations Executive, photographed as a lieutenant in the British Army. (The Churchill family)

Ivan Houston in uniform, wearing the sweater knitted for him by his grandmother. (Ivan Houston)

Ivan Houston in a sketch drawn by a Rome street artist, April 1945. (Ivan Houston)

Private Ivan Houston and his mother in Los Angeles after he enlisted. (Ivan Houston)

Gothic Line terrain: Serravezza, in the western Apennines. The Buffalo Soldiers attacked at night, in pouring rain, straight up the steep mountain slope on the right. (Ivan Houston)

Soldiers from the 92nd Infantry Division with a German prisoner, Lucca, Tuscany, September 1944. (ISREC, Lucca)

An American jeep stuck in the Italian mud, 1944. (Photo by Roger Viollet/Getty Images)

German paratroopers man an MG-42 machine gun commanding a view over a road on the Gothic Line, August 1944. (Photo by Atlantic Press/ullstein bild via Getty Images)

German paratroopers on the Italian front. (Photo by Roger Viollet/Getty Images)

Night-time artillery barrage by Allied forces supporting American patrol attacks on German positions in the Apennine mountains. (Photo by Margaret Bourke-White/The LIFE Picture Collection/Getty Images)

German soldiers carrying artillery shells through the Italian autumn mud, 1944. (Photo by ullstein bild/ullstein bild via Getty Images)

Italian women and children cheering the arrival of British armoured vehicles. Foiano della Chiana, July 1944. (Photo by Mondadori Portfolio via Getty Images)

outside Rimini, lined with vineyards, they had struck gold. The German major was carrying a complete set of plans for the defences on the eastern end of the Gothic Line.

The immediate concern for the partisans was simple: how to get the papers to the Allies as quickly as possible? By mid-August, their front line was still around Florence, so they told a partisan courier to take them to a fellow agent in Milan. From there they were escorted by a combination of couriers to the headquarters of the OSS across the Swiss border in Lugano. The lakeside town acted as the headquarters not just for the Office of Strategic Services but also as a main meeting and transit point for the British Special Operations Executive, based in Berne.

A few days later, on the western end of the Gothic Line, another group of partisans got lucky. They succeeded in stealing another set of plans that showed the German defences that stretched from Bologna in the centre towards the Mediterranean. These partisans were based in and around the old medieval walled town of Lucca in western Tuscany, twenty miles from the sea in the shadow of the Apennines. In late summer 1944, the weather was hot and calm, and the German soldiers patrolling around the town took cover from the afternoon sun in the shade of the palm, magnolia, and cypress trees. The Americans were still ten miles to the south, advancing steadily.

So when the partisans in Lucca got hold of the set of German plans, they had two choices. Take them across the Allied front lines ahead of them and risk capture by the Germans, immediate torture and execution, and the loss of the documents? Or take the safer route by smuggling them north to Switzerland? The disadvantage of this was having to cross miles of German-occupied territory, thus losing precious time. They chose the first option.

The plans were voluminous: heavy paper with detailed markings in coloured wax pencil. Any partisan carrying them had to imagine he would be stopped and searched by at least one German checkpoint or patrol, so it was out of the question to carry them in a bag, in the lining of a jacket, or taped around the legs. So the most important parts of the maps were cut into a long strip, showing the geographical line from La Spezia on the Mediterranean to Bologna. A partisan then divided the papers in two, folded the plans into tight compact squares, and put them in the soles of his boots, under the leather inlay beneath his socks. It meant he had to walk slowly lest the crunching sound of the papers give him away. Leaving Lucca before the curfew, he set off with his companions across the fields of corn, the orchards of lemons and peaches, and the stands of ilex and cypress trees interspersed with irrigation ditches. He crossed through territory controlled by the SS soldiers of Max Simon's 16th Reichsführer-SS Division, which was the part of the German 14th Army responsible for this part of the western sector of the Gothic Line. The Allied front line lay ahead of the partisan courier. This was ground occupied by the Indians of the Marathas deployed south of the river Arno, and by the Nisei of the 442nd between them and the sea. Once across the front, the small partisan group headed south for Siena and contacted the OSS. The plans headed immediately to General Mark Clark's HQ.[2]

## THE GERMANS AND THEIR DEFENSIVE POSITIONS

The plans confirmed what the American general had most hoped: Kesselring was expecting an attack at the western end of the Gothic Line, where it hit the Mediterranean. The weakest part of the German defences was exactly in the middle, where the 14th and 10th Armies interlinked in the mountains outside Bologna. British General Harold Alexander wanted to storm the line at this point, cut through the Apennines, and fan out with his armour into the plain of the river Po. The Allied landings in the south of France on Operation *Dragoon* – that both Churchill and Clark had bitterly resisted – had reduced the combined strength of the British 8th and American 5th Armies to some 150,000 men, or eighteen divisions. Up against them were two German armies which, with their reserves and an army corps in the Ligurian mountains above Genoa, consisted of nearly thirty divisions. So while both sides were unevenly matched in terms of men, the Allies had the massive advantage of air superiority, while the Germans held the high ground and had had ample time to prepare their defences. Although the Allies had a numerical superiority in tanks and artillery, the terrain counted against them: heavy artillery pieces had to be towed, driven, pushed, hauled, and dragged up the mountainous terrain of central Italy. Until the Allies crossed over into the plain of the Po, their superiority in tanks gave them only a small advantage. And the Germans' artillery was well dug in, camouflaged, and commanded every single main road, river, bridge, mountain approach, crossroads, town, and village.

The partisans were able to give a very clear intelligence picture, to both the OSS and General Clark's headquarters, of what life was like in the territory occupied by the Germans. Partisans and their families had been conscripted as forced labour for the Germans, so they could give an accurate appraisal of the exact strengths and weaknesses of the Gothic Line defences. In cities like Bologna, partisans reported that the German officer cadres were leading a busy and enjoyable social life. Italian Fascist officers and their sympathizers gave parties all the time: there was no shortage of wine, grappa, and vermouth, and no shortage of friendly Italian women who still thought that the war could swing back to the Germans' and Mussolini's favour. Collaborating Italian women frequently worked as prostitutes. There was little shortage of food for the Germans. Allied air attacks were frequent but caused as much damage and disruption to the civilian population as to the Germans, and weakened support for the British and Americans, mostly in the cities and towns that were hardest hit.

The plans and information smuggled across the lines contained information about the German high command structure too. From intercepted coded communications, cracked by Ultra, the Allies had already built up a clear picture of the commanders they were facing on the Gothic Line. One of the most capable German generals in front of them was Luftwaffe General der Fallschirmtruppe Richard Heidrich. He was a hugely experienced and highly decorated paratrooper who had fought as an infantryman in the First World

War, jumped with German airborne units in the invasions of France and Crete, fought in Russia, and parachuted again in advance of the Allied landings in Sicily. He'd fought at Anzio and, crucially, during the four battles of Monte Cassino. It was his men who had held up the Allied advance so doggedly during their attacks on the site of the Benedictine monastery. His *fallschirmjäger* (paratroopers), the so-called Green Devils, were among the best troops the Germans had, past masters of dug-in, defensive fighting.

The partisans reported that after withdrawing northward from Rome towards Florence, Heidrich had briefly based the headquarters of his 1st Parachute Corps in a Tuscan villa outside the town of Regello. The night before he and his HQ departed north, they hosted a large and grand party for the officers from their own and other German units. But the partisans had connections among the Tuscan waiters and gardeners, and via the OSS, the exact location of the villa and the time of the party was passed to the Allied Desert Air Force in Corsica. As the German paratroop officers relaxed after almost a year of constant combat, the sky overhead groaned and rumbled as American B-24 Liberators flew in and unloaded sticks of 500-pound bombs on the villa and its surroundings. The good news for the Allies was that Heidrich's garden party had been ruined. But the bad news, as passed on by the partisans, was that Heidrich's crack parachute corps had moved northeast and taken over the defences in the key coastal town of Rimini, one of the Allies' main targets.

The German paratroopers near the Adriatic town were doing more than preparing defensive positions. It was summer, and they were reportedly making the most of it – taking advantage of the sun to go swimming naked, occupying any number of hotels, and interspersing their preparations with forays into the countryside to pick tomatoes, grapes, and melons with which to augment their rations. One detachment of paratroopers, searching through a beachfront hotel in Rimini, found a letter from two women, sent from Germany. In early summer that year, the women had been planning to vacation in German-occupied Italy, which was a relatively safe destination until the Allies broke through the defensive lines outside Rome and headed north. Was it possible, the German women had asked in their letter, to go swimming in the nude in the sea at Rimini? Courteously, given that they were preparing for an enormous countrywide attack by the Allies, the German paratroopers wrote a letter back, saying that yes, everybody was swimming naked in the Adriatic that season.[3]

## THE GERMAN GENERALS

In the centre of the line, opposite the Marathas, were not only the 16th SS-Panzergrenadier Division but also a division of infantry from Berlin Brandenburg. Their morale was low, reported the partisans, mainly due to the eccentric and merciless leadership of their commanding officer, who was a tireless advocate of the tactical approach of fighting to the last man. The Allies knew Generalleutnant Harry Hoppe well. He was an Evangelical Christian from Braunschweig in eastern Prussia who stood five foot eight and weighed 126 pounds. He had been a soldier since 1914, when he enlisted as a private. Continually wounded, continually decorated, and continually promoted, by the summer of 1944 he was a major general in charge of the defence of Ancona on the Adriatic coast south of Rimini. He'd already won the Knight's Cross of the Iron Cross on the Russian Front, and he was to be mentioned in dispatches for his tenacious and highly skilful defence of the Adriatic port under a blistering attack by the Poles in late June. Nicknamed 'Stan Laurel' by his men, because of his lack of height and facial resemblance to the popular comedian, he had changed his name from Arthur to Harry in February 1943 as he thought it would make him more popular with his men. Whether it did is doubtful. A newly arrived detachment was hardly reassured when greeted with, 'You have come here to die and to be quick about it.'

Using clichés such as 'They Shall Not Pass' and 'Better Death than Captivity' in front of parades did not inspire confidence in his men, 1,000 of whom chose captivity over death when the unrelenting Poles of General Władysław Anders' II Corps overwhelmed them at Ancona. The survivors of the 278th Infantry Division were then transferred to central Italy, where they were aghast to discover that opposite them was another enemy just as hard as the Poles: the Marathas of the 21st Indian Brigade. And to make things worse, behind them were the partisans. Even the remorselessly upbeat Generalleutnant Hoppe was obliged to describe Easter 1944 in his diary as 'a sombre festival' after partisans blew up a Good Friday cinema performance, killing a number of his men as they celebrated the holiday. But contrary to morale, which was variable, the quality of German leadership across Italy was high. The style of generalship varied, with determined leaders like Heidrich, Hoppe, and the 16th SS-Panzergrenadiers' Max Simon. They led their men with a combination of tactical capability, inspiration, discipline and, in the case of the SS, ruthless devotion to a cause.

Yet morale among the German soldiers was variable. They knew they were well led, predominantly well equipped, and had control of the terrain. But by mid-1944, they were under no misapprehensions that their Italian allies were anything other than lacklustre and unreliable. Allied air strikes were a constant but predictable worry. But if and when everything went wrong, they knew from long experience since Sicily and North Africa that they could surrender to the Americans or British or Canadians and stand a good chance of making it to a POW stockade alive. Italy was not Russia, and the Allies were not the Red Army. Prisoners were taken. It was the Italian partisans who were the unknown, constant fear. It was impossible to tell where they would strike next. Any German vehicle travelling in a convoy that did not contain an armoured car or tank was a target. Small units based on isolated stretches of the line – and the Gothic Line snaked across some of Europe's most rugged, isolated mountainous terrain – had no idea who could be moving in front of their trenches, dugouts, or fortified houses in the darkness. Partisans? Wolves? Deer? Marathas or Gurkhas? It was impossible to tell.

But sometimes, out of the line it was impossible to relax and feel secure. Vicious reprisals against partisans and the civilian population had, since the massacre at Sant'Anna di Stazzema, become more frequent. So the partisans had no qualms about attacking the Germans wherever or whenever they found them. The individual political leadership of each partisan group, and the SOE and OSS officers who operated with them, continually reiterated to the partisans the operational imperatives stressed by Jock McCaffery, the head of the SOE in Berne: 'offensive military action and sabotage against German targets in support of the advancing Allies' war aims and strategic plan.'

So the Germans, in many cases, felt just as vulnerable to attack from behind as from the front. Way behind the Gothic Line were units stationed in the region of Liguria. This is a region of mountains that rise above the Mediterranean coast west of Genoa to the French border. The string of seaside towns – Savona, Imperia, San Remo – sit in the shadow of the mountains. Since the late 1870s, they had been the seaside resorts of choice for the inhabitants of northwest Italy; Bordighera, with its villas and carefully designed gardens, was a favourite of the British upper middle class. Each town had a long sandy beach with some rocky coves, a coastal railway line leading behind it, a little station, and then the town itself built up the gradual slopes that led into the limestone mountains. These were covered in harsh scrub of olive, ilex, and small oak trees.

Among the other German generals who led through a combination of bravery and enormous personal example was an officer who commanded a unit in this part of Italy. The 90th Panzergrenadier Division had been pulled back to the Gothic Line after the fighting at Cassino. It was commanded by Generalleutnant Ernst-Günther Baade. He had been a Rhodes scholar, winning a sports scholarship to study at Oxford University before the war, and was well known on the European equestrian circuit. He loved Scotland.[4] He frequently wore kilts, and, during the fighting at Monte Cassino, he announced the names of Allied POWs over the English and American radio frequencies so their unit commanders could know their men were alive. He had been wounded in North Africa during the fighting at Bir Hakeim, before the battle of El Alamein. Colleagues in the Afrika Korps remembered him as a legend, who was known to go into battle dressed in a Scottish kilt and carrying a claymore, a double-edged Scottish medieval broadsword. Wounded twice and decorated for gallantry nine times, he was adored by his men.

The Adriatic sector of the Gothic Line, from Pesaro to the Muraglione Pass near Florence, was under the command of an aristocratic Prussian officer, Generaloberst Heinrich von Vietinghoff, and his 10th Army. Having lied about his age (he was fifteen) to join the army during the First World War, he was a tank officer during the invasion of France in 1940, a general by the time Hitler's panzers pushed into Yugoslavia, and a tank corps commander in Army Group Centre during Operation *Barbarossa*. It was in Russia that he earned the nickname 'Panzerknacker', Tank Breaker. And it was in Italy, commanding the 10th Army on the Gustav Line, that he was awarded the Oak Leaves to accompany his Knight's Cross of the Iron Cross. It was he who reportedly developed the defensive concept of removing the 75mm guns and turrets of Panther tanks from their chassis and digging them into concrete revetments as a fixed gun emplacement. The turret mechanism and its traversing system was embedded in a concrete bunker at ground level, tactically sited, and then camouflaged. This allowed the tanks' firepower to be deployed on mountainous terrain in very strong defensive positions where tanks themselves do not have the capacity to manoeuvre.

The eastern end of the Adriatic sector was under the control of LXXVI Panzerkorps, commanded by General der Panzertruppe Traugott Herr, another tank officer who had fought in France and Russia, been wounded, and decorated for gallantry. He had five divisions – one panzergrenadier, three infantry, one mountain – and Richard Heidrich's paratrooper corps, itself with three more divisions. One of the infantry units, the 162nd, was primarily composed of Turkoman troops recruited from central Asia. Backing them up to the west, towards Florence, was General der Gebirgstruppe Valentin

Feurstein's LI Mountain Corps, which had only two actual *gerbirgsjäger* (mountain) divisions, and five line infantry divisions, one of them Italian.

From Bologna west to the Mediterranean was the fiefdom of General der Panzertruppe Joachim Lemelsen and his 14th Army. His deputy was another Anglophile and Oxford Rhodes scholar – General der Panzertruppe Frido von Senger und Etterlin, a Bavarian and devout Catholic, who was also a lay Benedictine; he commanded the army's XIV Panzer Corps. This was made up of one panzer division, one infantry division, and SS-Gruppenführer Max Simon with the 16th Reichsführer-SS Division, stationed west of Florence. To the far west, and north of the Gothic Line in the Mediterranean province of Liguria around Genoa, were two more German divisions and two Italian. In and around the mountains and passes on the French–Italian border was the German LXXV Corps. This was made up of three infantry divisions, one of which was the 90th Panzergrenadiers of the claymore-wielding Ernst-Günther Baade. Another four reserve divisions were spread behind the German lines between the Gothic Line and the Alps, making thirty-one divisions in total facing the Allies. Many were understrength.

In addition to the partisans' military operations behind the lines, they had been busy sabotaging the construction of some of the fortifications of the Gothic Line. The Germans had started building these around the time of the armistice, in September 1943, when Italy surrendered. They conscripted thousands of Italians as forced labour. Partisans, naturally, were among them. They couldn't make any difference to such factors as the layout of minefields, or the quality of weapons the Germans were using, but they could directly affect the building. Straw, hay, gravel, and the bare minimum of cement were used where possible, meaning that a pillbox made of the lowest quality concrete would buckle under Allied fire. Gun emplacements were built facing twenty or thirty degrees the wrong way, and only when German troops placed their MG-42s or their anti-tank weapons in them did they discover, too late, that they didn't have the necessary commanding view of approach roads and valleys. Barbed wire was stretched in front of trenches and gun positions, but it wasn't attached at either end to anything but a bush. Trenches were built on slopes that flooded easily in autumn and filled with snow in winter. Pillboxes were positioned by streams and rivers that would fill the concrete bunker with water through holes low on its sides. The partisans kept detailed notes of these soft spots in the German defences.

So across the Gothic Line the Germans waited. On the road towards Bologna, Walter Reder and his SS reconnaissance battalion headed towards the enormous mass of Monte Sole that overlooked the road north from Florence. Max Simon had deployed the remainder of the 16th Reichsführer-SS on the north side of the Arno, opposite the 34th US Infantry Division, on whose flanks were Sergeant Daniel Inouye and the 442nd RCT. General Harry Hoppe's battered but disciplined 278th Infantry Division was north of Florence, opposite the Maratha Light Infantry. General Ernst-Günther Baade and his 90th Panzergrenadiers were far to the northwest, spread across the Ligurian terrain right up to the outskirts of the city of Turin, in the shadow of the Alps. On the Adriatic coast at Rimini, the talented paratrooper General Richard Heidrich agreed with Kesselring's strategic evaluation that the Allies would attack in the centre or west of the Gothic Line. So in the third week of August, he went on leave. His paratroopers shook out across the city and surrounding countryside, preparing defensive positions that covered roads, open country, and the approach routes to the San Fortunato and Coriano ridges that dominated the flat land outside the port. Mortars, 88mm guns, and MG-42s were sited, minefields laid, anti-tank guns hidden inside haystacks and abandoned houses, and trenches dug.

In the church of San Lorenzo in Strada, outside the seaside suburb of Riccione, the Green Devils dug in. The building dominates the main road that leads northwest from Riccione to Rimini airfield, and then straight up the coast into the heart of the port itself. Any Allied attack up the seacoast would have to go through Riccione, and then directly at the church. Paratroopers from Heidrichs' 1st Fallschirmjäger Regiment took over the church in the third week of August. One of them was only seventeen that month. Jäger Helmut Bücher was born on Christmas Day 1926. He was from Otzenhausen, a town in the German Saarland that lies southwest of Frankfurt, only twenty miles from the border with eastern France. His hometown dated back to the days of Julius Caesar's wars in Germania in 30 BC, and just north of it is one of the oldest surviving Gothic settlements in Europe. Bücher had enlisted in the paratroopers when he turned seventeen, and it was a great source of pride to him that he had been posted to the 1st Fallschirmjäger Regiment. Only in late June that same year had he joined his unit. Most of his comrades were survivors of Monte Cassino. Several had parachuted into the vineyards of Crete in 1941. A few, a hard, central cadre, had been in Russia and France.

They dug trenches and a tunnel connecting the houses surrounding San Lorenzo in Strada to the crypt of the church; they had learned the technique in Russia and at Cassino. The defenders could run from one position to another without showing themselves, and vacate a house or building when it came under sustained tank or mortar fire, reappearing in the next house or garden or field or farm building. They knew from Cassino and the fighting in the mountain towns and villages of southern Italy that underground dugouts were vital. The Allies relied heavily on artillery bombardments to soften up a target: the German paratroopers would sit out the barrage, then the moment it stopped, emerge above ground and instantly get their MG-42 machine guns into prepared firing positions. They zeroed in on the tanks that often spearheaded the advance with anti-tank guns dug in up to a half mile away. The fall of shot of 81mm mortars was cross-mapped onto individual paths of advance, paths of retreat, and the areas of cover where the Allied infantry would hide and wait. The *fallschirmjäger* also prepared an escape route behind the church that would expose any Allied soldiers chasing them to the fire of tanks and machine guns stationed behind them as the next line of defence.

Helmut Bücher felt he was in the right place, at the right time, as he dug trenches, made a fire to heat food, carried belts of 7.92mm cartridges for the machine guns, and got ready for an attack his sergeant had told him could not be far away. He and colleagues walked the ground in front of and around their positions in the church and surrounding houses. They paced out distances – one, two, four, six hundred yards. Then they marked particular walls, low-hanging branches on notable trees, and the sides of visible houses with whitewash crosses. This would tell the defenders the exact range of their attackers once battle was joined. Bücher had told his parents in a letter that he thought he was defending all that was right and good about Germany. But as he prepared the position in front of the church outside Rimini, he wondered if he would see his eighteenth Christmas.[5]

# 9

## THE COMPLEXITIES OF COMMAND

### *General Leese and Operation* Olive

### Late August 1944

One of General Harold Alexander's most senior planning officers had devised a plan that involved the Americans and the British storming northward from Florence to Bologna and cutting the Gothic Line in half. Then they would flank left, right, and towards the centre into the plains of Lombardy that lay along the river Po. Once Bologna had fallen, the dreaded Apennines would be behind them. They could use their tanks to best advantage in the flat countryside. This plan focused on an attack in the centre, and it would be accompanied by diversionary attacks on both the Adriatic and Mediterranean coasts. The city of Rimini was the main prize in the east. But then the British commander of the 8th Army, Lieutenant General Oliver Leese, made the first of a series of strategic decisions that would ensure that the battle for the Gothic Line became a bloody, protracted affair. He insisted on attacking, and taking, the port of Rimini first.

Leese was an aristocratic British officer, the son of a baronet, who had been educated at Eton and then fought in the First World War on the Somme. He had served in the Coldstream Guards, the second-oldest regiment in the British Army. It was raised during the English Civil War in 1650 by Oliver Cromwell as part of his New Model Army, or Roundheads, who were fighting the Cavaliers, troops loyal to the monarchy of Kings Charles I and II. However, after the abdication of Cromwell's son and successor, Richard Cromwell, the Coldstreams changed sides, backed the monarchy, helped suppress an anti-royalist revolt, and were then chosen to be the king and royal household's personal bodyguard. By 1914, they were part of the prestigious Brigade of Guards, whose duties included guarding the monarch of England.

There was no more blue-blooded regiment in the British Army, and Leese fitted in perfectly. Guards officers were not just told to think they were better; in the 1920s many of them believed it as an article of faith. Surely the award of 107 different battle honours since the 1600s couldn't be wrong? They saw themselves as a military and social elite. Although Leese was indeed aristocratic, he was a good leader. He was kind, enjoyed a confident popularity with his men, and was certainly brave – he was born to play the part he did. He had been wounded three times in France in the First World War, the last time on the Somme in 1916. He was decorated twice for gallantry, the second time with the Distinguished Service Order, the British equivalent of the American Distinguished Service Cross.[1] He was a product of the British Empire, the upper echelons of the British class system, and was absolutely content with it. He'd never operated with any troops other than British or colonial ones. When war broke out in 1939, he was a colonel instructor at the British Army's staff college at Quetta in India: his experiences there simply confirmed his preconceptions.

He returned home and fought with the British Expeditionary Force in their doomed and ineffectual campaign against the German invasion of France, Holland, and Belgium. He left the beaches of Dunkirk. Eighteen months of home defence in England followed, and then in September 1942, Lieutenant General Bernard Montgomery asked for him to be transferred to North Africa. There, as an acting lieutenant general, he was given command of XXX Corps of the British 8th Army. Leese was not lacking in bravery, charm, connection, or leadership skills. Montgomery had instructed him at staff college in 1927 and 1928 and been impressed by him.[2] Leese had an easygoing, childlike sense of humour, which British soldiers warmed to, and in the manner of the eccentric British aristocracy, developed a personal and extra-curricular hobby while fighting in North Africa. He was fascinated by cacti. He made notes about the different types of cacti he found in the desert, and in the evenings when not drafting operational orders for his units, he quietly devised a way whereby, using electrically heated sand, they might be grown in large numbers in hothouses back in the chilly climate of England.

The British non-commissioned officers and private soldiers under his command, who had grown up with the divisive social realities of the English class system in the post-First World War period, understood Leese. They knew where they stood with him. The British generalship on the Western Front had so often been lacklustre at best and disastrous at worst that the generation of soldiers that followed in North Africa made the most of what they had. For some of them it seemed that a quietly eccentric, amiable, and aristocratic general who had been decorated for bravery was the best they were going to get. But other nationalities, American and Commonwealth, did not warm to Leese quite so easily.

The cacti-loving officer commanded XXX Corps across North Africa and in the invasion of Sicily, after which they were sent home to Britain to prepare for the invasion of northwest Europe. Leese went with them. Then Montgomery sent him a telegram ordering him back to Italy to take over the whole of the 8th Army. For the crucial month of late August to late September 1944, the success or failure of the Allied offensive on the Gothic Line was to lie with Leese. Despite being a protégée of General Montgomery, he lacked his strategic imagination and battlefield flexibility. Along with the American 5th Army, he had led the Allied forces in the fourth battle of Monte Cassino that finally broke the gridlock south of Rome. He should, therefore, have been the perfect foil to Mark Clark, and a well-suited accompaniment and counterpoint to his command style. But he and Clark did not see eye to eye. Leese, like many British soldiers, resented Clark for his handling of the debacle at Anzio that had cost so many lives. He also resented his grandstanding entry into Rome, mistaking it for personal triumphalism instead of the collective signalling of American victory that Clark believed it to be. The two generals should have cooperated better, but Leese's direct British superior, General Harold Alexander, was no favourite of Clark's either. Clark had once commented that Alexander 'was unsuited to high command'.[3]

But the most specific and focused criticism of Leese and his command style came not from the Americans but from the closest allies of the British – the Canadians.[4] The Canadian commander in Italy in summer 1944, Lieutenant General Henry 'Harry' Crerar, wrote in his diary about Oliver Leese and his Anglocentric view of generalship that 'in practice, no Canadian, American or other national commander, unless possessing quite phenomenal qualities, is ever rated as high (in their own opinion) as the British.'

The Canadians made fabulous soldiers. Yet despite their record of dogged, tenacious, and aggressive fighting in the appalling conditions in the battles around Monte Cassino, Leese thought that their leadership was substandard. He particularly found fault with Lieutenant General Tommy Burns, the commander of the 1st Canadian Corps. This senior officer had a notoriously brusque and anti-social manner with subordinates, which led to his quick-humoured Canadian soldiers nicknaming him 'Smiling Sunray'. (Sunray was the radio call sign of a unit's senior officer.) Leese was insecure about the Canadians. He thought they wouldn't do what they were told. He thought, simply, that he was better than them. They were independent of mind and of approach to soldiering, had almost no time for the colonialist attitude of the British Empire towards its subordinates – they rightly saw in Leese a typical product of Empire – and they fiercely resented criticism. So when Leese announced that he was going to carry out an investigation into the Canadians' (exceptional) performance in the battles in the Liri valley and on the Melfa River in May 1944, Burns and his chief of staff, Lieutenant General Ken Stuart, were incensed. Leese thought that various battalion- and brigade-level attacks could have been handled differently. The Canadians disagreed. Leese instructed Stuart to come up with a report on the capabilities of Burns and his senior officers. He said that it was likely that Burns would have to be replaced by a British general.

Not surprisingly, the Canadians closed ranks. Lieutenant General Stuart interviewed Canadian officers from brigadier down to the rank of captain and found that although the Canadians were quick to admit to tactical and logistical errors in the spring fighting – mainly based upon the appalling weather and the German tactical command of the high ground – they were an extremely cohesive division with high morale, and very determined. Stuart then turned the cards in his favour when he managed to persuade both Generals Clark and Alexander that the internal investigation was unnecessary, that the problem lay with Leese, and that the Canadians were not going to accept a British general to lead them. At a final meeting between Leese and Lieutenant General Stuart, where the latter calmly presented his findings, Leese lost his temper and accused the Canadians of trying to take over and command the 8th Army. Secretly, even Leese knew this was far too much. He had noted frequently in his diary since the end of 1943 that he admired the Canadians' fighting spirit and their commitment to the cause of defending the British Empire. But he could not admit to himself that on several occasions in Italy that year, a combination of the weather, the Germans' tactical and strategic skills, their men, equipment, and control of the terrain had, simply, defeated the Allies. And he was shooting himself in both feet by criticizing the Canadians. They were one of his trump cards, some of the best troops he had.

## THE CANADIANS FROM NEW WESTMINSTER

First into the attack on Rimini were going to be the British and Canadians; the second wave would be the rugged 5th Canadian Armoured Division. One of the regiments in this unit was the Westminster Regiment, whose soldiers came from the area of the same name – New Westminster, a town just outside Vancouver in the province of British Columbia, on Canada's Pacific coast. The Westminsters were frontiersmen – fishermen, lumberjacks, men who worked in sawmills. Above their town loomed the vastness of the mountains that march up the seaboard of the Pacific northwest. The unit sailed from Halifax, Nova Scotia, in June 1941, landed eleven days later in Liverpool, and then moved to a series of training camps in southern England. The British towns and countryside were filling up with Canadians, preceding the flood of Americans who would arrive after Pearl Harbor. The Canadians were billeted in army camps and in some of the huge country houses and estates that dotted England.[5] The Westminsters found themselves in countryside rather more genteel than that back home. They made camp at Pippingford Park, an English country house in the Ashdown Forest in Hampshire that dated back 300 years to the time of King Charles II. In the woods and fields of rural Hampshire, Surrey, and Norfolk, the 5th Division spent the next two and a half years training – and so missed the disastrous baptism by fire of the Canadian Army on the beaches of Dieppe in August 1942.

The Canadian generals were extremely keen that their soldiers gain combat experience and be seen to contribute to the Allied war effort. Winston Churchill, the leader of Combined Operations, Vice Admiral Lord Louis Mountbatten, and Lieutenant General Bernard Montgomery, then commanding Britain's South-Eastern District, were eager to carry out an amphibious landing on the northern coast of France. It would give the Allies crucial practice for a future invasion of northwest Europe, and as Churchill said in his diaries, 'I thought it most important that a large-scale operation should take place this summer, and military opinion seemed unanimous that until an operation on that scale was undertaken, no responsible general would take the responsibility of planning the main invasion.'

Marshal Joseph Stalin was exerting enormous pressure on the Allies to carry out a landing in occupied France: a year into Operation *Barbarossa*, he was desperate for at least thirty German divisions to be withdrawn from Russia. Allied naval intelligence reportedly wanted to use the raid as a cover so it could steal a German Enigma coding machine and codebooks from one of the headquarters in Dieppe. They would then pass them to the Bletchley Park decoding centre in southern England, where the Allies had made spectacular progress in decrypting the secrets of the German Enigma system. Lieutenant Commander Ian Fleming of British Naval Intelligence – who went on to create the character of James Bond – reportedly planned this operation. So on 19 August the raid took place. There had been a hint of doom: on 17 August, in the crossword of the *Daily Telegraph*, a clue appeared: 'French port'. The solution appeared the next day: 'Dieppe'. A senior Canadian intelligence officer, Lord Tweedsmuir, was told to investigate this apparent leak; he was the son of the author John Buchan, who had been governor general of Canada until his death in 1940. The conclusion was that the placing of the crossword clue was a coincidence. The disaster that was Operation *Jubilee* was not.

Six thousand Allied troops, 5,000 of them Canadian, went ashore on six open French beaches at dawn, unsupported by naval gunfire. Intelligence had said the target area in and around the coastal town of Dieppe was lightly defended and its beaches suitable for landings. Within ten hours, the entire force had been either killed, wounded, taken prisoner, or withdrawn by sea. There were significant successes – British commandos destroyed an artillery battery of six 150mm guns overlooking the beaches; intelligence was gathered on radar installations; significant lessons were learned about carrying out combined operations and amphibious landings. But at every strategic and almost every tactical level, it was a failure – the Royal Navy refused to commit cruisers and battleships as fire support because they thought they would be vulnerable to air attack, and their fire would hit French civilians. Landing craft and escort vessels got confused at sea and landed in the wrong place. Of one British Commando, 750 strong, only 18 men made it ashore in the right place on Yellow Beach. On Blue Beach alone, of 556 men from the Royal Canadian Regiment who landed, 200 were killed and 264 wounded or captured. They'd planned to land under cover of smokescreens and darkness, but the first blew away, the second cleared, and they were massacred by German machine guns as they hit the beach. Three dozen valuable landing craft were lost. Tanks landed on beaches got bogged down in soft shingle.

The RAF deployed forty-eight squadrons of Spitfires alone, some 550 aircraft, but they were operating at the extreme level of their range, and many could spend only five minutes over the target. Of 5,000 Canadians, 3,367 were killed, captured, or wounded. Operation *Jubilee* was an object lesson in how not to carry out an amphibious landing. The Canadians were at the centre of the furore that followed. The failure had little to do with the fact most of their troops were inexperienced – senior Allied officers determined subsequently that even the most experienced combat troops would almost certainly have proved incapable of storming in daylight open, exposed beaches covered by artillery, mortar, and machine guns. The Germans captured a set of invasion plans from an Allied officer who surrendered on a beach, and then tried – unsuccessfully – to bury his maps and documents under his feet in the shingle. German staff officers were astounded that an adversary would launch a divisional attack unsupported by artillery or naval gunfire, across exposed beaches, against an enemy that in many cases had been alerted to the forthcoming assault. Although senior Canadian officers had pressed hard for their men to be included in the plan, Canadian soldiers were left afterward with a sense of mistrust and suspicion of senior British and Commonwealth planning. So as the Westminster Regiment and the 5th Canadian Armoured Division trained for more than two years across the fields, villages, and parkland of southern England, the desperate lessons of Dieppe became ingrained in each unit's thinking. When was the next time they would be thrown headfirst into battle against well-prepared Germans by Allied staff officers who had made a shoddy plan?

## THE WESTMINSTERS GO TO WAR

On 15 November 1943, the Westminster Regiment set sail for Algiers. Of their six companies, A was commanded by Major John Keefer Mahony, known as 'Jack'. He was born in 1911 in New Westminster, educated at the local high school, and had a reputation as an athlete. He became a journalist, reporting for the *Vancouver Daily Province*, before joining the Westminsters and getting a commission in 1938. He sailed for England with the rest of the unit in November 1941. From Algiers, the battalion sailed to Naples and almost immediately moved up to the front in January 1944. Over the coming months in the fighting in Italy, the Westminster Regiment established a near record of any Allied unit for the greatest number of days spent in combat on the front line. Mahony estimated that between January and April alone, when they went headfirst into the fighting on the Liri River outside Monte Cassino, it was more than a hundred. By 3 May they came out of the line after the last battle of Cassino exhausted. They had a week's rest, and then the attack on the Gustav Line, the German defences north of Rome, began.

Along with the rest of the 5th Canadian Armoured Division, their mission was to cross the Liri and advance up the valley that stretched between two mountain ranges northwest of Cassino. The Liri valley was the main axis of approach to Rome. Taking it was vital. The Westminsters and a Canadian armoured reconnaissance unit, Lord Strathcona's Horse, were to lead the attack with an assault over the smaller Melfa River. So on the morning of 24 May a young Canadian lieutenant from Lord Strathcona's Horse roared forward with a troop of four light Honey tanks. Armed with 37mm cannon, these American armoured vehicles had proved hopelessly outgunned in North Africa by German Panther tanks, and had made easy targets for the German 88mm guns.

The tanks forded the shallow waters of the Melfa and took up positions on the west bank, facing the road to Rome. Lieutenant Edward J. Perkins and his sergeant, Clifford Macey, got the troop into defensive positions facing 270 degrees, and waited while Mahony led A Company across the river behind them to support and enlarge the bridgehead.[6] The problem was that the Germans not only had machine guns, tanks, and self-propelled guns on the west bank, they also still had them on the east bank waiting to cross the river. Both these German units opened fire on A Company of the Westminsters as Mahony led them across the river on foot onto the west bank, and then as he got them positioned in a loose semi-circle. The company immediately started taking casualties and, apart from the tanks' light cannon, had almost nothing with which to hit back at the German 88s. Like the Indians and the British, the Canadians were armed with Lee–Enfields, Bren guns, and a mix of Sten and Thompson submachine guns. As German shells and bullets sang overhead, thwacked into the ground, or smashed into the rocks, the Westminsters tried to dig into the soggy ground with their entrenching tools. Mahony seemed to be everywhere, encouraging, marking targets, identifying the source of German fire.

Surrounding the small bridgehead, the Germans had two 88mm self-propelled guns, a battery of anti-aircraft weapons, machine guns, and more than 100 infantry. Against the armour, the Canadians had only cumbersome British PIAT anti-tank rocket launchers. They were heavy, spring-propelled drainpipes with a forward stand on which the firer rested the launcher's weight. Thirty-two pounds, inaccurate, loathsome to carry, and requiring considerable physical strength to use, the PIAT was a disastrous invention. To cock the heavy spring, the operator had to stand up and use his booted foot to depress it, so exposing himself to enemy fire at the crucial, most vulnerable moment when he needed to reload it. The British had produced such exceptional weapons as the Lee–Enfield rifle, the Bren gun, and the 25-pounder anti-tank gun, but the PIAT was not one of them. However, Mahony and his men had no choice but to use the weapons they had. Using the heavy rocket launcher, they knocked out the anti-aircraft guns and one of the 88s, all the while under heavy fire. Then the Germans counterattacked. A Company had crossed the Melfa 132 strong, but by this point only 60 were left unwounded. Three out of four of Mahony's officers were wounded. At one point a section was pinned down under machine-gun fire, but the calm, level-headed officer from British Columbia crawled forward, threw smoke grenades to cover their withdrawal, and managed to extricate the ten men, losing only one.

The Germans counterattacked again, knowing that the weakened company and the four light tanks were the only toehold the entire Allied armies had on the western side of the river. Mahony was wounded twice in the leg, as well as in the head, but overnight he commanded his company and beat off repeated German attacks, holding off the enemy until the Westminsters were reinforced and relieved the following morning. A later citation summed up the action with characteristic understatement:

> Major Mahony personally led his company down to and across the river . . . Although the crossing was made in full view of and under heavy fire from the enemy machine-gun posts on the right rear and left front, he personally directed each section into its proper position on the west bank with the greatest coolness and confidence. With absolute fearlessness and disregard for his own safety, Major Mahony personally directed the fire of his PIATs throughout this action, encouraging and exhorting his men. Mahony was wounded in the head and twice in the leg, but he refused medical attention and continued to direct the defence of the bridgehead, never allowing the thought of withdrawal to enter his mind. His example was followed closely by his men, and the Germans were defeated in their efforts to destroy the bridgehead. His defence of the perimeter against overwhelming odds under the severest battle conditions was crucial to the outcome of the

Battle of Liri Valley. Only when reinforcements arrived would Mahony allow his wounds to be dressed.[7]

Jack Mahony received the Victoria Cross on 31 July from King George VI. Lieutenant Perkins from Lord Strathcona's Horse was awarded the Distinguished Service Order and promotion to captain; for a young subaltern, the award of a DSO, normally reserved for ranks of major and above, meant he had probably come close to being cited for a VC. Sergeant Macey got the Distinguished Conduct Medal. The monarch was travelling incognito in Italy, disguised as a fictitious 'General Collingwood', and other recipients of honours he handed out included Oliver Leese, whom the king knighted in the field. Mahony was still semi-crippled by his wounds and could hardly stand up when George VI pinned the bronze cross with its dark maroon ribbon on his tunic.

In the Liri valley, the Canadians had led the way. But a week later, it was their turn to rest and refit as the Allied advance moved up towards Rome. The regiment was pulled back to two small villages behind the lines. As May turned to June, the late spring to early summer, A Company's main adversaries stopped being enemy fire, artillery, or mines, and became diarrhoea, the malaria mosquito, and jaundice. Every night, the troops would climb under an awkward mosquito net; some of them took Atabrine tablets, which caused paranoia and excessive mood swings, not behaviour that self-possessed and confident Canadian combat soldiers needed.

Another persistent problem for them and all the troops on both sides was sunburn. The Mediterranean from May to September is hot, the sun unforgiving. Sun cream for Allied troops fighting in North Africa and Italy was not in regular production or indeed commercial development at that stage of the war, although Benjamin Green, an American airman who was to become a pharmacist, invented one of the first sun creams that became available only to American troops serving in the Pacific. It had a very limited protection factor and worked by blocking ultraviolet radiation. It was called Red Vet Pet (short for red veterinary petrolatum) and was akin to putting red petroleum jelly on the skin, like a scarlet Vaseline. (Coppertone acquired the patent in the early 1950s.) But for British soldiers and American GIs in summer in Italy, there was little to protect their faces, arms, and necks. Olive oil was sometimes offered by sympathetic Italian civilians, which resulted in soldiers quickly finding themselves covered in a sticky amalgam of olive oil and dust, which, though hideously uncomfortable, provided some protection against the sun. On the opposite side, some units of the German Army were issued a very basic white sun cream that had been developed for vacationers in the 1930s.

The weather was hot as May turned into June, and the Westminsters found streams and rivers to bathe in. There was shade under ilex and chestnut trees. Local Italians, particularly in the countryside, were beyond generous with red and white wine, apricots, melons, and peaches. Diarrhoea and dysentery didn't take orders, though, and struck constantly, so many men filled their canteens with wine rather than risk drinking water from the rivers. The stalking spectre of war and fighting and combat stood back from the Westminsters for a few weeks, and looked elsewhere for victims.

## THE DIFFERENT ALLIED PLANS OF ATTACK

It was no surprise the Allies couldn't agree on a cohesive plan for the opening battle of the Gothic Line. The British commander, Oliver Leese, didn't completely trust the senior officers of one of the main component parts of his army – the Canadians – and intensely disliked his fellow army commander Mark Clark. In addition, they were making a plan to attack a well-commanded German force dug in to positions of their own choosing. Some of the senior Allied officers thought they were courting disaster. Different factors had pushed them inexorably towards a confrontation with Kesselring on a defended line on terrain of his own making. There was the failure at Anzio, Mark Clark's entry into Rome, the invasion of southern France, and the escape northward of the German 10th Army. Now the disagreements among Clark, Leese, and the Canadians seemed to be compounding the Allies' problems, pushing them farther into uncharted, dangerous terrain where the enemy could always blindside or second-guess them.

One thing, however, united the ambitious American Clark and the debonair but rigid British Guardsman Leese. They both deeply resented the way their armies had been stripped of seven divisions in the lead-up to the invasion of southern France, a redeployment both thought a diversionary waste of resources. By late August, the American and French forces fighting their way up the Rhone valley had not succeeded in diverting a single German brigade, let alone a division, from Normandy. In Italy, Leese and Clark knew the British and Americans were going to need every man they could get for the attack on the Gothic Line. And they were just about to lose some more of their very best fighters, men who in three months of combat had proved invaluable.

Leese, Clark, and their planning staffs had proposed a number of different attack options to General Harold Alexander. Not surprisingly, all sides disagreed. The British favoured a concentration of forces on one fixed objective – a strategic modus operandi the Americans thought was the brainchild of the trench warfare on the Western Front. Clark and the Americans wanted to push directly at the weakest point in the line, probe for resistance, and then exploit their tactical successes. Leese thought that this approach had been tried twice before by Clark, with disastrous results. Once, during the American attack on the Gari River south of Cassino, which had proved a bloodbath. And second, on a larger scale at Anzio, where the unopposed landings had provided the perfect opportunity for an immediate and flexible tactical exploitation of the battlefield situation. Instead, under Clark's direction, the American General John Lucas had ordered his men to dig in and consolidate the bridgehead, allowing the Germans time to counterattack and turn Anzio into the five-month debacle it had proved, where the blood of some of the best soldiers in the American and British armies had been poured needlessly into the sand.

Clark's first plan for the Gothic Line involved the British 8th and American 5th Armies attacking together in a single push northward through the Apennine mountains, from Florence to Bologna. The plans that the partisans had captured from the Germans and smuggled across the line showed that Kesselring's weakest point was in the centre around the San Giorgio Pass, near Bologna. So it made sense to attack there. But this scheme was rejected by Leese. He told General Władysław Anders, the legendary commander of II Polish Corps, that he wanted to fight up the Adriatic coast, while the Americans fought in the middle. He meant that he didn't want to fight alongside Clark's command, but this put him in a difficult command position. If he was going to attack Rimini with a separate 8th Army command, the troops at his disposal were going to be some of the most independent and idiosyncratic in Italy. Leese would command three different corps: one Canadian, one Polish, and one made up of New Zealanders and Greeks. There was some relief – the latter also contained the 1st British Armoured Division, made up of fellow Guardsmen. But the Greeks and New Zealanders were almost as independent as the Canadians and the Poles. Leese's British sense of superiority was about to be put to the most severe test.

Anders' Polish troops had won the final battle of Monte Cassino. Their commander had fought in Poland and Russia, had been wounded eight times, and would be decorated twenty-eight times for gallantry by ten countries, including his own. On both the Allied and German sides, the senior commanders who were alive, capable, and in control tended to have long service experience, to have been wounded in the First or Second World War, and to be decorated.

So to counter Mark Clark's strategy, Leese proposed an alternative plan. The British 8th Army, based around its three separate corps, would attack up the Adriatic coast towards the town of Rimini. This would force Albert Kesselring to move additional forces westward from Tuscany. The Americans would then attack the centre of the line, around Bologna, and a mixed multi-national force – South Africans, the Nisei, newly arrived Brazilians, and a racially segregated

African-American division – would advance up the Mediterranean coast in the west. The plan for the attack on Rimini was code-named 'Operation *Olive*'. Clark and Alexander approved it. It required almost the whole of the British 8th Army to be transferred from central Italy to the west. Leese was delighted. He was finally, as he saw it, properly in charge. Like so many British officers who had served with the 8th Army under Montgomery in North Africa, he had, as one senior officer would later say, 'a great deal of desert sand in his boots'. [8] He missed the flexibility of movement and open spaces of North Africa.

Many British commanders were exhausted by the blood, mud, and terrain that had accompanied the winter and spring slog up Italy, by the freezing, flooded rivers, the heavily defended mountains that slowed offensive operations to a crawl and restricted the Allies' ability to exploit their huge numerical advantage in armor. There had been precious relief with the fast summer dash north from Rome to Florence. But they pined for the desert, for its vast space that had afforded such extensive freedom of operational movement. In Italy, their operations were far more dictated by the terrain and by the German defenders who held it. If the Allies could break through the Apennines at Bologna, and outflank the Germans at Rimini, and then flank left into the wide flatlands of the Po valley, the flat terrain, and their enormous superiority in armour and air power, they could regain their tactical and strategic advantage.

Under Operation *Olive*, and as a compromise to the Americans, Clark's 5th Army in the centre would take control over an additional four divisions of British troops. Lieutenant General Sidney Kirkman's XIII Corps was chosen. This strengthened army would then attack towards Bologna directly through the Apennines. Once through the mountains, the XIIIth would swing towards the area north of Rimini, as the 8th Army advanced to the south, trapping the Germans in a pincer. Clark would push north from Florence through the San Giorgio and Futa Passes to Bologna. Once this city was taken, the road to the Po valley would be open and the Apennines cracked, and all the

German forces east of Bologna would be trapped by the Americans on the left and the 8th Army on the right. Such was the plan. Kesselring himself admitted that if Bologna fell, all of his forces to the east of it – effectively half the troops under his command – were doomed.

The Allies knew very well the enormous difficulties of attacking German defensive lines. In the winter of 1943, they had been stopped at Mignano Gap, south of Monte Cassino. The Allies had been able to advance only six miles in seven weeks, constantly stalled by the rain, the terrain, the mud, and the strength of the German opposition. A New Zealand infantry officer serving in the 8th Army, Captain Frederick Majdalany, wrote at the time, 'If the cost of breaking this temporary line is remembered, and the time it took to do it, an idea may be gained of what was going to be involved when the finest German troops, the geography of Italy, and the full fury of mid-winter conspired together in defence – as now they are about to do.' He was talking about the forthcoming attack on the Gustav Line, but nearly a year later, on the eve of the attack on Rimini, and with autumn coming, conditions were the same. On 22 May 1944, an eternally optimistic Leese had written to his wife, Margaret, before the battle for another of the German defensive lines south of Rome, 'Tomorrow, I hope and pray the Canadians will break the Adolf Hitler Line. Then we shall have finished with organized lines for a bit. They are expensive to deal with.'

He had the largest and toughest one yet to come.

# 10

## A Multi-national Assault
### Ten Armies on the Gothic Line

### August 25, 1944

With seven experienced divisions pulled from their command, Lieutenant Generals Mark Clark and Oliver Leese had divided their forces into three. The British, Canadian, and Polish corps were to attack Rimini. The Americans, strengthened by Sidney Kirkman's XIII Corps, were to strike towards Bologna. And on the Mediterranean coast, the multi-national army of all the remaining Allied troops in Italy would push straight up the left flank, through the mountains overlooking it, to the key ports of La Spezia and then Genoa. Behind the lines, across the breadth of Italy, SOE and OSS agents would parachute with arms and supplies to lead the partisans in an enormous assault on the Germans from behind. The strategic aims were simple. To prevent Kesselring's two German armies from escaping into France, Austria, or Yugoslavia by destroying them on the ground or taking their surrender. To exploit through the Apennines and Gothic Line defences, flank left into the Po valley, and head towards Venice and Trieste, thence to Ljubljana and Vienna, reaching the latter before the Red Army. And finally, to help the different partisan groups save the Italian economic infrastructure – the dams, hydroelectric plants, factories – from destruction by the retreating Germans, so that Italy would have a functioning economy after the war ended.

In practice, the Italian economy meant northern Italy, so the Allied covert missions were concentrated in a long line westward from Liguria, Turin, via Milan to Venice. The large number of SOE and OSS detachments would also try, to the greatest extent possible, to oversee and channel the political aspirations of the different partisan groups. The Allies wanted to make sure that the post-war political apparatus was one of their choosing, was non-communist, and stood a decent chance of contributing to post-war stability, rather than civil war.

## THE ATTACK IN THE WEST: THE NISEI HEAD NORTH

In the west, the US 34th Infantry Division was tasked with holding the extreme end of the Allied line and fighting up towards La Spezia. Sergeant Daniel Inouye and the rest of the 442nd Regimental Combat Team were, by mid-August, recuperating after six weeks of constant advances, and four major battles, that had taken them as far as the Mediterranean where the Arno flows into the sea. They were preparing to head north to hit the Gothic Line where it met the Mediterranean. The fighting had been tough: Inouye was quickly discovering the contradictions, fear, massive elation, successes, and simple tragic human sadness that are facts of life during wartime.

One morning he had been on patrol in the Tuscan countryside, leading his squad in the sunshine along a gentle slope towards a farmhouse that seemed deserted. They got to about thirty yards from it when an MG-42 machine gun opened up from one of the windows. Inouye's lead scout was cut almost in half by bullets. The Nisei hit the ground as the machine gun fired 'steady, disciplined bursts of six' at them. They fired a bazooka rocket into the house, which detonated, and then charged, throwing hand grenades through the windows. They burst into the house and found two Germans torn to pieces by the bazooka. A third German was still alive, thrown back against the wall of the room semi-conscious, one of his legs completely broken.

Inouye approached, his finger on the trigger of his M1 Garand, which still had three rounds left in its magazine. The German muttered '*kamerad*' twice and smiled.[1]

Then the German reached inside his battledress tunic. Was he going for a gun? Inouye hesitated. The Nisei sergeant had no time to make up his mind. He made a split-second decision and fired the last three .30-06 rounds from his rifle into the German soldier's chest, the heavy bullets smacking him up against the wall. As the man slid sideways, dead, his hand fell out of his tunic. A photograph that he had been reaching for slipped from his fingers – a picture of an attractive woman and two small children. A handwritten inscription on it said '*Deine dich liebende Frau, Heidi*' (Your most loving wife, Heidi).

The incident caused Sergeant Daniel Inouye a massive crisis of conscience. Here he was, a respectable Japanese-American son from a household where any form of violence was abhorred. Where, as he said to the unit's padre later, the family had an obligation to every sick cat and dog. He believed in the mantra 'Thou shalt not kill'. But here was another Inouye, a capable, tough squad leader, proud to be a soldier. He felt there were two sides to him. The padre was succinct: 'We are fighting because we have to – our enemy *does* believe in killing . . . You must fight – and yes, and kill – to protect the kind of life that helped you grow up to hate killing.'

Walking afterward in the darkness, Inouye reconciled himself, remembering his father's plea not to bring dishonour on the family name. Feeling more resolved, he strode off into the dark back to his tent, utterly confident he knew which side honour was on.

Hardly had the crisis passed than he suddenly found himself medevaced to a hospital in Rome, as his unit prepared to move north to attack the Gothic Line. Under local anaesthetic, he watched surgeons operate on him, and then recovered in a bed next to other American soldiers wounded in combat. They crowded around Inouye, staring at the swathes of bandages covering both his feet. They offered chocolate and cookies from the parcels they had received from home. Cigarettes were proffered. What, they asked, had happened to him?

Bullet wounds? A land mine? The desperately embarrassed Japanese-American sergeant could hardly bear to reply. Two days before, in a defensive position after a patrol, he'd taken off his combat boots and been knocked back by the smell of infected flesh. A passing medic took one look, and within an hour he was on his way south to Rome, with two badly infected ingrown toenails. The moment he explained to the wounded combat veterans around him on the hospital ward what had happened, they took one look at him, said nothing, avoided eye contact, and didn't speak to him again.

Two nights later, Daniel Inouye broke out of the hospital and went AWOL. He bribed the ward orderly with fifty dollars he had won playing dice, and spent two days and three nights hitching rides north, trying to avoid the military police. When he arrived back with Easy Company of the 2nd Battalion, his captain called him over and told him the hospital wanted to court-martial him. Then he hesitated and assured Inouye the unit would have a swift field trial, find him innocent, and he could accompany it northward. For the 442nd RCT was boarding Liberty ships in the port of Livorno. They'd gotten to the very edge of the Gothic Line positions, the first Allied troops to do so, but now were being pulled out of the line. Like so many of the other experienced Allied troops in Italy, they were being sent north to France. The Gothic Line would have to wait. To Inouye and his men, it seemed completely senseless.

## THE BUFFALO SOLDIERS ARRIVE

The 442nd RCT was replaced by allies from three unexpected quarters: South Africans, a Brazilian Regimental Combat Team, and some fellow Americans who, like the Nisei, were no strangers to racial segregation. The US 92nd Infantry Division arrived on the line that stretched along the river Arno. Nicknamed the 'Buffalo Soldiers', they were all black Americans, with a very small handful of white officers. Italian Fascist spies and German scouts from the SS units of the 16th Panzergrenadier Division, dug in opposite the US 34th and the 92nd, reported back.

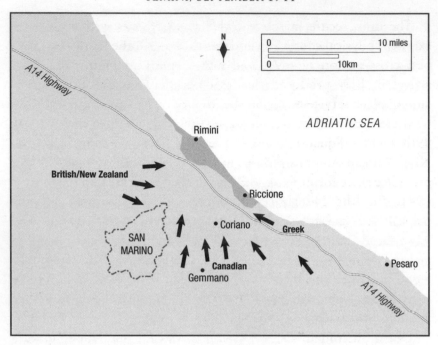

Their opponents must have sounded like something from a National Socialist nightmare: Japanese-Americans, black Americans, a mix of white and black South Africans, and Brazilians. Recruited mostly from the Deep South of the United States, some of the soldiers from the 92nd couldn't read or write. The 370th Regimental Combat Team, commanded by Colonel Raymond G. Sherman, went abroad as the advance guard of the 92nd Infantry Division. This combat team was formed at Fort Huachuca in Arizona on 4 April 1944. During the period of intensive training for its movement overseas, men failing tests in the 370th were transferred out to other units and replaced by men with higher qualifications and capabilities. Many of these were volunteers. The whole combat team, consisting of the 370th Infantry, the 598th Field Artillery Battalion, and detachments from each of the special units of the 92nd Division, including the headquarters company, sailed from Hampton Roads, Virginia, on 15 July 1944. Transshipping at Oran in Algeria, it arrived at Naples on 30 July.

The unit, secure in the knowledge that it was well trained, in excellent physical condition, and was made up of the 92nd Division's best cross-section of men, had high hopes and high morale. Its arrival in Italy produced flurries of excitement and anticipation among black service troops in the Mediterranean area equalled only by those produced by the arrival of the Tuskegee Airmen from the 99th Fighter Squadron and the 332nd Fighter Group. Like the Nisei, African-American troops had faced consistent opposition and prejudice since forming up as a unit in Fort Huachuca in Arizona in 1941. But the Nisei faced discrimination not because of race per se, but because their race was that of their country's enemy. The 92nd faced discrimination because they were black – out of pure racism. Even the American Red Cross collected racially segregated blood, as white and black troops were not then allowed to receive transfusions from each other. The 92nd Division was determined to prove its critics wrong.

One of their men was Ivan Houston, a six-foot-tall nineteen-year-old athlete and boxer from Los Angeles, who'd majored in sports at the University of California. Houston's father had served with another racially segregated division in the First World War. By the time the Second World War came around, the 92nd had been given the nickname the 'Buffalo Soldiers', after the description used by Native Americans for black soldiers in the US Army in the 1870s. Houston became the clerk of D Company of the 366th Regiment shortly before they shipped out from Hampton Roads in Virginia. He had no idea where they were heading. They crossed the Atlantic and landed at the port of Oran in Algeria in July. Led by Lieutenant Colonel Clarence Doggett from Alabama, a white officer whom Houston and the other men respected, the 366th proceeded to the Bay of Naples on 1 August 1944. As they arrived, Houston and his colleagues reckoned they could only be en route to the front.

Many of the black troops came from dirt-poor backgrounds from rural Georgia, Mississippi, and Alabama, but none of them had ever seen such poverty as they witnessed in Naples in 1944. The harbour was full of ships that had been hit by air attacks and were half sunk; the port was full of dirty, hungry people, and as the African-American soldiers disembarked, ragged, grimy teenage boys ran along the line, trying to sell their sisters for soap. Naples was starving.

The Buffalo Soldiers trekked towards the front on foot and in trucks, moving northwest through countryside whose natural beauty had been removed by the savage fighting that had ground over it that year. Many trees had no leaves left, the branches stripped by artillery fire. Houston noticed little beauty on the route north, although he was taken aback by the random nature of environmental and human survival in wartime. Next to a clump of shattered trees, branches and trunks pitted with artillery shrapnel, leaves blown to dust, he saw some lemon trees standing untouched, their yellow fruit immaculate.

The 366th had made it to Tuscany, in front of the river Arno, by the last week of August. The area was teeming with different nationalities. Houston had grown up with Japanese Americans in California and felt at home with the 442nd RCT, which were very briefly next to them on the Arno Line. Like the Nisei, the men from the 92nd thought the idea of sending the Japanese-American unit to France, now that they were within touching distance of the Gothic Line, to be completely nonsensical. A Brazilian regimental combat team arrived behind the Buffalo Soldiers, the South Americans' uniforms bearing the unit patch of a boa constrictor smoking a pipe. The men from the Brazilian Expeditionary Force spoke almost no English, but they seemed to dovetail culturally and linguistically with the Italians. The South Africans had also arrived, and Houston and his colleagues noticed instantly that every white South African officer had a black orderly. The Italians found the men from the 92nd fascinating and called them 'the Good Giants'. They would call out 'Tikedesi' to them, imitating their American accents, their way of saying 'Take it easy'.

As the boiling-hot month of August started to wind to its end, and across the whole of Italy hundreds of thousands of men were hours away from going into action on the Gothic Line, the men of the 92nd kept themselves busy. They smoked, but as enlisted men they were not allowed to drink alcohol. Some GIs flicked their cigarette ash into their Coca-Cola bottles, hoping for a nicotine-induced high. The medics sipped their ethanol. From time to time there was captured German brandy and cognac, taken off prisoners, drunk out of sight of NCOs or officers. M1 Garands, M1 carbines, .45 Thompsons, .30 Browning machine guns, and Browning Automatic Rifles were cleaned again and again. The clock ticked down as the sun of summer burned on.

To the east of this racial melting pot on the Arno, the 1st Battalion of the Maratha Light Infantry had advanced into Florence and then refitted. As part of the 21st Infantry Brigade, itself part of 8th Indian Division, they were now under the command of the British XIII Corps that had been detached from the 8th Army to serve under General Mark Clark. Captain Eustace D'Souza and his men left their tented camp outside Florence in the third week of August, heading for a laying-up position just behind a new front line north of the city on the Gothic Line itself. The division moved twelve miles to the east, into the Pontassieve area. Here the River Sieve flows down in a great bend along the foothills of the Apennines. Within this bend the enemy held a series of high spurs that constituted the outworks of the Gothic Line, barring entry into the narrow valleys by which the main roads climb over the crests of the mountains. Due east of Florence, the first contours of this high ground are rounded and gracious, tree clad and heavily cultivated, but as the ridges fuse into the foothills, they tend to become sharp, rugged, and irregular. The Indian front covered the intermediate stage of this transformation, in which thickly wooded hills rose about 1,300 feet above the river, and in which the rolling countryside had begun to yield to narrow summits and little crooked valleys.

Meanwhile, to their right, the majority of the 8th Army had just been moved from the middle of Italy to the east. Kesselring was still convinced that the main Allied attack would come either in the centre towards Bologna or in the west. An Allied deception plan, code-named 'Operation *Ulster*', had worked much better than expected:

bombing raids on the outskirts of Bologna had helped persuade the Germans that the city was to be the focus of the Allies' impending attack. The Germans had somehow missed the movement of eleven infantry divisions, with their accompanying artillery and engineer vehicles. Not to mention hundreds of tanks. It was late August in north-central Italy; the countryside was at its driest. Convoys of vehicles raised dust clouds that could be seen for miles. But somehow the telltale sound of ringing church bells – often used by Italian Fascist collaborators to signal the impending arrival of Allied troops – was absent. One reason was that the Germans had almost non-existent aerial reconnaissance capability. Second, their forward troops were by now all dug in to their positions on the Gothic Line. Third, the troops took their lead from their commanding officers. Generaloberst Heinrich von Vietinghoff, commanding the 10th Army on the Adriatic front, and General Heidrich, the paratroop commander in Rimini, were absent. They were still on leave.

So when, at dawn on 25 August, the first units of the British 8th Army crossed the Metauro River on Bailey bridges, and attacked German outposts east of Rimini under the cover of mortar and artillery fire, alarm bells did not ring. The Germans reported simply that the Allies were advancing to occupy ground vacated by withdrawing German soldiers. They also didn't attach any significance to Indian units moving up from the south, or Polish cavalry units heading north from Pesaro. Lieutenant General Oliver Leese had won his Distinguished Service Order on the Somme leading his men in covert raids on German trenches; now, with 100,000 men, twenty-seven years later, he repeated this approach. In the opening hours of the attack on the Gothic Line, he had achieved complete surprise. From Rimini in the east, to Carrara in the west, the Allies moved forward under artillery and mortar barrages. In the far west, near the Mediterranean, Private 1st Class Ivan Houston said simply that 'the whole front seemed to explode'.

# 1 1

## WITH INFANTRY AND TANKS

*The Canadians on the Foglia River*

### 26 August 1944

The Westminster Regiment spent the night before the attack on Rimini in a mulberry grove. Each of their vehicles was assigned its own tree under which the men stretched burlap and hessian camouflage strips to cover their Universal Carriers. These were three-and-a-half-ton vehicles, open topped, with half an inch of armour, that held four men and were normally used to carry heavy weapons like machine guns and mortars. The vehicle mounted a Bren gun in the front, and because they were officially a semi-motorized unit, the Westminsters travelled in them. On the morning of the attack, the men found that mulberries had dropped out of the trees onto their vehicles, leaving purple juice. It reminded some of the men of a night earlier that summer when the unit had parked in a field of watermelons, and gone into action the following day, in the words of one officer, 'very sticky'.

Like the rest of the 8th Army, the Westminster Regiment was travelling incognito as part of the massive deception operation designed to hide their eastward movement from the Germans. So the men had taken off their 'Canada' shoulder badges, divisional flashes

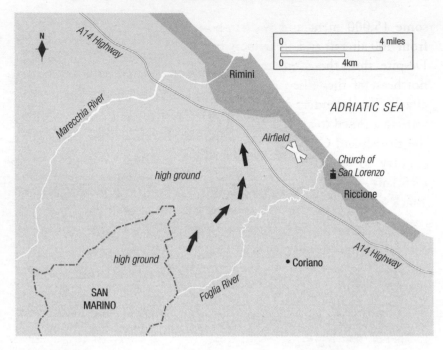

and unit insignia, and painted out the maple leaf marking on their vehicles. The move into battle seemed very low-key, especially for a unit that had fought its way up Italy for a year. It felt something of an anti-climax. The open Bren gun carriers trundled across their start line outside the small village of Jesi, ten miles southwest of Rimini, at five o'clock in the afternoon of 26 August. At first their advance was uneventful, deceptively quiet, and unopposed. They rolled through warm fields and down dusty roads.

The British and Canadian soldiers who had crossed the Metauro River the previous night had managed to surprise the Germans. From the officers in General Leese's headquarters down to the individual infantry platoons that forded the clear summer waters on foot, by rubber boat, and over Bailey bridges, it seemed extraordinary. If the opening salvos of Operation *Olive* had been a silent night attack by a couple of companies, 250 men, perhaps, then surprise would have been understandable. But this operation involved two entire divisions, some 15,000 men, and was supported by an aerial bombardment from 400 aircraft and an artillery barrage of an estimated 1,502 guns. Despite this, the German headquarters in Rimini, fifteen miles northeast of the Allied start line, made no log of a huge infantry attack. The defenders of the port, and the surrounding countryside, were so attuned to air attacks and artillery barrages that they assumed the British and Canadians were just advancing across mostly empty country to close the distance between their front line and the Germans'. Kesselring's headquarters were still expecting the main attack to come towards Bologna, in the centre of the line, so were suspicious of Allied diversions. But unbeknownst to them, three entire army corps – Canadian, British, and Polish – were coming directly at them.

The Westminsters moved northwest past the village of Montecchio, which the Germans had razed to the ground to provide open arcs of fire from the slopes overlooking it. Still nothing happened. Over the radio net, the regiment could hear other units ahead that were in contact with the enemy. They sent patrols out in front to test the German defences. There was no response. Was the Gothic Line one enormous bluff by the Germans? wondered some of the Westminster officers. Where was the enemy? For four days of almost phoney war, the regiment advanced very slowly, hundreds of yards an hour, men poised as lookouts, cartridges in the breeches of their Lee–Enfield rifles. They refuelled, ate, dug in, slept. The radio net was crackling and squawking non-stop with 'sitreps' from units ahead. But the Westminsters proceeded untouched. As often on the verge of combat, men thought of the most mundane things.

One Canadian officer with a supporting artillery unit had one main thing on his mind. When British and Canadian officers were issued long-barrel .38 calibre Smith & Wesson revolvers, they were often told that .38 calibre ammunition was very scarce. This officer had been issued his eight bullets and had never dared to even practice firing, lest he end up with a revolver and no shells. So he was desperate to find ammunition for his sidearm. The priority of another tank officer – who had been awarded the Distinguished Service Order for extreme bravery in combat around Monte Cassino – was to make repeated daily entries in his diary, hoping his wife would write to him.

On 27 August Lieutenant General Oliver Leese had broadcast a message to all ranks of the 8th Army from his tactical headquarters behind the lines. He described the attack on Rimini as 'the last lap' and said that 'victory in the coming battles means the beginning of the end for the German Armies in Italy'. Kesselring's headquarters intercepted the message immediately. But it was only on the following day, three whole days after the start of the attack, that the Germans realized that the assault towards Rimini constituted the main Allied offensive. Kesselring ordered three divisions of reinforcements to drive as fast as they could towards the outskirts of the city. But they wouldn't be able to reach their positions before 30 August, and the Allies were moving fast to encircle the port and the ground around it. All they had to do was take the high ground of two key ridges at Coriano and San Fortunato before the German reinforcements arrived.

Just after two o'clock in the afternoon of 30 August, the Westminsters drove through a small village just short of their main target, the Foglia River, which flows southwest of Rimini. In the village churchyard was a row of white crosses, with mounds of fresh dark red earth dug just hours before. On each cross was the name of a Canadian soldier from the Loyal Edmonton Regiment. Battle was very close. The unit drove through some trees and found themselves on a slope looking downward to the Foglia: at six in the morning, a lot of the men walked forward to look at the battle ahead of them. 'It was a unique position from which one could literally see for miles across the Foglia, and the whole scene reminded the watchers in the rear of a sand table model, rather than the real thing.'[1]

Then the war intervened. In swift succession, a truckload of mortar ammunition was hit by a German shell; a second one wounded three men. Within an hour, the Westminsters' two leading companies had made it across the Foglia and were furiously digging in. Night fell, shelling continued, nobody slept. The following day was very hot, and in their foxholes just across the river, the Canadians were under German shellfire all day. Three more were killed. The men could move between the dugouts only by crawling on their stomachs. All day, in temperatures over ninety degrees, the men sweated it out under fire, and then when night fell, they moved off into the attack, cautiously patrolling forward in single file under a clear sky in bright moonlight. By the side of the road, a German gun emplacement was still smoking, the weapon knocked out. Ahead of the battalion, a reconnaissance patrol creeping along the road suddenly saw the clear, almost blue moonlight bouncing off something metallic. The Canadians froze. Up ahead they saw what had reflected the light: German steel helmets. The patrol opened fire with their Bren gun, Thompsons, and rifles, killing four of the ambush party, wounding another one, and forcing the rest to flee northward.

Shortly afterward, the Westminsters marched into a nearby town, guarded by another smoking emplacement, its weapon destroyed. The men settled in for the night, trying to form an all-around defence, as firing continued over their heads, from all sides, and from within the town itself. A German tank broke through in the night. When dawn broke on the soft hills and forests around them, the Canadians realized they were on the outskirts of a village and surrounded. The battalion was spread across the bottom and slopes of a shallow valley, with the Germans behind and in front of them. In the hot day of confused combat that followed, it was hard for both sides to distinguish between each other. Many of the Germans were wearing Afrika Korps-style uniforms, identical in colouring to the Canadians'.

A Canadian anti-tank gun crew opened fire on a haystack that seemed to be moving: it fell apart, revealing a 75mm German PaK gun. The men from British Columbia destroyed it with two shells.

## SNIPERS IN ITALY IN 1944

The Westminsters' sniper and scouts platoon, meanwhile, was in its element. Its second in command was Sergeant Len Bailey. He had already been decorated with the Military Medal outside Monte Cassino, and had been the soldier who had crawled to the rescue of the wounded Major Mahony on the Melfa River. Half Native American, and half Canadian trapper, Bailey came from the Rocky Mountains above New Westminster. He made a perfect sniper, and his background gave him the flair for silent, tactical movement across difficult terrain, exemplary shooting skills, knowledge of the countryside and terrain, and the huge patience and powers of observation that being a good sniper required. He commanded men who excelled at fast-moving individual and small-group actions in the middle of a confused and complex battlefield.

The Canadian snipers, even by the individualistic standards of their fellow-countrymen, eschewed conventional uniforms and appearance. Bailey's platoon boasted men carrying Bowie knives, bandannas wrapped over their heads. They often wore camouflaged airborne Denison jump-smocks they'd been issued or exchanged with British paratroopers, sometimes for trophies such as captured Luger pistols. Their basic weapon was in time to be regarded as one of the world's finest sniper rifles.[2] This was the British .303 Lee–Enfield No.4 Mark 1, with a three-and-a-half times magnification telescopic sight. The advantage that this weapon enjoyed over the American Springfields, German Mausers and Russian Mosin-Nagants was that the Lee–Enfields were specifically adapted as sniper rifles. Most other armies simply took an issue service rifle and fitted a telescopic sight to it. The Lee–Enfield was custom-adapted to the task, with a barrel that was re-fitted into the stock, a cheek rest added to the butt, scope pads fitted, and the telescopic sight mounted in one fitted unit.[3] The weapon was tough and reliable in combat, and with ten rounds in its magazine it enjoyed a higher rate of fire than its German, Russian or American equivalents, whose magazines all held only five rounds.

Italy's terrain was perfectly suited to snipers. Hills, forests, trees, church steeples, small buildings hidden in narrow streets, mountain peaks all gave the sniper somewhere to lie up and hide and wait for the enemy. As the front line in Italy was moving constantly, a German sniper could wait behind while his colleagues withdrew – or operate ahead of them – and thus be in perfect position for when the Allies arrived. Photo after photo of American, British, Polish, Indian and Canadian troops fighting through towns and villages all the way up Italy shows patrols of wary, ultra-cautious soldiers creeping through the rubble of half-destroyed streets, eyes pinned for a sniper's positions.

The Germans, having the upper hand of holding pre-prepared defensive positions, were best placed to deploy snipers who would conceal themselves carefully, remembering the sniper's mantra: sniping is one part shooting and ten parts camouflage.

Snipers often operated in pairs, where one man would fire, and the other observe through binoculars. Equipment carried tended to be light: rifle, ammunition, entrenching tool, a knife, food, water and medical supplies. The observer would usually carry a light automatic weapon or rifle himself for fire-support if the sniper position was discovered. Snipers would advance forward of their front lines at night, and dig themselves into positions in hedgerows, fields, at crossroads, on hillsides, on the edge of treelines that bordered the numerous woods and forests of central and northern Italy. A capable sniper could easily pin down an entire thirty-man platoon, particularly if his position was well-camouflaged, and well-enough prepared to protect him from artillery or mortar fire. Operating on a fluid and ill-defined front line also increased the sniper's chances of hitting enemy soldiers. Snipers concealed themselves inside haystacks, in church steeples (which always made escape treacherous) and inside the rooms of small stone houses. They would fire from the rear of the room, so no muzzle blast was visible through the window. They lay in the high oak trees of the Apennines, they dug into cover under large, shady trees with low-hanging foliage, or even hid themselves inside destroyed armoured vehicles.

A Scottish officer from the Queen's Own Cameron Highlanders, operating in Tuscany, described the activities of some of the unit's snipers in July and August 1944:

> The two weeks which followed were perhaps the most personally successful ones we ever had in Italy. We suffered only four or five casualties and

inflicted about thirty on the Germans, as well as taking twenty eight prisoners. They were weeks of gay swashbuckling bravado, almost piratical insolence, and daring individual effort. A German sauntering into the village of Castellucio to buy vino suddenly drops dead in the road. Corporal Cameron of the snipers shoots two more as they hang out their washing at a house in Le Balze. Another German stoops to wash the dust from his face in the cool waters of the Arno. There is a sharp crack and his body plops into the gently flowing stream.[4]

Meanwhile, back on the Westminsters' battlefield outside Rimini, a German soldier was taken prisoner by one of the snipers: he tried to escape several times until the Canadian sharpshooter took off the man's trousers and underpants, marching him in half naked. The fighting continued all morning and afternoon. Then the night was lit by the glow of burning haystacks and 'brewed-up' tanks; the sky over Rimini, with its outskirts burning from air raids, glowed orange. The moon shone down through smoke that moved like a vast curtain of wafting cordite across the battlefield. The Westminsters moved under cover of darkness to try to break out of their encircled position. It was the men's third night without sleep. They marched forward and at dawn found themselves in a slightly higher valley but still surrounded. The Germans now brought every weapon they had to bear on the Canadians. Along with mortars, 75mm anti-tank guns, 88s, and machine guns mounted on tripods in a 'sustained fire' role, there were the hated Nebelwerfers. Nicknamed 'Moaning Minnies', these were German multiple-barrel launchers that fired five 21cm rockets, which made a howling sound when in flight. Under the heavy German fire, one Canadian sergeant major closed his mouth so hard as a shell exploded near him that he bit through the stem of his pipe.

As the sun came up, their commanding officers realized it was vital to get the men out of the exposed position, so for that entire day they fought their way forward, still clinging stubbornly to their northeastward access of advance. Their objective now was to get out of the hilly country where they were surrounded and try to cut the coast road that led southeast from Rimini. This would cut off the Germans retreating from the Polish advance ten miles farther south. Along with a squadron of Canadian tanks and four 105mm self-propelled guns, the lead company of the Westminsters headed out, with Sergeant Bailey and his snipers and scouts in the lead.

As they pushed up towards the coast road – narrowly avoiding an incident of friendly fire with fellow Canadian infantry – the rest of their battalion followed inland in parallel. After yet another night on the move, another whole day of fighting followed. Two German Mark IV Panthers roared straight through the Westminsters' lines at one point, trying to escape; one of the Canadian sergeants responsible for directing the flow of battlefield traffic simply guided the German tanks into a parking area. The slight loss of speed by the two enemy vehicles caused them to arrive late at a nearby bridge, which by then had been blown up. They wheezed to a halt, and two Canadian anti-tank gunners knocked them out. While Sergeant Bailey, now at the head of A Company, moved towards the coast road, B and C Companies of the Westminsters entered the village of Misano, which lay directly between their start line and the main road that led along the coast to Rimini. The village was taken without a single man killed or wounded, but German shellfire was landing with considerable accuracy in the areas just behind the front units. Sergeant Bailey's platoon commander, a former Royal Canadian Mounted Policeman, was killed along with one of the snipers when a German shell blew their scout car apart. Sergeant Bailey was now in charge in the scouts and snipers.

The confusion of battle was all around them. They were in the middle of an area the German troops had vacated hours before: company, battalion, and divisional signs in German seemed to be everywhere. At one point, an enemy Opel truck drove straight into the middle of the ground that C Company of the Westminsters had just taken. The exhausted Canadian soldiers were astounded when they surrounded the truck and discovered that it was bringing hot rations to the German soldiers who had just surrendered and retreated.

The truck also contained beer. The men from British Columbia wolfed down the hot food – their first in three days – and drank the beer, which they reported tasted like 'low-grade spring water'. Hardly had they finished this surprise meal than A Company, now accompanied by a whole squadron of sixteen Sherman tanks, arrived in support. The village of Misano was now under extremely heavy shellfire.

The Westminsters were confronted not just by German anti-tank weapons and 88mms but also by the 75mm guns of Panther tanks whose turrets were buried in cement emplacements almost at ground level, with land mines and machine-gun positions in front of them. These carefully dug-in emplacements were positioned along the high ground on the Coriano Ridge, which stretched southwest of Rimini and directly overlooked the line of advance of the Canadian corps. This ridge was also manned by General Heidrich's *fallschirmjäger*, the 1st German Parachute Division. To the Canadians' left were the British V and X Corps, heading towards Rimini directly from the west; on their right flank, heading up the Adriatic coast, was II Polish Corps. Just behind the main Allied front line was a New Zealand division and a brigade of Greek mountain troops. The Westminsters were desperately trying to push forward out of the shadow of the Coriano Ridge to the coast road that led along the Adriatic towards Rimini, passing through the suburb of Riccione just outside Rimini airfield. Trying to attack forward, they found that the only usable road went straight along the top of a steep embankment that led for more than half a mile directly under the view of the German artillery. The lightly armoured Universal Carriers were easy targets. Overturned by explosions or driven off the road to avoid the incoming artillery rounds, the Canadian advance stalled as their tank support halted. They needed engineers to bridge at least two small rivers that lay in their path. The men from B Company were taking cover in a ditch, lying head to toe, the soles of the hobnailed boots of one man lying inches in front of the face of the next man down the line. An explosion picked up the body of the company commander's batman and drove him backward with terrific force, his feet slamming his major's tin helmet over his ears. Despite this very heavy incoming fire, the Westminsters decided to push forward.

Sergeant Bailey and his sniper section saw that his colleagues were under fire not only from mortars, machine guns, and artillery but also from a German sniper. He decided to do something about it. The whole of his battalion could see him as he crawled out from his position. He wriggled on his stomach through the mud, dust, and earth of the mortar and artillery barrage, and physically stalked the German sniper, coming up behind his position, reaching into his dugout, and lifting him out, in full view of several hundred of his comrades. It was just what they needed. The three companies, unescorted by armour, reached the edges of the Coriano Ridge, which ran like a spine southwest, dominating the countryside around it. It was to stand over the fighting for the British and Canadians as they advanced towards Rimini that week. But once astride the ridge, the Westminsters were suddenly ordered to halt and were pulled out of the line. Another Canadian battalion took over from them. In the words of the Westminster Regiment war diary, they 'pulled back and just lay down and collectively went to sleep'.

They had been fighting and moving for five days, from the morning of 30 August to the morning of 5 September. Each man had had an average of ninety minutes of sleep per day, most of them less. Their uniforms were covered in mud, dust, sweat, the blood of the enemy and the blood of their colleagues, and hundreds of tiny golden pieces of chaff and ears of wheat from running and fighting through cornfields that were being blown apart by high explosives. They'd taken casualties too: ten men had died, sixty had been wounded, and thirty were evacuated to the hospital with jaundice – one of the primary symptoms of hepatitis. The battalion was pulled out of the line for two days to rest.

There was one benefit to the land around Rimini, though. The Canadian soldiers had been digging trenches and foxholes in vineyards up the length of Italy since the late autumn of 1943. Like all the Allied and German soldiers, crouching down under vines, digging holes in the earth underneath the trellises, they'd tasted a lot of grapes.

And the results of eating such a surfeit of soft fruit had too often been widespread diarrhoea. But not in the vineyards outside Rimini, where the white grapes were seedless. To a man, the Canadians discovered that the grapes that made the local white wine, Colli di Rimini Biancame, had no ill side effects.[5]

## THE ALLIED ADVANCE STALLS

Then autumn suddenly played its hand. The rains came. In a foretaste of the winter that was to come, the hot Italian summer broke and the troops in and around Rimini were flooded and half drowned under characteristically Italian torrential rain. Half a month's rainfall seemed to drop out of the sky in four hours. The sandy, red loam of the vineyards turned to a fine liquid glue. The roads submerged in mud: the earth could not cope with the water and the huge traffic of tanks, self-propelled guns, armoured personnel carriers, trucks, scout cars, and jeeps of two modern armies at war. Small soggy lakes formed on the flat fields. The soldiers were sodden. Moving tanks became almost impossible – although the German Panthers and Tigers, with their wider tracks, had a slight advantage over the Allied Churchills and Shermans. The dried-up streams and white stony riverbeds that zigzagged across the battlefield now roared full of water. A Canadian artillery officer saw the transformation from hot and dry to wet and cold as instantaneous:

> We sought shelter in Italian houses or barns. Some fellows dug holes in small haystacks which were often set on fire by German tracer bullets. Some tank troopers took shelter from shell fire and rain by sleeping under their tanks only to have the tank slowly sink into the mud at night and pin them underneath. We tried digging shallow fox holes about 18 inches deep to escape the shrapnel only to have the hole fill with water during the night. The rains lasted about a week and it was a hellish time. We never had dry clothes or feet. Every day we hoped that we would come down with jaundice which meant we would be shipped back to a hospital for

several weeks. The outbreak of jaundice was severe and upwards of 100 O.R.'s [Other Ranks] and officers were evacuated. Some of our men 'cracked up' and had to be taken out of the line. Still others thought that shooting themselves in the foot would be a way of getting into the hospital. When the rains finally quit and the hot dry weather returned, the 8th Army, including our 5th Canadian Armoured Division, re-opened the offensive. Our objective was Coriano Ridge.[6]

Between 26 August and 4 September the Canadians – including the Westminsters – moved their 1st Infantry and 5th Armoured Divisions forward fifteen miles. They were halted by three things. First, by the main body of the German artillery and infantry reinforcements dug in on the two ridges at Coriano and San Fortunato. The Allies couldn't move towards Rimini before these two pieces of high ground were taken because the German guns could reach out across the whole Allied axis of advance.

The San Fortunato Ridge also prevented them from exploiting north and west of Rimini into the plains of Lombardy. The bulk of the German Gothic Line defences outside Rimini were on these two stretches of high ground. Second, the Adriatic coastal road and the suburb of Riccione were heavily defended by the 1st German Parachute Division. Third, Lieutenant General Oliver Leese had fallen into the trap the Germans had laid for him. Like Mark Clark at Rome in June that year, Leese should have ordered his men to bypass Rimini in a fluid semi-circular outflanking movement. And then concentrated on getting into the flat land of the Po valley before the autumn rains came, and moved troops to occupy Rimini last. He would also have been able to trap the German forces south and southeast of the city. Yet he chose to do the opposite. The Allies didn't need Rimini for any strategic value – they already had a huge deep-water port at Anconca, captured by the Poles in July. They needed strategically valuable land, not symbolic towns with no tactical value. They could have outflanked Rimini but instead found themselves forced into three defensive corridors of the Germans' design, overlooked by two long stretches of high ground studded with artillery positions. One German staff officer, Oberstleutnant Horst Pretzell, was to write that 'the battle of Rimini, as characterised by concentration of materiel in a confined area, will take its place in history as an example of a battle of attrition in the grand style. For the first time the German troops could conduct defensive operations in a major battle as laid down in the German manual of Field Service Operations.'[7]

The newly boggy ground seemed all too reminiscent of the Western Front, the change in the weather making the Allied plan a faint reminder of the appalling strategy and tactics of those days. The sharp-witted British and Canadian generals moving in on the port were not slow to realize this and were determined to do something about it.

Without their realizing it, the Canadians' rapid advance had pushed the Germans completely off balance. Although the three British divisions advancing on the Canadians' left flank, bearing into Rimini from due west, were getting bogged down, the Germans were about to pull out. General Traugott Herr, in command of the LXXVI Panzerkorps, with eight divisions under his command, was considering pulling his entire force back to a line north of Rimini. This would have left the crucial left flank, the western approaches to Rimini, wide open for the Allies to flank into the plains beyond. Leese insisted the Canadians and British and Poles move straight towards the Adriatic port instead of flank left. As both the Canadian and British advance suddenly stalled, the chief of staff of the German 10th Army unwittingly saved the day for Kesselring. General Fritz Wentzell saw that Rimini was lost, but the strategically vital land to the west of it was not. He could see that the Allies' advance, which seemed in places like a juggernaut, could be blocked at two crucial points. So he took action without telling either Kesselring or, more importantly, his direct superior, Generaloberst Heinrich von Vietinghoff, the notorious 'Panzerknacker'. He ordered two highly capable regiments, one from his 5th Alpine Division, the other from the 29th Panzergrenadier Division, to reinforce the two most strategically vital points on the line. These were the hill and village of

Gemmano, and the centre of the Coriano Ridge, which together commanded the whole western approach to Rimini. In one move, the general had ensured the Allies were blocked.

While the exhausted Westminsters were fast asleep, the first battle of Coriano began. Canadian infantry and cavalry attacked the town of Besanigo, while the three regiments of the British 1st Armoured Division went straight at Coriano Ridge. Each had fifty-two tanks. On the first day, the British tank squadrons from the Queen's Bays, the 10th Royal Hussars, and the 9th Queen's Royal Lancers lost seventy-seven Shermans destroyed or immobilized by either 88mm and 75mm anti-tank guns or dug-in German Panther tank turrets. These were the defensive positions of the Gothic Line at their most brutal. The Germans had won the first battle of Coriano.[8]

Meanwhile, the Canadians were advancing up the Adriatic coast road towards Rimini. Its large airfield sits on a southeastern flank: any attack into Rimini must go not only through the airfield but also through the seaside town of Riccione that sits before it. And commanding the approaches to both this town and the airfield is a crucial crossroads in front of which sits the church of San Lorenzo in Strada. Seventeen-year-old Helmut Bücher and his *fallschirmjäger* colleagues were waiting.

# 12

## GREEN DEVILS ON
## THE ADRIATIC

*The German Defence and the Fall of Rimini*

### September 5, 1944

Leaving the suburban town of Riccione on the Adriatic coast and heading northwest into Rimini, Highway 16 turns to the right a few hundred yards short of the southern boundary of Miramare airfield. The road curves to swing around the eastern boundary of the airstrip, which is the side lying closest to the sea. Just before it turns, this main road intersects with two others, Via Vittorio Veneto, which joins it from the left, and Via Flaminia. Overlooking this junction, and commanding the approaches to it, the airfield, and the outskirts of Rimini, is a small church. There have been buildings on the site of San Lorenzo in Strada for at least seventeen hundred years – Roman remains dating back to the fourth century AD were excavated in fields behind it in the 1930s.

The 1st Battalion of the 3rd Fallschirmjäger Regiment had prepared the position well. In open country to the side of Via Flaminia, a Panther turret with a 75mm gun was dug into a field with a concrete revetment. It was almost invisible. Helmut Bücher and his fellow paratroopers knew it was there only because they had paced out the distance to it across the fields, and because the crew of the gun had been coming over to the church in preceding days to join the paratroopers for meals. There were mortars and machine guns in the houses behind the church. Another Panther turret was in a stand of fig trees, behind them and to the right, aiming straight down the road approaching the church. It could hit any Allied armour at distances of around a mile. The three 88mm anti-aircraft guns positioned around the church and the road junction were aimed south and west; they were capable of busting through the frontal armour of any Allied tank at 1,000 yards. The arcs of fire and ranges of the entire defensive company battle group had been worked out up to half a mile in front of and to the side of the San Lorenzo crossroads. The German airborne soldiers had the land marked out south, west towards Coriano, and east up to Rimini and the sea. They had dug a small fortress. The far eastern end of the Gothic Line was located only miles away, at the port of Pesaro. The Germans knew how crucial it was to hold the southern approaches to Rimini and the coastal plain west and north of it: the key defensive points were the San Fortunato and Coriano Ridges, and in the south the approach road to Rimini, which went straight through San Lorenzo in Strada.[1]

Before dawn had broken on 3 September, Canada's 1st Infantry Division and 5th Armoured Division had crossed the Conca River southwest of Rimini. The tempestuous rain that had suddenly poured out of the sky had stopped almost as soon as it had begun. The sun was now shining. The Royal Canadian Regiment, an infantry unit from the country's eastern provinces, was moving up Highway 16, the southern approach road. They were in the same Universal Bren Carriers as the Westminsters, whom they had just replaced. They had fought their way up through the suburb of Riccione, sidetracked under fire through defended houses near the beach, until their progress was held up by a blown bridge. Pinned down by MG-42s situated in houses near the sea, they moved inland across irrigation ditches and through orchards of lemon trees, trying to outflank them. They had moved farther away from the beach, and become caught up in a complex multi-battalion firefight on the lower slopes of the Misano Ridge, and then stopped. They had moved too far west of their axis of advance, which was meant to go straight up Highway 16. So during the night of 4 September they trudged back towards the tarmac of the road that approached the airport, reaching it just after first light. The men were exhausted. By the morning of 5 September the Germans had inflicted 300 casualties on this and the two other infantry battalions in their brigade.

Luckily, the weather was holding. Their company and platoon commanders organized them into the tactical formations that would advance up the road towards San Lorenzo in Strada and Rimini airfield. Early on the morning of the 5th, they set off. The first troops the Royal Canadian Regiment met as they pushed up Highway 16 were Turkoman troops from the German 162nd Division. These were mostly Red Army conscripts who had decided to join the German Army after being captured during Operation *Barbarossa* in 1941. It was preferable to facing a certain death from starvation in a POW stockade. The Turkomans surrendered quickly, their machine-gun positions left lying empty in the lanky bamboo-like shrubs at the side of the road. The Royal Canadian Regiment squads were relieved; this was going to be easier than they thought. They walked forward in long single lines on both sides of the road, the Bren carriers in the middle of the tarmac. Up ahead in the distance, their NCOs said there was a road junction. A lieutenant from the battalion's B Company and one of his section corporals were in the lead of the column. Suddenly, eleven huge thumping blasts roared from every point of the compass in front of them, and the almost instantaneous screeching whistle of incoming artillery, mortar, anti-tank, and tank shells. The air around them, the sky, the road, and the line of advance disintegrated. The incoming shells blasted chunks out of the trees and the tarmac, and blew the flimsy carriers into the air and onto their backs, burning instantly. Most of the men in range of the blasts were shredded like liver kicked through a colander, or hit by viperous scythes of shrapnel. The Royal Canadian Regiment had been on the line long enough to know instantly what was happening: they had walked straight into a massive ambush. Then the German MG-42 machine guns opened up, and it was as though the air in front of the Canadians was being torn apart in a series of high-speed ripping noises, bodies of soldiers blasted backward and sideways into the ditch or onto the surface of the road. The advance came to a sudden halt.

The German MG-42 belt-fed machine gun had one major flaw. Its rate of fire was so high that its barrel had a tendency to overheat after firing two to three hundred rounds and would start to glow red-hot. So the soldier firing it had to change the barrel, and this meant leaning forward, unlocking a retaining lever ahead of the cartridge ejection vent on the right of the weapon, sliding the hot barrel backward and out of its sleeve, and pushing in another one. In the hands of an experienced user, this series of small actions would take about twenty seconds; with a platoon of Russian soldiers charging at you, it could be done in fewer than ten. But it still meant that the soldiers being shot at by the machine gun, if experienced, had a tiny period of respite when they knew they weren't going to get hit. By September 1944, the Allies had been on the receiving end of the MG-42 all the way up Italy and knew what they were up against. So for the men of the Royal Canadian Regiment attacking the church at San Lorenzo in Strada, it was the moment they could stand up and charge forward, or throw a hand grenade. But the sudden wall of enemy fire had taken them by surprise. The battalion hit the ground and stayed there. The Universal Bren Carriers were blown up like small toy cars kicked aside and torn apart by orange fire. The Canadian infantrymen were face down on the tarmac, in the ditch. Or in the field beside it, their faces pressed as far as it was physically possible to press them, without breaking a bone, into the earth or the grass or the gravel. The air continued to be torn apart.

A thousand yards away, Jäger Helmut Bücher was inside the church, his Mauser K98 rifle kicking into his shoulder with every shot he fired.

But he knew that he was at the maximum extent of his weapon's range, so after one magazine of five cartridges was used up, he held his fire. The paratroopers had pushed the pews inside the church up against the walls as added protection against tank fire. Most of the company was outside. There were sixty-one men in and around the church. A semi-circle of deep foxholes had been dug around the front of the building, each one holding a dugout into which the soldiers could dive when incoming artillery shells, mortar fire, or aircraft ranged in. The paratroopers had dug a tunnel from the kitchen of a building behind the church to the altar itself, where they had placed an MG-42 firing straight out of the wooden front doors. There were foxholes in the orchards and fields across the road, the two Panther turrets firing from left and right flanks, the 88mms from just behind and above them, the mortars coughing their thumping retort as they pushed 81mm rounds into the air. As the Canadians went to ground, the MG-42s ceased fire immediately. The sudden silence inside and in front of the church was palpable; on the floor of the church a last spray of ejected brass cartridge cases and black metal belt-retaining clips bounced and tinkled across the tiles. The air was hot and full of cordite and smoke from the anti-aircraft guns. Men swigged water. When the German officers looked through their binoculars at the Canadian advance a half mile away, it was a bull's-eye of orange flame and black smoke in the centre of their lenses. Men flicked left and right like flitting ants. The German guns ceased fire. The *fallschirmjäger* knew from experience exactly what the Allied soldiers would do next. First would come smoke shells to cover their position as they re-organized. Then there would be mortar bombs. Then four, maybe eight tanks would emerge from the smoke and drive straight at the entrenched positions, with two platoons or a company of infantry behind them.

And so it proved. The Canadians attacked twice that afternoon of the 5th. Then as the sun started to go down in the sky over Rimini, fighter-bombers from the Allied Desert Air Force roared in over the trees behind the Canadians, hitting the church and the positions in front of it with 20mm cannon fire and rockets. At dusk, the Royal

Canadian Regiment attacked again. To their horror, as the platoons advanced up the road, the Germans paratroopers seemed to reappear from the very rocket craters the fighter-bombers had blown in the ground. The *fallschirmjäger* had learned their techniques at Cassino, under the weight of thousands of pounds of bombs dropped by American and British aircraft. If anybody knew how to fortify themselves in dug-in positions, it was them.

The Canadians attacked again that night, and a lieutenant of the Royal Canadian Regiment led his platoon straight through the front door of the church but was killed by a German *panzerfaust*, a single-shot anti-tank rocket. One of his section corporals followed behind him, killed four German paratroopers with his Thompson submachine gun, and narrowly avoided being killed when a fifth paratrooper ran out of ammunition. Lance Corporal Rodesse Duhaime, one of thirteen children from Espanola in Northern Ontario, was awarded the Military Medal and promoted to sergeant afterwards.[2] Meanwhile, the German tank turrets and anti-tank weapons could not fire on the church for fear of hitting their own men. The Canadians were pushed back: the limited space inside the church and at its entrance allowed only five or six men to fight effectively without blocking each other's field of fire. The anti-tank guns and the dug-in Panther tanks kept any vehicles from approaching – the Canadians bought up tanks, as the Germans predicted. But none of them got closer than 700 yards at any point of the compass. As night fell, five burning Shermans sat in the fields next to the smouldering hulls of the Universal Carriers. The Canadian advance faltered – the platoon commander from B Company personally led two attacks into the church, but the distance between him and his battalion was too great – at least half a mile – and fire support was impossible. By dawn on 6 September the Canadian attack up Highway 16 had ground to a halt.

Rain then started pouring down. It reminded the Allies that the two days of renewed sunshine had been a surprise. There would be more sunshine to come in September. But the downpour that soaked the exhausted Canadians and German paratroopers who were still alive at Lorenzo in Strada on the morning of the 6th reminded them that this was the pattern of things to come until the spring. The church on the crossroads that still held out on the morning after the attack was just one Gothic Line battalion objective, held by half a German company of perhaps eighty or ninety men, three 88mm guns, two Panther turrets, six 81mm mortars, two PaK 75mm anti-tank guns, and five MG-42s. The surrounding battle for the Coriano and San Fortunato ridges involved six divisions.

The Germans had pushed back the first Allied attack after the quick-thinking General Wentzell had provided two large battalions of reinforcements to the key points of Gemmano and Coriano. Now Lieutenant General Oliver Leese had to launch another attack on both. Two days before, on the evening of 4 September, a British battalion had sent one platoon of thirty men on a reconnaissance of the key position of Gemmano village, which lay on top of a ridge north of Coriano, overlooking the valleys below that led to Rimini.

The platoon moved around, assessed the potential strength of the Germans, reported back to divisional headquarters that there was probably a battalion of Germans there, and left Gemmano to its own devices. Lieutenant General Leese therefore ordered his main British attacking force to proceed towards Coriano and Rimini, ignoring Gemmano. It was to be his second key mistake in the strategic handling of Operation *Olive*, a clunking, rigid plan that was proving inflexible on the ground. Gemmano was a fortress. It was manned by three capable battalions of the 100th Gebirgsjäger, a regiment of anti-aircraft artillery – which meant 88mms – and a regiment of field artillery. There were 4,500 men overlooking the main Allied line of advance. It had to be taken before Coriano itself could fall. The severity of the fighting was comparable to Monte Cassino – and it was totally unnecessary. The Germans had been given three days to build up their strength on the ridge while the British and Canadians had been failing to take Coriano, five miles farther south, and failing to advance along Highway 16 beyond San Lorenzo in Strada. It took four British attacks, and ten days, to take Gemmano. The Germans lost 900 dead and 1,500 wounded and missing. Every British battalion that attacked the ridge suffered more than 100 casualties. At the centre of the village of Gemmano was a stone cross, which was finally captured by a British platoon from the Lincolnshire Regiment. 'All around the bullet-chipped cross on Pt.449, the dead, khaki and field-grey, lay heaped, unburied, in score upon score; at their centre a soldier of the Lincolns whose hands were still frozen in death round the cross itself, which he had reached in his battalion's first attack. Few regiments of 8th Army had ever known fiercer fighting than that of Gemmano.'[3] Major General Arthur 'Hol' Holworthy, a veteran Gurkha officer who was commanding the 4th Indian Division at that point in Italy, was more brutal and succinct in his diary: 'A good show. Gemmano full of dead and smells like another Cassino.'

Allied bombers and guns then dropped 500 tons of bombs and artillery shells on Coriano Ridge on the night of 12 September. At five o'clock in the morning, the Westminsters, who had spent six days resting, moved up into the line. They were accompanied by some of the best infantry and cavalry units the Canadian forces had brought to Italy. Nine hundred smoke shells were fired onto the German positions, but the Westminsters came under immediate and heavy shellfire. But with the tanks of the Strathcona's Horse ahead of them, they pushed forward, using the techniques that they had perfected earlier that month, as well as in the Liri Valley. Sergeant Len Bailey, the sniper who was commanding the scouts and sniper platoon, perfected a method of approaching a German position while accompanied by a tank. On the edge of the Coriano position, a German machine gun was situated in one of the lower rooms of a house, firing out of the window. Bailey 'stalked' his way up to the door. Unable to break in because of the machine-gun fire, he radioed a sniper colleague, who contacted their tank support on the radio net: a Sherman of the Strathconas simply drove up to the door of the house and fired its 75mm main armament through it.

The next day the weather broke again. The Westminsters were preparing for another week of fighting in sodden ground in wet uniforms, on roads and hillsides that turned to soggy bogs, where streams swelled to rivers overnight, where mud appeared everywhere there had been mere dust the previous day. But suddenly they were drawn out of the line again, sent back to Riccione, and told they were due another period of 'rest and recuperation'. It all sounded suspiciously easy. Something was wrong. It was as though the senior command was about to launch them in the vanguard of the last assault on the centre of Rimini, defended as it was by the surviving battalions of General Richard Heidrich's *fallschirmjäger*. They were, after all, one of the most combat-experienced battalions in the Canadian Army and thus the logical choice to go into the breach first. But no. They arrived on the soggy, rainy windswept beach at Riccione, south of Rimini.

Then they moved inland. A mobile bath unit appeared, which was always a sign that they were going to be out of the line for at least forty-eight hours. Then they began training again – this time with flamethrowers. Things were deceptively peaceful. The regimental diary summed up their one wish: 'As long as the Westminsters had been in Italy, there had always been the wistful thought that . . . if the "one more ridge" directly in front of them could be captured, the regiment would emerge in flat country where the Germans would not be looking down and accurately directing fire at them . . . At last that "one more ridge" became a reality. It was the San Fortunato, southwest of Rimini, and it commanded the coastal entrance to the plains of Lombardy.' Two days later, the unit's commander went forward and stood on the ridge, which had just fallen to the Canadians. He returned smiling, saying that as far as he could see from San Fortunato, 'It's as flat as a pool table.'

Rimini fell on the morning of 21 September. Greek, Canadian, and New Zealand units had battled back German paratroopers from both sides of the airfield, swung right, and pushed into the centre of the city. The church at San Lorenzo had fallen too, to a concentrated tank assault. The Germans had pulled out, pouring north to avoid being outflanked by the Allied success in – finally – taking

San Fortunato Ridge. At 7:45 a.m., the mayor of Rimini officially surrendered to the 3rd Greek Mountain Brigade. Winston Churchill, very mindful of the need to keep Greece onside as an ally just as the Russians were entering Bulgaria, had decided that they should have the privilege of taking the city, to avenge the loss of Athens to the Germans in 1941. It was for this reason that the Westminsters had been halted and taken out of the line. The month-long battle had cost the Allies 14,000 casualties, of whom 4,500 were Canadian, along with 660 tanks. Allied casualties approximated 140 dead and 600 wounded every day in the last week of the battle. The Germans lost 7,000 dead and wounded, and another 7,000 'disappeared' or went missing. Their 10th Army was reduced to a shell – of its nineteen list divisions, by the end of the battle of Rimini and Operation *Olive*, only ten of them were above half strength, most considerably below.

And the final casualty of the supposedly grand battle of mobile warfare that was meant to be the sweep to the Adriatic? Its very architect, Lieutenant General Oliver Leese. Shortly after the fall of Rimini, he was sent to command 11th Army Group in Southeast Asia. This included the highly individual and capable 14th Army, commanded by the legendary Lieutenant General William 'Bill' Slim, the architect of British victory in Burma. On arrival, Slim made note in his diary of Leese's style of command and management: 'He and his staff were rather inclined to thrust Eighth Army down our throats.'

# 13

## MULES, BULLDOZERS, AND BAILEY BRIDGES

### *The Indians on the Apennines*

The Allied plan for the assault on the Gothic Line specified that once the 8th Army had taken Rimini and was operating in the countryside near the Adriatic coast, then the American 5th Army would attack across the Apennines in the centre. Their main objectives would be the city of Bologna and the flatlands of the Po valley that lay beyond it. Kesselring had already worked out that if this move was successful, half of his forces would be trapped between Bologna and the Adriatic by 5th and 8th Armies. The strike on Bologna was given to 2nd Corps of the American 5th Army, which would carry out the main attack; they were supported on their flank by Lieutenant General Stanley Kirkman's XIII British Corps, which would attack over the mountains on their right. XIII Corps consisted of three divisions: the 1st British, the 6th British Armoured, and the 8th Indian. The 8th had three infantry brigades, one of which was the 21st. This was made up of a British infantry battalion from the Royal West Kents and two Indian ones – the Punjabis and the 1st Battalion of the Maratha Light Infantry.

For Captain Eustace D'Souza and his men, it was another early autumn in Italy. The weather was still hot. They were still wearing shorts. In front of them were the Apennines, rising to a height of 5,000 feet and forming a vast barrier that sat like a huge wall between them and the flat plain of the River Po that lay on the other side. They would have to fight their way up and across. For the young captain from Bombay and many of his men it brought back jarring, violent memories of the second battle for Monte Cassino earlier that year. After their rapid summer advance across the warm and dusty Tuscan uplands, the Marathas were to be thrown back into mountain warfare. Despite the sunny weather and blue skies, it was only a matter of time before the rains closed in and the men were back in the land of winter mud. D'Souza knew that the first positions on the Gothic Line that the Marathas would encounter were on the slopes he was looking at. This was what he and the men had come all the way from India for. The fight for God and Empire, for the man his Marathas described as 'the King Emperor'. For D'Souza, everything on the path from the dusty hockey field in Bombay to officer academy to the example set by his family and school had led to this point.

The Indian soldiers were preparing themselves for another advance. They were sharpening knives and 'pulling-through' the barrels of their Lee–Enfields with the scraps of rifle-cleaning cloth the army called 'four-by-two'. Each piece of this flannel fit the barrel perfectly. They thumbed .45 rounds into Thompson magazines, settled grenades and Bren magazines in their pouches, and sat laughing and teasing each other, chatting, one man making tea, another holding his rifle muzzle up to the sky to check the cleanliness on the inside of the barrel. D'Souza watched them, and then went to join the officers looking at the maps of the terrain that lay in front of them.

There were three main roads going north and northeast from Florence across the Apennines towards Bologna, and all of them followed valleys up to the crest of the mountains and down the other side. In each valley was a river that flowed down into the Po valley on the reverse slope facing away from the Indians. The Allies had to capture these three roads and valleys and the mountains that overlooked them, because they formed the backbone of the Gothic Line in this central sector. The mountains were 5,000 feet high in some places, and parts of them were semi-vertical. The Allies gave code names to these three main roads they had to take north towards Bologna: Star, Arrow, and Sword. On the reverse slope of the Apennines, these roads descended into the Po valley down the valleys of three rivers running almost in parallel. These were the Sieve, the Lamone, and the Senio. Route Star ran down the valley of the Sieve and hit the flatland of the Po valley at the town of Forli. Starting from their position on the south of the mountains, the Marathas were going to attack up and over them on Route Star and clear the positions of the Gothic Line on the crest and reverse slope. Then they would head down the valley of the Sieve, into the Po valley, take Forli, and hook up with the 8th Army advancing west from the flatlands around Rimini. That was the backbone of the plan that Captain D'Souza and his English and Indian colleagues were looking at as they stood in front of the Apennines at the beginning of the second week in September.

Up and over the Apennines, into the flatlands of the Po, and then turn left for Bologna. On paper, it looked simple. Allied commanders were still optimistically confident it could be achieved by October, before the rain, mud, and then the snow would make transport, communications, and fighting next to impossible. They had learned their lessons about fighting in the Italian autumn and winter the year before, so they knew they had to be across the Apennines and into the Po valley before the end of October, at the latest.

But as D'Souza went off to find some .45 ammunition for his Webley pistol and cartridges for his Thompson submachine gun, he reckoned the Allies were being over-optimistic. He'd seen the desperately slow progress made in front of Monte Cassino that spring, the mountains and rivers like the Sangro blocking the Marathas for weeks in a sea of mud and waves of rain, and infantry attacks that crawled forward with heavy casualties. Here were the Apennines, the highest mountain peaks in the whole country, defended by the best soldiers in the SS, the Wehrmacht Heer, and the Luftwaffe, with the most laboriously prepared positions in the whole Italian campaign. This was going to be tough mountain fighting. In his orders, he had told the NCOs and the junior Indian non-commissioned officers, the *havildars* and *jemadars,* that the unit would be heavily supported by engineers and sappers on the forthcoming assault. By late 1944, no unit advancing up Italy was complete without the technical help vital to getting across the rivers, peaks, and ravines. Three items had become war-winning assets for the Allies: bulldozers, Bailey bridges, and mules. And from where D'Souza was standing in front of the Apennines, mules were now the most important, and often the only, form of transport that could haul supplies across the rock faces, gulleys, and tiny paths of the mountain slopes.

By autumn 1944, the Allies were using around 30,000 of the dogged pack animals in Italy. The Royal Indian Army Service Corps was in charge of the Indian Mule Companies attached to battalions like the Maratha Light Infantry. The animals under their charge came from three sources: they had been brought over from Tunisia to Sicily in 1943, captured from the Germans on the advance up Italy, or imported from the Middle East. The Americans used some 11,000 mules and 4,000 horses. The advantages of mules was simple: they could walk, climb, and scramble over mountain routes where no vehicles could go, and they could transport anything from wounded men to ammunition, food, and even pack howitzers broken down into parts. Like the Americans, the British, and the Germans, the Indians tried to find only brown, dark grey, or black mules. White or light-skinned ones were highly visible at night. The Americans discovered that a grey mule, sprayed or painted with a solution of purple potassium permanganate, would hold a much darker colour for up to two months, or one month in the autumn rains. The Indian mule handlers were devoted to their charges, with the brand of a crow's foot on the off-side of their necks, indicating they belonged to the British Army.

> Mules were in great demand in these hills. They performed wonders and earned the undying gratitude of the fighting troops whom they served. Daily they carried food, water and ammunition along paths exposed to incessant shell and mortar fire. One Sikh mule unit attached to a British battalion established a proud record. No mule was ever left unattended or allowed to break away from a supply column under fire. The Sikhs' tendency to treat their mules like potential Derby winners led one officer to estimate casualties to be higher among the drivers than among the mules. When fire was directed on them the Sikhs would bring their animals' heads together and would stand in front of them. One Sikh muleteer sheltered his mules in the corner of two walls while eighteen shells exploded around him.[1]

For an army that in so many ways relied on enormous industrial mobilization, some of the Allies' key weapons and equipment were remarkably simple. Bulldozers and Bailey bridges were two of them. A battalion like the Marathas would be on the start line of an infantry assault, similar to the one where D'Souza and his men waited to make their up-and-over crossing on Route Star. They would be in a tented camp, or billeted in and around an Italian village. If the local population had fled, they would occupy their houses and barns; if not, they would find any cover available in stables and outbuildings. The Marathas had slept in more cow barns than they could remember since arriving at Taranto. The men would march to their forward position from the last point on a road or track accessible to trucks and jeeps. This was called the 'truck-head' or 'jeep-head'. A day or two behind them as they advanced would be sappers and road construction units. These men would build any form of track or path or road they could, so that the forward fighting troops could be re-supplied as easily as possible, casualties evacuated swiftly, and, if necessary the fighting companies could withdraw. From the point where vehicles could go no farther, mules took over.

The Maratha Light Infantry was supported by companies of Indian sappers and miners, a Canadian drilling section, Italian pioneer companies, and a number of specialized mechanical units. Bulldozers dug, pushed, scraped, and shaped the earth, filling shell craters, clearing revetments and obstacles, and digging a large hole in the time it took an Indian light infantryman to down a cup of hot tea. In one feat of engineering farther south, these gangs had cleared a track accessible to vehicles from a mountain path down into a river bottom, a drop of 400 feet. In the Apennines, the tracks followed old footpaths along the steep hillsides, winding in and out of gullies and then climbing up the beds of mountain streams to heights of three or 4,000 feet above the valleys. The engineers had to deal with giant boulders, crumbling surfaces, rocky ledges, patches of scrub, and heavy forest, and they used bulldozers, picks and shovels, and high explosives to do it. It would take ninety engineers a day and a half to build five miles of tank track; thirty men three days to build a couple of miles of pathway that a jeep could drive down. Much of this work was done at night, often under fire, in the rain, and without knowing whether the engineers would be attacked at any moment from above, behind, or in front. The engineering parties had platoons that provided defence, but at night it was impossible to secure a perimeter in the Italian mountains without a man every five yards. Constructing a Bailey bridge over fast-flowing – often raging – rivers was physical labour incarnate.

To begin with, all parties got soaking wet, often in spring or winter, and stayed soaking wet for sometimes two days. While in the river, or on its banks, the engineers laying the bridges were routinely covered in mud; there was also the ever-present danger of being swept away by the current. Bailey bridges are hugely heavy sections of steel that can be attached together, rolled across a river on pontoons, and be used to ford any river with gradients on both banks that sometimes appear unfeasible.

The manpower required to support a single battalion like the Marathas was huge. The ratio of infantrymen at bayonet-point in an attack to the number of engineers, pioneers, sappers, artillerymen, drivers, medical staff, cooks, and administrative staff was sometimes one to four. A letter to his men from Major General Dudley Russell, the commanding officer of the 8th Indian Division who had spent twenty-five years in the Indian Army, summed up the joint effort required in an attack:

> Behind the indomitable infantry that clambered and won the peaks, the entire Division worked in high gear. The smoothness of the ancillary services was the yardstick of the speed of the attack. Next to the battle line, both literally and in priority, came the mule trains, the patient animals and the indefatigable drivers who followed wherever the fighting men went. They fetched food, water, ammunition and blankets, and took back litters of wounded. Day by day Indian sappers drove the jeep-head deeper into the hills. Winding up the mountain slopes for mile after mile, the narrow tracks looked like threads of cotton against the brown mountainsides. The Divisional Provosts in an unbroken tour of duty policed these routes in order that the traffic might flow steadily and without jam. Signallers laid hundreds of miles of cable; no sooner had the infantry dug in than the telephones began to buzz. At vehicle-head the stretcher-bearers lifted the wounded from the litter mules and laid them carefully on specially fitted jeeps which edged cautiously down the mountain side. The 'Q' Services worked twenty-four hours in each day, replenishing sub-dumps from main dumps apportioning and delivering supplies by jeep, mule, and man pack.[2]

Russell was extremely popular with his men: he was nicknamed 'the Pasha' (chief) partly because he spoke fluent Pashto, one of the languages of the Indian North-West Frontier. He had served with the Royal West Kents in the First World War, then joined the Indian Army in 1917. He was awarded the Military Cross in Iraq in 1919; served in India until 1938, by which time he was a lieutenant colonel; and then in 1940 served as a senior staff officer with an Indian division in Eritrea. In 1941, he negotiated the surrender at Amba Alagi of the Italian forces in Eritrea. Russell then led a brigade in Syria and at both battles of El Alamein. He had been in charge of the 8th Indian Division since they arrived at Taranto. He understood Indian soldiers and encouraged his men with a combination of exhortation – 'Step up, keep stepping up' – and thanks. Like his men, he knew that attacking the Apennines head-on was not going to be any form of picnic.

On 11 September the Marathas crossed their start line. The advance was at first up gentle slopes. Columns of jeeps and mules barged and bumped alongside them. Vineyards and cultivated fields lay by the side of the roads and Italian men and women paused, leaning on their hoes and pitchforks, as the Indian soldiers passed, the *scrunch-scrunch* of their boots on the stone tracks announcing their passing. Cows stared from the pastures. The Indians, who came from a country where cows are sacred, were fascinated by them. Innumerable times in battle they had watched as cows behaved imperturbedly under shellfire and with the deafening noise of battle around them. Some soldiers thought they had no sense of hearing, nerves, or of self-preservation. In the late summer heat, the Indians moved continually forward up the slope towards battle. Innumerable small tributaries of the river Sieve seemed everywhere – the march was constantly broken by clambering, wading, and scrabbling through streams and small rivers. Three miles north of the river Sieve itself, they suddenly found strongly wired and entrenched positions that had been abandoned. The men halted. The officers conferred. The formations of companies and platoons spread out in the afternoon sun, the high peaks of the Apennines rising directly in front of the men of the Maratha Light Infantry. They had finally arrived on the Gothic Line.

There were three main mountain peaks right in front of the men of the 8th Indian Division. On the left was Le Scalette, Alpe di Vitigliano in the centre, and Femina Morta on the right. They rose straight above the surrounding countryside, devoid of trees, steep slopes leading towards them. There was scree, rock, and patches of bare grass leading up to razor-backed crests, 3,000 feet above, which marched straight up to the three main peaks. They ran from seven o'clock to two o'clock, from southwest to northeast, and the mountains offered no cover at all. It was perfect defensive country, and the Indians knew that the Germans were waiting. General Russell allocated Alpe di Vitigliano to the 21st Brigade: two ridges that led onto it, Monte Citerna and Monte Stiletto, were the first objectives. The 1st Battalion of the Marathas was briefed to seize the approach ground, so, as light fell on 12 September, they began to climb. After scrabbling uphill for seven hours, they hit the first German positions on the southwestern slopes of Monte Citerna. The men hit the ground and consolidated their line. Then for miles all along the Apennines, a massive artillery barrage screamed inbound and exploded along the front, as the British 13th and 2nd US Corps moved in to the attack.

As the shells screamed in, the Marathas moved hard left, ducking down and running sideways along the slopes of Monte Citerna towards one of its sub-peaks, Monte Verruca. The unit chosen to spearhead the attack on this was C Company. D'Souza was its second in command. He moved back as fast as he could to get the men into position as the company commander, an Anglo-Indian major, got ready for the attack. Neil Pettingell had won the Military Cross earlier that year near Cassino and understood exactly how his Indian soldiers operated, how the Germans thought tactically, and how to match the two together. Major General Russell was watching C Company's attack through binoculars from 1,000 yards away on the slopes below them. Pettingell had carried out a detailed reconnaissance of both the target and his company's line of attack, crawling with two men up and across the slopes of Monte Verruca; he found it was going to be impossible to put more than eighteen men at one time into the attack as the slope was so steep and the width of the line extremely narrow. His company of 130 men was therefore going to have to go into the attack eighteen at a time, and the astute officer had pre-arranged an individual fire-support artillery mission for each assault group.

The lead platoon crossed the start line at twenty minutes past four in the afternoon. Eustace D'Souza was with the company's headquarters group, detailed to lead the second platoon. The lead group headed straight for a group of three MG-42 positions that Pettingell had spotted on his recce crawl. Behind the Marathas were their favourite comrades-in-arms from the 14th Canadian Armoured Brigade. The Indians sent a series of pre-arranged radio signals, and the Canadian Shermans opened up from 800 yards away at the first objective until the Indian light infantrymen were only fifteen yards from it. Their gunfire was deadly accurate. Hardly had the last 75mm shell exploded than the Marathas charged, killing four Germans immediately, at which point the remaining fifteen threw their hands in the air. The Canadian tanks then opened fire again as another twenty men charged forward. But the MG-42 positions they were targeting were lying vertically dug in on the slope: in military terminology they were in defilade, meaning it was impossible for the Shermans to fire along their deployed axis. The Marathas hardly faltered. 'Naik Nathu Dhanuwade dived into the scrub, clambered like a chamois, and reappeared above the German redoubt, upon which he showered grenades until resistance ceased. The third platoon followed through as though upon exercise.'[3]

The artillery then blasted Monte Verucca with smoke shells, as the ninety Indians now deployed on the small enemy objective charged through it and up the hill like mountain goats. A half mile below them, their commanding officer was astounded. Watching his men through binoculars finish off a perfect textbook operation, Major General Dudley Russell had one comment: 'I wish His Majesty had been here to see it.'

The smoke from the shells was still drifting around the gulleys and ravines four hours later at midnight, when A Company of the Marathas reached the summit of Monte Verucca. Three days later, the Indians captured a German who had been on the mountain. On him they found a letter he hadn't had time to mail: 'September 13th was my birthday, and I shall never forget this one. Tommy attacked and I had a hairsbreadth escape from capture. I have never run so fast as I did then, and up a mountainside. I had received two parcels from home, but everything was left behind. . . .'[4]

From the top of Monte Verruca, the Marathas started to march northeast and climb towards Le Scalette. By noon, the exhausted Indians were standing on its summit, having taken it without any opposition. The high Apennine wind snapped at the uniform shorts of the Indian soldiers, covered with mud, dust, sweat, earth, cordite smoke, and in some cases blood. They stared northward as their officers and NCOs prepared for the next march. They had just captured their first objective on the Gothic Line. A week later, Major General Russell sent every man in his division a message, congratulating them on everything they had achieved since they had arrived at Taranto a year earlier. He signed off with a typically personal exhortation: 'This retrospect is pleasant, the prospect is inspiring. Keep right on to the end of the road.'

Captured German officers, under questioning, said that the reason they lost the high ground on Monte Verruca, La Stilette, and then Alpe di Vitigliano was that the 10th and 14th German Armies had lost contact with each other; others said that the Germans had been waiting for reserves to arrive. The Allies estimated that it was a combination of both, compounded by the excellent tactical skills of the Indians, their cooperation with the Canadian tanks, and the enormous aerial support the Allied Desert Air Force provided.

Never have the Allied air forces intervened in greater strength and with greater effectiveness. All day long the sky above the mountain peaks was filled with the thunder of aircraft, sallying and returning, with never an enemy machine to challenge them. Along the narrow valleys, as on the bare crests, the fighter bombers, the mediums and the heavies, struck devastating blows. The enemy lived like a beast in this hole, in terror of what awaited him. By day he dared not move. After dark when his horse-drawn transport dashed along the roads, with urgent supplies, the night bombers swooped with destruction . . .

# 14

## ALIENATING THE ITALIAN POPULATION

### *The Massacre at Marzabotto*

#### Late September 1944

Knowing that the attack on the Gothic Line was imminent, Kesselring wanted his best units to be rested. So Max Simon's 16th SS-Panzergrenadiers had been taken out of the line on 8 August, vacating its barracks in Pisa and heading northwest. The men were given a month to rest and refit. On the night of 11/12 August, the day before the killings in the mountains at Sant'Anna di Stazzema, SS-Sturmbannführer Walter Reder and his reconnaissance battalion arrived in the town of Carrara along with the rest of his division. The SS stationed their men in the seaside Tuscan town, in its marina, and in the outlying towns of Ruosina, Isola di Carrara, and Seravezza, which lay in the shadow of the marble quarries on the surrounding mountains. Its senior officers took over the ochre-coloured old Villa Barsanti in a suburb. On 19 August the reconnaissance unit killed fifty-four prisoners in the reprisal at San Terenzo Monte. When the Allies attacked Rimini on 25 August the whole division was put on standby but stayed put behind the line. All through the battle of Rimini they waited. In front of them on the west coast of Italy, the Nisei, then the Buffalo Soldiers, the South Africans, and the Brazilians were in combat, fighting hard to push up the Tuscan coast. Before the Japanese Americans were taken out of the line in August, the SS men had been in combat against the Nisei of the 442nd Regimental Combat Team around St Vincente and Cecina in southern Tuscany.

The Japanese Americans had proved a tenacious and evasive enemy. The Reichsführer-SS were used to the Red Army's way of fighting, of human wave assaults preceded by rolling artillery barrages, then mortar bombardments, then a line, three deep, of often drunk infantrymen charging at them. The 442nd used a more tactically adept three-pronged assault technique. The 3.5-inch bazooka team would be with the Garand riflemen in the middle of the squad: the moment they came under fire, one or more rockets would be fired at the enemy location, supported by rifle fire. Then, as the Browning Automatic Rifle and possibly a .30 Browning belt-fed machine gun fired from the left or right flank, the riflemen would crawl, run, duck, dive, or race to the side of the target, if a machine-gun nest, or to the front or back, if a house. Then grenades were thrown in. With this attacking technique, out of a ten-man section, only five or six men were on their feet and visible at any one time.

As their officers' plans changed with the speed of the campaign around them, the German soldiers thrived on reports from their scouts — exaggerated gossip and hearsay from Fascist Italian soldiers, rumours from prisoners and other units that had been in the line before them, and briefings from their superiors. Italian partisans will skin you alive if you're caught; Canadians and New Zealanders are hard as nails and sometimes don't take prisoners; Moroccan mountain troops will rape you like they did the Italian men, women, and children around Cassino. You can hear Americans in the dark because they all chew gum; Italian peasant women want sex all the time and African-American soldiers are here to degrade Western civilization. The British are honourable and brave, the Indians little monkeys with big knives who kill for fun. And cut your head off afterward. Many of these prejudices and rumours made for easy anti-Allied propaganda. One Italian poster showed a black American soldier in a slouch hat with his arm draped around a marble statue, 'looting' the country's artistic heritage. And then the Japanese arrived. The first rumours about them spread after they arrived in Naples, from Italian spies. To begin with, the Germans thought that Japanese soldiers who had been captured in the Pacific were being drafted into American units. Then, when they realized that the number of Japanese soldiers surrendering in the Pacific wouldn't fill a rifle company, they changed tack. By the time the 442nd RCT arrived on the line in June, the Germans learned that these were Americans of Japanese ancestry. The handful of prisoners they took confirmed this.

The Italians and the Russians were the subject of more accurate and informed prejudice, in many cases based upon the personal experiences of Reder and the men from the Reichsführer-SS. Like many of his fellow officers, Reder was aware of Mussolini's well-known critique in 1934 of the Third Reich's position on race: 'Thirty centuries of history allow us to look with supreme pity on certain doctrines which are preached beyond the Alps by the descendants of those who were illiterate when Rome had Caesar, Virgil and Augustus.'[1]

In military practice, Reder, like many SS and Wehrmacht colleagues, thought the Italian Fascist military hierarchy untrustworthy and unreliable at best. Fascist troops loyal to Mussolini were eager to participate in *rastrellamente* actions and torture prisoners, but when it came to real combat? Reder would far rather have Turkomans or Cossacks. You knew where you stood with them. And as for the Russians themselves, nothing Walter Reder had experienced in twenty-one months of continuous combat in their country made him think they were anything other than brainwashed, powerless sheep with deadly, destructive leaders. Good fighters, yes. But Bolshevism, he thought, was simply against the natural order of things. Russians? It was like the Italian Fascist propaganda poster popular that year across northern Italy, which showed a long, slow train of railway cars curling through a frozen, blighted forest landscape somewhere in the east. The bodies of women and children lie tossed into the snow by the tracks. On the top of the last railway wagon sits a Russian guard, in helmet and greatcoat, clutching a rifle. Except he is a grinning skeleton. The caption? 'Russians bring death.' And on this matter, SS-Hauptsturmführer Walter Reder, his superiors, and several of the Allied leaders were going to see eye to eye far more than they could have imagined.

But finally, in his lexicon of opinion and prejudice, Reder did have a soft spot for the Spaniards, whom he saw as glorified Mexican bandits, fighting a just and valid civil war against communism and republicanism. On the front outside Leningrad, and in the fighting around Kharkov, Reder's battle cry when leading his men into action against Russian trenches had been, 'Caramba, carajo, ein whisky!'[2]

The moment Generalfeldmarschall Kesselring realized the attacks on Rimini constituted the main assault on the Gothic Line, he moved as fast as he could to protect his front and to destroy any partisan threats behind him. At the beginning of September, knowing that an attack on Bologna could be imminent, he issued orders to SS-Gruppenführer Max Simon. Overlooking the city was an enormous massif that dominated approach roads to it. Italian Fascist spies told the Germans it was the base of the partisan brigade Stella Rossa. If Allied troops pushing north from Florence to Bologna with artillery could occupy Monte Sole with the help of the partisans, the Germans would lose control of the high ground overlooking the central fulcrum of the Gothic Line defences. They had to take towns and villages on the mountain from partisan control, and hold them.

So on 26 September, Max Simon summoned SS-Sturmbannführer Walter Reder to the headquarters of the Reichsführer-SS division in the town of Reggio Emilia.[3] He briefed him and other regimental commanders. The one-armed officer had never heard of the Monte Sole area, the Red Star Brigade, or its leader who used the *nom de guerre* Lupo, 'Wolf'. Simon was succinct: there were partisans and their support network to be destroyed, and Hauptsturmführer Reder's unit, Aufklärungsabteilung 16, Reconnaissance Battalion 16, was given the task of doing it. He returned to Carrara by road and gathered his company and platoon commanders together. They would sweep up two sides of the mountain from the south and west, taking control of each village they moved through. At the top of the huge mountain was a hamlet called Marzabotto.

—■·O·■—

Dawn on 29 September arrived around six in the morning, a grey, mountain day of mist and drizzle. The dry heat of the Italian summer was already a memory, and the rainy autumn skies offered the SS unit better protection against Allied air attack. Nevertheless, from operational necessity and habit, they cut branches from the orange, pine, and olive trees growing at the side of the roads around Carrara to lay on top of their vehicles as camouflage; large bundles of dry hay and straw were put on the half-tracks and trucks. Men kept their eyes peeled at the sky, watchful for prowling Spitfires, Kittyhawks, and Mustang fighters from the Allied Desert Air Force, based in Corsica and on airstrips south of Florence.

The drive to their attack position took an hour. The SS started up the lower slopes of Monte Sole, and around ten o'clock, as the first troops attacked partisan positions in the lower villages, SS-Gruppenführer Simon arrived to see how the operation was going. The SS had already captured twelve prisoners, and Max Simon wanted to know what they would reveal under interrogation. German casualties, Reder noted, were high for an operation against partisans: the SS had taken forty wounded and twenty-four killed in four hours. This was not an operation against a few partisans and their village folk; the Red Star was putting up a stiff fight. By the middle of the afternoon, Reder sent his second in command, a captain, farther up the muddy tracks and pitted, broken road to where his combat platoons were fighting halfway up the hillside. The captain returned with part of a partisan's uniform, an epaulette bearing a red star.

The Germans showed it to a partisan prisoner, who identified it as belonging to Lupo. The SS were convinced they had killed the guerrillas' leader.

The fighting continued through the night, as the partisans moved farther up the mountain and the SS, using mortars and half-tracked armoured vehicles mounted with machine guns and 20mm cannon, tried to encircle them. The Reichsführer-SS took more casualties. As they advanced, they realized they were up against a full brigade of partisans, 1,500–2,000 strong. The SOE and OSS had sent couriers instructing them to mass on the Monte Sole plateau so they could support the American drive towards Bologna through the valleys below them.

On the morning of 30 September, Reder received orders to move some of his men southeast to the town of Lagaro, where Americans were pushing through on the road to Bologna. He left his second in command on Monte Sole, along with more junior officers who were commanding platoons and companies as they spread through the hamlets and villages that marched up the slopes. The men moved through the cover of oak and scrub pines, and then towards the top of the mountain, where the treeline vanished and they were exposed to the full force of the wind and elements. In front of them, at the top, was the scattered 'collective' village of Marzabotto. Around it were two separate municipal areas, Grizzana Morandi and Monzuno, each containing a number of scattered houses and hamlets. These included Caprara, Casaglia, and Cerpiana.

The lines of SS men moved up the mountain in a typical anti-partisan *rastrellamento*. Monte Sole is big – almost fifty square miles of slope, wooded thickets, barns, and squat, stone houses set around small fields and patches of crops. The operation took five days. Rations and fresh units of men arrived from Carrara. The SS slept in the barns and houses they occupied, while their fellow soldiers kept guard. After four years of war, this was a normal operation to them. Every position was cleared of partisans – the Germans killed almost all of them, took a select few prisoners, while those who escaped alive scattered farther

A group of women in Italy during the Second World War, circa 1944. (Photo by George Rodger/ The LIFE Picture Collection/Getty Images)

A machine gunner and two riflemen cover a building occupied by five Germans, as an assault squad of the US 10th Mountain Division flushes them out. (Bettmann via Getty Images)

A South African tank passes a knocked-out German troop carrier on the road to Montepulciano, Italy, June 1944. (Photo by Paul Popper/Popperfoto/Getty Images)

British Prime Minister Winston Churchill uses binoculars to watch an attack on a German-held position on the Gothic Line in August 1944. He is accompanied by British General Sir Harold Alexander. (Photo by Capt. Gade/ IWM via Getty Images)

Allied pack mules pass an overturned truck near the Gothic Line in Italy, September 1944. (Photo by Photo12/UIG/Getty Images)

A British 105mm self-propelled gun negotiates a hairpin bend on a mountain road near Mondaino, during the advance against the Gothic Line, 6 September 1944. (Photo by Sgt Dawson/IWM via Getty Images)

Italian partisans after the liberation of Florence, August 1944. (Istituto Storico della Resistenza Toscana)

Italian partisans with captured German weapons. An MG-42 machine gun in the foreground, Paola Ordano behind. (ISREC, Imperia)

Partisan Paola Ordano in her shorts, with Beretta submachine gun, Imperia, April 1945. (ISREC, Imperia)

The liberation of Milan. Italian Partisans parade on 6 May, 1945. (Photo by Keystone-France/Gamma-Keystone via Getty Images)

The end: 1 May 1945. Italian crowds and Allied soldiers as Trieste is liberated. (IRSML, Trieste)

New Zealand soldiers liberate Trieste, 1 May 1945. (IRSML, Trieste)

Allied soldiers and Yugoslav soldiers and partisans confer over a map, Trieste, 1 May 1945.
(IRSML, Trieste)

African-American soldiers of the 92nd Infantry Division pursue retreating Germans along the Gothic Line. (Photo by PhotoQuest/Getty Images)

President Clinton upgrades Daniel Inouye's DSC to a Congressional Medal of Honor, June 2000. (The Daniel K. Inouye Institute)

Ivan Houston re-visits Tuscany in 2015: behind him is an Italian re-enactor in American Second World War uniform. (Ivan Houston)

towards the top of the Monte Solo massif. From its windy, chilly summit, the spires and rooftops of Bologna were visible. For the partisans and civilians who made it to the summit by the day of 3 September, there was nowhere else to run. They joined the terrified population of the hamlet of Casaglia di Monte Sole who took refuge in the church of Santa Maria Assunta and knelt in the few rows of wooden pews. The village priest, Don Ubaldo Marchioni, and three older people led them in prayer. Then the SS arrived.

They broke down the stout wooden door of the church, opened fire with MP-40 machine pistols and threw in grenades. A belt-fed machine gun was then fired through the church doorway. To the left of and behind the church was the cemetery, where more villagers had gathered. The German soldiers grabbed another priest, Father Giovanni Fornasini, and cut off his head. MG-42 machine guns, firing long, high-speed bursts of 7.92mm rounds, raked the terrified crowd huddled in the cemetery. The bullets smacked into the villagers, who were blown backward on top of each other. There was a lot of blood. Nearly 200 people died there. Another 550 were killed in the three neighbouring villages, including Marzabotto itself, 250 of them children, and five Catholic priests. A conflicting version says that only fifty people were killed in Marzabotto itself, and that the majority of the dead in the villages of Caprara, Casaglia, and Cerpiana were partisans.[4]

SS-Sturmbannführer Reder tallied up the deaths of 728 'bandits' in his after-action report. The survivors and partisan groups that arrived on the mountain in the following days and weeks said that up to 1,835 people died, but this included all the armed partisans killed in the five-day *rastrellamento*. This number of dead fighters was estimated to be as high as 720. Both the Fascist authorities in Bologna and their loyal local newspaper, *Il Resto del Carlino*, downplayed the number of civilian deaths and exaggerated the body count of the partisans who had reportedly been killed. The Catholic Church, partisans in Bologna, and every anti-fascist civilian within miles poured gasoline on the flames of rumour until the figure of 3,000 dead was being passed around.

Reder himself reported that he arrived back in the village of Cerpiano on Monte Sole only on the night of 4/5 October, after driving from combat positions near the road to Bologna where Americans were advancing. He said he got to Monte Sole at 5:00 a.m. Only then did he realize that all of the houses and the church had been burned in Casaglia. The five-day *rastrellamento* was a military operation, he said, not a reprisal. He knew by this stage that reprisals served as nothing more than recruitment operations for the partisans and were of no tactical or strategic value at all. He had spent long enough in Russia to learn that, and Marzabotto had been a military action where civilians had died as well. In areas out of Fascist control and influence, the Italian civilian population was now foursquare united behind the Allies and the partisans. The alienation reinforced by Sant'Anna di Stazzema was now cemented. But Reder said that for his men, the operation had been a matter of war and combat, where death is natural. And as for the deaths on the mountainside, he thought they were simply the rotten fruits of such a war.[5]

The days when his ultimate commander, Generalfeldmarschall Kesselring, could balance the finer subtleties between a reprisal and a military operation were gone. In March 1944, when partisans blew up SS soldiers in Via Rasella, SS-Obersturmbannführer Herbert Kappler and the general in charge of the German Army in Rome had sat up all night drinking brandy and telephoning each other every hour to make sure they got the numbers right on the execution lists. Six months later, Rome had fallen, the Germans were retreating, and Kesselring didn't care whether the killings on Monte Sole massif were a reprisal or a military operation. He had a crumbling front line to hold.[6]

And it was now, as the weather turned dramatically from summer to autumn, that his choice of defensive positions and subsequent control of the terrain became so important. The decision by Lieutenant General Oliver Leese not to exploit the attack on the Fortunato Ridge in the early days of Operation *Olive* had been a completely unexpected bonus, allowing his troops to escape west. The Allies' over-optimism about an early end to the fighting in northern Italy turned to ashes when exposed to Leese's inability to grasp the tactical and strategic moment, which was then compounded by his underestimation of the effects of flooding and heavy rain on the flatlands of the Po valley. Not having pushed forward nearly as fast as expected, the Allies were now victims of the weather for the second winter running, up against Germans in strong defensive positions. Kesselring knew that, if he could hold Bologna until the snow came to the Apennines, the war in Italy would last at least until the early spring of 1945. He knew now that the Allies couldn't invade the Balkans, but he was also aware that there were three cards on the table stacked against him. First, the partisans were getting better armed, better organized, and more numerous by the day. There were 100,000 of them now. It was of immense concern to the Allies which faction was in the political ascendant – Communists, Liberals, Christian Democrats – but Kesselring cared not a fig. To him they were all just armed Italians who wanted to kill his men and push his armies out of Italy.

Second, Kesselring had expected the Allied armies to be more weakened by the unnecessary transfer to France of seven of their more experienced divisions. Yet the most unexpected units in his opponent's ranks were in some cases running rings around his men. The Indians, Poles, and Canadians he had known would fight like determined, steely-eyed gladiators – that was the kind of soldiers they were. But he was getting reports about black Americans, Japanese, and Brazilians going head-to-head with the SS and panzergrenadiers and winning the day. Surprised by the attack on Rimini, he had moved forces from the centre to reinforce it, which meant that now he was having to try to pull them back to hold the line in front of Bologna. And meanwhile, up the west coast slogged this determined force made up of men he had never dreamed of encountering in action. He could only thank the gods hourly for the terrain and the weather.

The third factor was totally beyond his control. It was now the beginning of October. The British, Canadian, and American advance across northwest Europe had slowed. Their lines of supply were overstretched, and the ammunition for soldiers in trenches in central

Holland and the gas for tanks thirty miles from the German border still had to be trucked from the Normandy beachheads. Operation *Market-Garden*, Montgomery's airborne extravaganza designed to cross the Lower Rhine with a carpet of paratroopers and flank into northern Germany by October, had just failed. The Russians were crossing Poland and entering Romania, and Kesselring could almost intuit what the Allies were thinking. They would first want to rid Italy of Mussolini and his followers and make sure a powerful partisan grouping came to the fore, one they backed politically. In practice Kesselring knew this meant any party except the Communists. Then they would want to keep Marshal Tito's Yugoslav partisans off Italian soil, and use Yugoslavia itself as a buffer between Italy and the Russians. They would much rather sue for peace and do a deal with the Germans than allow the Soviets any closer into Europe. This meant that the longer Kesselring could hold the Allies on the Gothic Line, the stronger a position the Germans would be in when it came time to hammer out a peace settlement with the British and Americans. Kesselring could feel the post-war wind coming – but all this, he knew, would have to wait for spring. With the weather and terrain on his side, Oliver Leese's armour bogged in up to its tank tracks in the mud of the soggy Po valley, he was going to make the Allies fight. And winter was coming.

# 15

## FIGHTING GERMAN ARTILLERY AND JIM CROW

### *The Buffalo Soldiers in Tuscany*

### September–October 1944

Private Ivan Houston and the rest of the 370th Regimental Combat Team of the 92nd Infantry Division were the first black American Army unit to go into action in the Second World War. So when they arrived near the 5th Army's front line on the south banks of the Arno on 24 August, senior officers, soldiers from other units, and war correspondents showed enormous interest in them. The Buffalo Soldiers had moved up to a thirty-five-mile-wide front extending east from the Mediterranean Sea, on the far west of the Allied front line. Given the number of veteran divisions that had been diverted to the fighting in southern France, American and British senior commanders were reportedly delighted to have the 92nd with them.

The 370th RCT formed part of the American 5th Army's IV Corps, a seriously understrength formation that was desperately trying to patch together its numbers in time for the assault on the Gothic Line, which had already begun in the east. Anti-aircraft units had been equipped with infantry weapons and formed into ad hoc rifle battalions. One Allied officer noted that they were 'a polyglot task force of American and British anti-aircraft gunners acting as infantry, with Italian Partisans, Brazilians and coloured American troops fighting by their side and we learned that different peoples can fight well together.'

When the 370th first went into the line on the night of 23 August, white officers accompanied them, intensely curious to see how this new unit would function under combat conditions. Would they bolt and run at the first enemy shot? Would they prove effortlessly determined and brave? Would they obey orders? How was America's first black ground combat unit going to acquit itself? A US Amy one-star general, accompanied by a group of journalists and a camera crew, arrived to see them. Lieutenant General Mark Clark followed. Clark, who at Anzio had shown himself to be unafraid of frontline combat conditions, frequently visiting his men in their foxholes, was relieved to see the black soldiers. He used the occasion to indulge in a piece of histrionic grandstanding that drew attention to himself as a commander while at the same time endearing him enormously to his combat troops. It typified his personal and operational dichotomy. When he arrived to see the unit, a senior officer told Clark that one main problem the 370th were experiencing was that some of its more capable officers were being promoted too slowly.

'Give me an example,' the general is reported to have said. So the officer – a colonel – called over a black American first lieutenant who was an acting company commander, telling Clark that the officer was overdue for promotion. General Clark then turned to a captain who was accompanying his party, 'borrowed' the officer's twin bars of rank from his shoulders, and pinned them on the black lieutenant. News of the incident spread very fast among the men of the 92nd – as Clark intended – and was a huge boost for unit morale among the untried and untested division.[1]

Four days later, the 370th Regimental Combat Team's spirits received another lift. It made its first 'contact' with the enemy and came under fire. The headquarters of one of its three battalions was bombed in the night, the 598th Artillery that provided fire support for the 370th fired its first rounds at the enemy, and on 30 August, a patrol of Buffalo Soldiers crossed the Arno. It destroyed a machine-gun post and captured two prisoners. The 370th RCT was operational. Then along with the rest of IV Corps, the unit crossed the wide, shallow waters of the Arno on 1 September.

Six foot one, black, carrying the battalion's maps, and of considerable interest to the Brazilians, the British, the white Americans, South Africans, and especially to the Italians around him, Private Ivan Houston waded the Arno along with his unit. The soldiers were briefed that in the enemy line opposite them were the panzergrenadiers of the 16th SS-Panzergrenadier Division, as well as a composite unit of Germans from Alsace in eastern France, captured Poles, and Italian Fascist troops. Houston was less worried about which German troops he was going to come up against than about the constant artillery fire. His battalion headed north from the Arno towards the Tuscan town of Lucca. In between the Arno and this old walled city were two bits of high ground, Monte Pisano and Monte Albano, which IV Corps had been ordered to take, occupy, and hold, as they dominated all the high ground overlooking Lucca itself.

Houston and his battalion headquarters moved through four villages the other side of the river. In each of them, the welcome from Italian civilians was immense – old men, women, children, and people of all ages showered them with wine, kisses, grapes, and flowers. They held on to the soldiers' vehicles, hugging the GIs, greeting them in Italian, some of the women crying, others kissing the Americans, others just watching and waving. Old men ran alongside the trucks and jeeps, pouring red wine from earthenware jugs. Children jumped up and down in the road. 'Here were White Italians greeting Negro Americans as liberators and showering us with love, while in our own country we remained second-class citizens in all respects,' noted Houston in his diary.[2]

The American vehicles rumbled slowly through the four villages between the Arno and Monte Pisano. Outside one village, Houston had just given a tin of chopped ham and eggs from his K-rations to a starving priest, thin, sunken of eye and gaunt of cheek, embarrassed to be asking for food. Suddenly he and his colleagues heard the loud muzzle report of an 88mm gun as it fired, followed by the hiss of the incoming shell. The soldiers jumped out of their truck and landed hard and fast in the prone position by the road as the 88mm shells exploded with heavy, air-displacing percussive *whummpps*. Houston and the other GIs all had their faces in the dirt. Except for one of their number, a soldier who had been asleep in the truck when the 88 fired. Described by Houston as 'a slow-moving, slow-talking Southern farm boy', Private Hiram MacBeth remained in the truck, sound asleep through the bombardment.

As Houston realized for the first time that the enemy was actually trying to kill *him,* MacBeth slumbered on, waking only when they reached battalion headquarters. Houston paused in Pisa, which was still being fought over, and found himself taking cover at the bottom of the walls of the Leaning Tower. Next to him, keeping his head down, was a Nisei soldier. He and Houston had no time to reflect on how the two of them had ended up here in Italy fighting for America – raising your head four inches too far could get it shot off by a German sniper.

The German artillery kept coming in. From 88mm anti-aircraft guns, 105mm field howitzers, self-propelled cannon, and even a pair of 150mm guns that the Germans had put on a spit of land outside La Spezia harbour, fifteen miles north. Every time a tank or jeep or truck moved, raising any form of dust, shells landed. Private Houston noted in the battalion log that between the 370th Battalion's arrival on the line in August 1944 and the moment the war ended, there was not one whole day when they were not under some kind of artillery fire: in the advance to Lucca, he counted 500 incoming rounds in one day. Taking cover in mid-September in a deserted Italian villa, he counted 127 shells landing in his vicinity. He could hear the boom of the German weapon firing the round, the roar as it travelled, and the hiss of its incoming trajectory. Houston's father had served with an artillery unit of black American soldiers in the First World War, and he had told his son the noise of shells passing overhead was like a freight train. Thirty years later, it was exactly the same.

The unit's regimental aid post was next to battalion headquarters where Private Houston was stationed. As his colleagues fought their way hand to hand into the village of Ripafratta, which lay between the Arno and Lucca, the young private saw the results of artillery fire first-hand. Medics brought in the body of the 370th's executive officer, Major Aubrey Biggs, one of the unit's white leaders and its first officer casualty. Houston saw from the blood-splashed mess of saw-edged cranial bone and the state of the man's skull that he'd been killed by shrapnel. Two privates who were friends of Houston's were then also hit: one died in the other's arms, as his friend begged him to hang on until medical help arrived. The second man was then also hit by artillery. After four days in action, every single man in the unit had seen what the German artillery could do — Houston was with battalion headquarters in a deserted villa when two enormous shells fired by German howitzers from a range of ten miles landed in the building's elegant dusty garden. Neither exploded, although they left enormous cone-shaped holes in the ground. Houston and his fellow soldiers stood around thinking how lucky they had been. Sometimes those wounded or killed by artillery bore almost no marks at all — the tiniest piece of shrapnel was enough to tear into a man's body, and if it found an artery, vein, or major organ, it frequently proved lethal.

'Shrapnel' is the generic name given to the red-hot pieces of torn metal from the casing of a shell, ranging from a fifth the size of a little fingernail to great blooming flowers of molten metal the size of a man's hand, edges curled and razor sharp. When the shell explodes, its casing tears apart, and the pieces of metal fly through the air almost at the speed of sound. It was named after Major General Henry Shrapnel, a British artillery officer and inventor who in 1784 invented a cannonball that was filled with lead shot, designed to blow up in midair. By 1803, the British Army had taken his design further and produced an elongated projectile, which they named the 'Shrapnel shell'. His inventions were used by the British in wars against the Dutch, and then against Napoleon.

But sometimes the explosion of an artillery round did no damage at all. Ivan Houston and a colleague were taking cover behind a wall outside Lucca one day when an 88mm landed just the other side of it: there was an enormous explosion, the two men were thrown up into the air by the blast, but then, said Houston, they were dropped back down to earth very gently, completely unhurt.

The infantry of the 370th, which had taken to riding on the backs of the accompanying Sherman tanks of the 1st US Armoured Division, soon realized it was safer being on foot. Tanks attracted shells. Clinging to the backs of tanks as they went into action was a risky business, too: yes, it saved footslogging, but the perils of being swiped off by a revolving turret, burning yourself on the exhaust, and simply being thrown off, risking a broken limb on the lumpy, bumpy terrain were ever present.

Meanwhile, the Germans would post observers in any high building they could find, particularly the church in every town and village. They thought the Allies would not fire on them. They were also retreating from one piece of high ground to another, meaning they always had observers who could watch the American advance. By the end of the day on 3 September the 1st and 2nd Battalions of the 370th had advanced over and marched around the high ground at Monte Pisano. The next stop was the medieval town of Lucca on the plain below.

## THE FALL OF LUCCA AND THE ADVANCE TO THE SERCHIO RIVER

The 370th Regimental Combat Team approached the town from the south and southwest. Behind them was the 100th Battalion of the Nisei, the last of the Japanese-American units still fighting on the line, before they were sent to France. Accompanying them were the Sherman tanks of the 1st Armoured Division, and in reserve were the South Africans and the Brazilians. Houston, along with 3rd Battalion headquarters and K Company, moved towards the small hamlet of Cerasomma, which lies on the railway that leads due west from Lucca to the sea. Where the track crosses the road from Viareggio to Lucca,

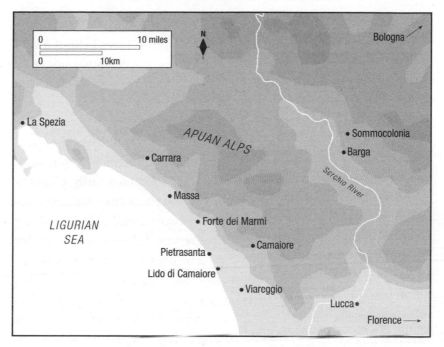

there was a large old house, built in the eighteenth century, surrounded by gardens of magnolia, palm, and pine trees. A tiled balcony looks out on the gardens at the back, while in front a colonnade of pillars provides shade over a terrace and patio. Villa Orsini is Tuscan Risorgimento architecture at its most elegant.

Battalion HQ of the 3rd/370th moved in and made it their temporary home. Outside the front door, the road leads right across the level crossing down to Viareggio, and left to Lucca. The regimental commander, Colonel Clarence W. Daugette Jr., and his second in command were en route to the villa when another artillery barrage caught them and the headquarters party in the open – they were pinned down for six hours before they could move into the new HQ at Villa Orsini as dark fell. Compiling the casualty list for the battalion that night, the officers saw that six men had been killed and at least thirty had been wounded. These included a disproportionately high number of junior officers and senior non-commissioned officers, the soldiers who were always at the front leading and encouraging their men. The operational spine of the 370th was made up of these men: they had been the first into training at Fort Huachuca, the best qualified on command and skills courses, and were the soldiers the junior ranks looked up to and, now, in their first month of combat, were following into battle.

Houston knew the 370th RCT was good – its soldiers were well trained, but the junior leadership of the division was being wounded or killed very quickly, and the officers and NCOs were lasting only a matter of days. It was, he noted, 'devastating'. Sufficient replacements weren't available, as the number of soldiers from the 92nd who had scored sufficiently well on the Army General Classification Test was low, and so all the best men had been sent with the 370th to the front line first. The reserves were not of the same standard as the men from the 1st, 2nd, and 3rd Battalions now surrounding Lucca, and the regiment's officers were desperately concerned about how this was going to affect the 92nd's performance in battle on the Gothic Line, at a time when the black American soldiers were under the scrutiny of everybody in the 5th Army. They were the first black combat infantry unit deployed in the Second World War, made up of men who had been systematically discriminated against, as had their families and relatives, for four generations. They had arrived in an important theatre of operations at a time when the US Army needed every man it could get, and the 370th RCT had been posted to a stretch of the line that was as vital, and well-defended, as any other. The men of the 370th knew they had a lot to prove, and their officers, both black and white, and senior and junior NCOs were determined that the unit give as good an account of itself as possible. It was not just German artillery the men were up against. Their military performance was being evaluated on their training and combat conduct, as well as through a prism comprised of expectations based upon race. But when it came to it, they were a combat unit as capable as any other, they had received the same training in the same places with the same equipment, and now in Italy they were facing the same obstacles and enemy as other Allied soldiers. Combat, the

Germans, and the Gothic Line were not interested in ethnicity, race, or creed: it was universal soldiering skills that counted.

The unit had expected to have to fight hand to hand for the walled city of Lucca, a Roman and medieval city with stone and earth walls thirty feet high surrounding it on all sides. There were four gates, which one entered through stone arches. Outside the walls was a clear area of flat grass that stretched more than 100 yards on all sides. The town had been built to be defended. From the top of its walls, machine guns and infantrymen would have made short work of any attackers. The 370th had requested flamethrowers as additional support for their attack. But when the combat companies of the 3rd Battalion moved east along the road from Villa Orsini and moved in from the south of the town, they found the city deserted. The Germans had pulled back to the far side of the Serchio River, into the Apennines, the heart of the Gothic Line.

On the morning of 10 September, two things were immediately noticeable to every man in the 370th Regimental Combat Team who stood in the late autumn sun looking up at the Apennine mountains. First, the incessant German artillery that had marked every hour of their time on the line since late August had stopped. The explosive punctuations that had disrupted every minute of every hour suddenly ceased. The second was that the mountains were going to prove formidable obstacles to attack.

To the north of Lucca, the Apennine range of Tuscany begins. Between 1,500 and 6,000 feet high, the mountains rise steeply upward from the coastal plain along the Mediterranean. In the first valley that runs parallel to the coast, where the mountains start, is the Serchio River. It flows down from the mountains absolutely in parallel with the seaside, about fifteen miles inland. Mountains rise up on both sides of it, and the Germans had made these the backbone of their most westerly Gothic Line defences. For attacking troops, it was pointless trying to capture and hold the cities and towns on the Mediterranean coast – Carrara, La Spezia – if they couldn't take and hold the mountains that overlooked them, from which artillery and mortar fire could be hurled at will down onto the plain that ran along the sea. And the only way to take the mountain peaks was to take the road that snaked north through the Serchio valley at their base. As well as the towns and villages that lay on this road. The Germans had established defensive positions all the way along its length, and as they withdrew northward, they were demolishing bridges, blowing up the narrow roads, dynamiting rock faces to cause landslides, and leaving behind barbed wire, booby traps, and land mines. The 370th Regimental Combat Team, backed up by the Brazilians, the 1st Armoured Division, some attached British units, and the South Africans, were given the mission of taking the valley and the key mountains that rose above it. In the west of Italy, it was the best-defended stretch of the Gothic Line before it ran into the Mediterranean Sea.

At the last moment, the Buffalo Soldiers suddenly discovered they were going to attack it without the support of the tanks that had accompanied them all the way north from the Arno. Far to the east, parts of the US 5th Army had broken through Il Giogo Pass on 18 September, a crucial mountain bottleneck on the Gothic Line south of Bologna. The Shermans of the 1st Armoured were told to prepare to move towards the centre of the Allied line in support.

The Serchio River rushed heavy and high past the men of the 370th a week later as they made a night-time advance up the only stretch of road in the valley the Germans hadn't destroyed. Their target was a hill their HQ had code-named 'Mexico' that rose above them. It had a heavy stone castle on top, was defended by artillery, mortars, and machine guns, and seemed to be impregnable to the artillery fire that the Buffalo Soldiers had been laying onto it all day. An attack by three companies, supported by artillery and engineers, went in, the black American soldiers climbing, scrambling, walking, running, and in some places crawling up its steep slopes. The officers in the 5th Army who wanted to see how the Buffalo Soldiers fought should have been there that day, noted several of its officers and NCOs. At one point the Germans were bringing artillery to bear almost on their own dugouts on the top of the hill, so close were the men of the 370th. But three repeated attacks over thirty-six hours failed to dislodge the Germans, who were heavily and cleverly dug in. Still, the Buffalo Soldiers were not giving up: there were more than fifty wounded piling up in the regimental aid post. Private Houston was at the battalion HQ and led two casualties off the hill. One had shot off his own thumb so he could be medevaced out of the line. But he was an exception.

On the summit of 'Mexico', Sergeant Charles 'Schoolboy' Patterson from Fort Wayne, Indiana, led the charge. He destroyed three MG-42 positions with hand grenades, but the incoming fire from five *other* machine-gun nests farther up the summit – which had pinned down a whole company of the 3rd Battalion – prevented him from moving forward. He was to be awarded the Silver Star for bravery in pressing home the attack. But 'Mexico' proved to be an objective that the men couldn't take, so instead of wasting more soldiers, the commander of the 1st Armoured Division ordered the men off the slopes and posted them on surrounding high ground with mortars and heavy machine guns. These kept up a constant stream of fire on the Germans dug in on 'Mexico', who were now surrounded. Four companies from the 370th had taken two dozen dead and fifty injured in three separate attacks, by night and day, that had lasted forty-eight hours. The Germans pulled out a week later. The soldiers of the 370th had now proved themselves in combat, but they had taken very significant losses of very significant men – their junior officers and NCOs.

They had advanced into the Gothic Line and cut the key Highway 12 that ran east–west between Tuscany and the coast. They were now embedded deep within the Serchio valley, up against the German defensive positions. They had to take and break these to be able to clear the mountains above the valley, which would in turn allow them to clear the coast, which ran parallel to them the other side of the mountain range. In the far east of Italy, the fighting around Rimini and in the Po valley for cities like Ravenna was to decide the fate of the Adriatic end of the Gothic Line. Bologna would decide the middle. But in the west, the winner or loser would be the side that won the Serchio valley and the mountains that rose on both sides above it.

# 16

## AT THE POINT OF THE LINE

### *The Attack on Seravezza*

### 10 October 1944

The beginning of October 1944 saw the Russians and the Allies closing in on the Germans and Japanese. The Red Army had entered Yugoslavia and Hungary but had done nothing to help the Polish Home Army during the Warsaw Uprising, which the Germans had just crushed. In mainland Greece, British forces took Corinth and then liberated Athens, while the Americans were already fighting inside the German border for the town of Aachen. Churchill and Stalin met for the first day of the Moscow Conference on 9 October where they intended to decide the make-up of post-war Europe. In the Far East, the Americans had landed in the Philippines and were two weeks away from a major naval victory over the Imperial Japanese Navy at Leyte Gulf. But both the Japanese and the Germans were resisting stubbornly: few thought the war in Europe would be over by Christmas, and nobody wanted to predict how long it would continue in the Pacific. An invasion of mainland Japan seemed to be a possibility. General Harold Alexander's optimistic predictions of that summer, that the Allies could be through the Gothic Line before October, now rang terribly hollow. They were still short of 60 per cent of their main objectives on the line, it was nearly the middle of October, and winter was approaching fast.

On the far west of the Gothic Line, near the Mediterranean, Mark Clark thought that the German defences of the Serchio River valley could be taken at the same time as another assault on Bologna in the centre. Then the mixed multi-national task force could advance up the Mediterranean coast. So two days after the Germans withdrew from the high ground that included 'Mexico', Brazilians arrived to take over part of the ground held by the Buffalo Soldiers of the 370th, who were to be pulled back out of the line for rest and recuperation. When the South American troops arrived for the unit handover, communication proved a major obstacle. The Brazilian commander spoke Portuguese, a little Spanish, and a little Italian; the American regimental commander spoke only English. The only person in battalion headquarters whoo could speak any Spanish was Private Houston. Through a combination of patience and four languages, the Brazilian officer and Houston worked out the complexities of the replacement. Most of the 370th were then pulled south out of the line, through the muddy, rain-spattered white-water torrent of the Serchio River, and back south for a shower, a change of clothes, and food that was actually hot, eaten in clothes that were dry, in a location that wasn't under artillery fire.

By this point, the men from the 370th who had arrived on the Arno on 24 August had been under constant artillery fire for nearly fifty days straight and had fought several stiff battles, often at night, against defensive positions, achieved while climbing nearly sheer mountains carrying sixty pounds of equipment, wearing sodden uniforms in conditions so dark the men couldn't see their comrades in front of them. Many of them had seen the physical and organizational centres of their military existence – reliable officers and NCOs – blown into small pieces by artillery, shot dead, or hideously wounded. Most of the black soldiers had had only ten weeks' combat training before leaving the United States, were poorly educated, and their upbringing had left them with little trust in any form of authority. It was extraordinary that their prowess against dug-in, experienced German troops was so positive. The creed of the Buffalo Soldier was establishing itself.

By 9 October, the 370th's advance up the Mediterranean coast and along the mountains that ran above it had reached the town of Pietrasanta, two miles inland from the sea. Once again, the high ground overlooking the town had to be taken. This time, it was a feature called Monte Cauala, which overlooked the small town of Seravezza at the confluence of the Sera and Vezza Rivers. A road some three miles long led from Pietrasanta up into the hills towards the junction of the two, and the lower slopes of Monte Cauala. Not surprisingly, every foot of it was under the observation of the Germans on the mountain, whose mortars and artillery were well within range of the northern suburb of Pietrasanta where the 370th was preparing for the oncoming attack.

Private Ivan Houston, M1 Garand slung over his shoulder, curious as to his surroundings, was walking through the tree-lined streets in the north part of the town. German artillery opened fire from above Seravezza: the sound of it was now so regular and routine the soldiers often hit the ground instinctively without realizing they had done it. Houston ducked into a warehouse that stored huge slabs of the marble that was quarried from the mountains above Carrara. The German shells exploded near the slabs and their shrapnel hit the hard, white marble, shattering shards of it into hundreds of tiny splinters of stone – each of which, the battalion headquarters man noted, could kill a soldier in a second. He left fast. Houston preferred the British response to German artillery. Later that day, he came across an English patrol that had made tea during a German bombardment, and he was invited to join them. As they drank their afternoon beverage, Lee–Enfield rifles and a Bren gun leaning against the trunks of the orange trees lining the streets, the air around them seemed to explode.

All four companies of the 370th Regimental Combat Team's 3rd Battalion – India, Kilo, Lima, and Mike – were briefed to take part in the attack on Monte Cauala by the regimental commander, Colonel Raymond Sherman. Along with battalion headquarters, Ivan Houston moved out early in the evening of 11 October. The night was black as pitch. There was a wild thunderstorm. Rain poured down in sheets. The soldiers in the line stumbled along the narrow, winding mountain trail they had been told to use, as the main road from Pietrasanta to Seravezza was under constant artillery and machine-gun fire. The mountain path was that in name only – mules would have had difficulty negotiating it, Houston noted in the battalion log. The rain kept pouring. The only illumination the men had was the flashes of lightning that crackled out of the thunderstorm. Each man held on to his colleague in front to save himself from getting lost, or falling off the track, and it took more than four hours to march one mile, stumbling along. The battalion orderly was carrying everything on his back – his trusted M1 rifle, a sleeping roll, and the half of a tent that each man hefted as part of his equipment. Called a 'shelter half', it enabled two soldiers to pair up and erect a two-man shelter. Houston had its poles and pegs, shovel, a bandolier of extra ammunition for his Garand, his bayonet, medical supplies, and rations of cheese and biscuits. There was a lot of shelling, machine-gun fire whipping constantly down the road that ran along the Sera River, which had risen to a torrent.

At no point did any man have any feeling that the Germans they were facing were a spent force – they were very good, far from being a broken army, thought Houston as he stumbled along the sodden trail. Soaked to the skin, slipping into the mud at every second step, almost blind in the darkness, he wondered how on earth he and his colleagues stood the slightest chance of defeating the Germans and occupying the high ground ahead. And then after that, if they were successful, they had to repeat the operation again and again, hill after hill, all the way up the Serchio valley, mountain by mountain, as the towns on the coast fell in tandem, all the way up the Tuscan coast. Only then could they break through the Gothic Line and start pushing the Germans backward. Since leaving Lucca, the pace of operations had changed from the fast-moving skirmishing in hot autumn weather that had seen different objectives fall every other day; operations where the men's morale was constantly boosted by the weather, by the feeling of success and achievement at taking positions, by the novelty of what they were doing, by the countryside around them, and by the basic physical and mental factors that make soldiers feel human – being dry, warm at night, sleeping in clothes that were not sodden, eating hot food, being in contact with their colleagues. And for the black American troops, who for the first time had left a country where they were so often treated as second class, here were Italians revelling in their presence as liberators. And the unit was getting things done. There were triumphs. The men felt good about themselves, and about their place in the war.

Now things had changed. The terrain and the weather made the fighting a war of uphill attrition, of near-vertical assaults on mountain positions, in cold, rain, mud, and mist, where the attacking force was at a huge disadvantage. The German defenders of the Gothic Line had planned it exactly thus: their tactical forethought and their command of the terrain now combined with the lousy weather to make their positions doubly hard to attack. This was how they had foreseen the defensive concept of the Gothic Line working out in practice. And conditions would worsen, too, for the Allies. Winter, which would bring a halt to such offensive operations, was coming.

The 3rd Battalion couldn't ford the Sera River that night – it was a coursing flood of brown water speeding along, carrying logs, branches, and vegetation with it. So the men stumbled around in the dark until they found an abandoned shack. Finally out of the pouring rain, they collapsed inside until daybreak, sleeping in sodden clothes, piles of drenched equipment around them. The attack on Monte Cauala would wait until the next day. So when light came, and the grey lines of rain were still pushing down, they wound their way into Seravezza and found the battalion command post. The regimental commander, Colonel Raymond Sherman, had followed the men across the mountain track and directed the scattered groups of troops as they arrived to their positions – Houston found his headquarters emplacement in an abandoned school. Now that it was daylight, the Germans on the mountain above could see the Americans in the town below. They opened fire on them with mortars, machine guns, and the light artillery they had been able to get to the top of the mountain. The streets of Seravezza turned into a free-fire zone. The 3rd Battalion of the 370th spent the day taking cover, while establishing observation posts to watch the mountains, and a position where they would cross the Sera River that night.

The day was made up of mortar bombs, rain, machine-gun fire, and shells. Monte Cauala loomed over the small Tuscan town as the black American soldiers prepared for battle. They were the tip of the Allied advance on the western end of the Gothic Line. The eyes of 5th Army command were on them.

At eleven o'clock that night, Ivan Houston, numbed by another day of artillery fire, lowered his already-sodden six-foot frame in its dripping wet battledress into the freezing waters of the Sera River. It was a miserable way to go into battle. Any part of him that hadn't been wet through before now was, apart from his Garand. On the other side of the river, the men walked towards the lower slopes of Monte Cauala and scrambled up wooden ladders that allowed them to climb over the most inaccessible sections of the rock face. The rocks were wet and sharp, and the drenched men encountered even more physical discomfort as the rock faces cut and gouged knees, hands, elbows, and legs as they climbed. Finally they reached ground that, while not easy, at least wasn't vertical. Humping their equipment, keeping their eyes as closely fixed on the man in front of them as they could, ears instinctively tuned to the sound of incoming artillery and the burping wrench of MG-42s, they trudged upward to their objective. Eight hours later, at seven-thirty in the morning, wet, exhausted, hungry, sodden equipment and boots chafing, rubbing, and cutting into their tired bodies, three combat companies and battalion headquarters had made it to the top. Daylight found them totally exposed to the Germans' fire, so the Buffalo Soldiers attacked. It was a heroic moment.

The fighting continued all day: K, L, and M Companies were dug in at various positions across the huge swathe of open space at the top of the mountain, and the Germans launched attacks at them from three directions. The Americans on the summit were mortaring the Germans approaching on the surrounding slopes and across its plateau. Machine-gun fire criss-crossed in several different directions, up, down, and across the summit and slopes of the mountain. The American companies were split up – during their climb some men had lagged behind, become wounded, or fallen from the rocks. Composite units of small groups of soldiers formed quickly, launched squad-level attacks, and then took cover. The regimental headquarters at the foot of the mountain was suddenly attacked by a platoon of Germans. The Buffalo Soldiers at the top sent down runners desperately asking for rations and, most vitally, ammunition to be transported to the top. It was a huge bit of ground, 2,500 feet high, and communication between the different companies, platoons, and squads was all but impossible as the German attacks zigzagged and weaved through the constantly changing American positions. The individual German and American soldiers, and their squads, platoons, and half companies, charged and withdrew and took cover and ducked and ran backward and forward, opened fire, were shot and wounded, or lived to fight another hour. They were like hundreds of constantly intersecting ants. Over and through them stitched an incessant stream of machine-gun fire from the German MG-42s and the American Brownings, mortars, rifle grenades, submachine-gun bullets, and hand grenades.

Down below at battalion HQ, Private Ivan Houston volunteered to help carry badly needed ammunition up the mountain. Each metal case contained 400 rounds of .30 cal ammunition for rifles and machine guns, and weighed twenty-five pounds. He slung his rifle over his shoulder and picked up a case of ammunition in each hand, walking towards the base of the hill, ducking and running to keep out of the multiple lines of fire. Bullets whizzed and sped past him like hissing fireflies at the speed of sound, and when they hit a rock they bounced off into the distance with an explosive metallic ricochet. Houston, along with twelve other men, stumbled back towards the fire-drenched slopes, staggering heavily and missing his footing as he had no use of his hands. And suddenly, for the first time since arriving in Italy, he actually saw a German soldier– in fact, two of them. As he looked up, he saw a pair of German soldiers firing a belt-fed machine gun. It was the first time he had seen his foe. Every day for more than fifty days he had been on the receiving end of their artillery fire, but here, finally, was the enemy in person.

One of the German soldiers reeled back, hit by American fire, and the other soldier carried him away and vanished. Houston, jarred out of the moment of watching the enemy, carried on climbing just as another artillery barrage starting hitting the bottom of the mountain. The ammunition detail advanced onward, as mortars and machine guns started zeroing in on them. Houston was hit by hot shrapnel that burned quickly through his uniform and scorched his skin: luckily for him, it had reached the extreme end of its range, and he was not hurt. He staggered onward with his fifty pounds of ammunition. Then more men in the ammunition party were hit, the artillery intensified, and it became impossible to continue. Houston returned back down the mountain, bitterly regretting not being able to go any farther. Other soldiers came towards him, withdrawing from positions farther up the slope as the Germans' counterattacks continued. 'It became,' said Houston, with characteristic understatement, 'a mess'.

One thing did cause the 370th's attack to waver, despite extraordinary persistence and bravery by units on the slopes and summit: an incident of friendly fire, a 'blue-on-blue'. Around four o'clock in the afternoon of 12 October, as two half companies were battling on the summit, American artillery fire fell short and hit two of the 3rd Battalion's other companies dug in at the bottom of the slope. The American soldiers poured out of their foxholes to avoid their own shells, and found the way forward towards Monte Cauala blocked by a German counterattack. So they turned back and moved fast into Seravezza, preparing to defend the town as the Germans threatened to storm into it. One American major at the base of the mountain was heard saying, 'Men coming off the hill should be hit on their head with a rifle butt.' That was easy to say. Individual units on the top of the mountain were still in action, as were men on the slopes. The half companies at the bottom had turned back for Seravezza: American artillery was hitting both sides, and the Germans were launching multiple counterattacks. With a few units still fighting on the summit and slopes, the whole battalion pulled back into Seravezza, disorganized, units fragmented, with crucial command and control structures dissipating.

The enemy counterattack into Seravezza did not come: the 370th failed to retake Monte Cauala. There were seventy-three wounded, including five officers and, surprisingly, given a battalion of well-trained and combat-experienced soldiers fighting for twenty-four hours against a numerically superior and well-dug-in enemy, only three dead. The Germans had won the battle again, defending positions of their own choosing, on terrain they had prepared in advance. They had held the day. The western end of the Gothic Line was standing.

## THE BUFFALO SOLDIERS AND THEIR AFTER-ACTION REPORT

Across Italy, British, Canadian, Polish, American soldiers, as well as units of fifteen other nationalities, had been storming up well-defended hills and mountains in the middle of the night since September 1943, taking huge casualties. The four battles of Monte Cassino, and the thousands of Allied casualties, were just a few examples of what happens when you send men up mountains against well-dug-in and experienced soldiers. In the battle for Gemmano outside Rimini, every Allied battalion lost at least 100–150 dead. In the attack on Point 447 on the same ridge, the British and Canadians lost one 198 dead alone. In one night in Ortona, the Canadian battalion lost 318 men.

The main casualty from the battle for Seravezza and Monte Cauala was the morale of the 92nd Infantry Division, and particularly of the men from the 370th Regimental Combat Team who fought the battle. Another casualty was the external perception of the combat performance of the Buffalo Soldiers. Many officers, NCOs, and enlisted men behaved with exceptional bravery: Private Jake McInnis of K Company personally killed twelve Germans while defending a position on the summit of Monte Cauala with his Browning Automatic Rifle. Later wounded, he was taken to the regimental aid post but asked to return to battle. He was awarded the Silver Star. The 370th's executive officer at Seravezza was Lieutenant Colonel John J. Phelan. His predecessor was the unit's first officer casualty, whose body, wounded by shrapnel, Houston had seen. Phelan had been with the 3rd Battalion for six months and commented, 'During my period of observation, I have heard of just as many acts of individual heroism among Negro troops as among white'.

On Monte Cauala, Captain Charles F. Gandy, commander of Company F, though mortally wounded, led the stand until 3:00 a.m. the following morning when the units withdrew on regimental orders. A platoon of Company L, under Lieutenant Reuben L. Horner, fought off eight enemy counterattacks on Monte Strettoia while awaiting support from another unit that failed to locate it. This platoon remained until it used up all its ammunition. The 370th was in the spotlight: they were new, black soldiers who, out of necessity caused by the transfer of troops to France, were put on one of the most tricky, sensitive, and visible parts of the line, at one of the most crucial moments of the battle, with only ten weeks' training, six weeks' combat experience, under the eyes not just of the Americans and British but also other minority and colonial troops. The pressure was immense, the lessons learned about command and control huge, and the need for good officers and NCOs and replacements paramount. A unit that had almost been set up to fail, to take a fall, had in fact proved much better than expected. And months of combat still lay ahead.

After its first full month in action, a report from IV Corps estimated the 370th Regimental Combat Team had advanced some twenty miles, lost nineteen men killed in action, had 248 sick, wounded, or injured, and twenty-three 'missing', which meant presumed dead or captured by the enemy. (The casualty figures were erroneously low.) They had captured around 280 of the enemy. And at divisional level, another report on the 370th after its first month in the line was encouraging: 'In combat missions they will go wherever led. They will stay as long as their leaders, anywhere.'

And the chief of staff of IV Corps, a one-star general, reported that the performance of the 370th in the first few days, 'while not without a number of incidents which would have been avoided by more seasoned troops, was on the average as satisfactory as might be expected from a similar untried and inexperienced unit. There is no question of their will to learn, alertness and attention to duty; the nervousness exhibited is natural and may well be overcome in time . . . The combat team showed every sign of building a splendid record of accomplishment.'

# Part Four

## BEHIND THE LINE

# 17

---

# BEHIND ENEMY LINES

## The SOE and OSS Missions in the North

### November 1944

Bogged down by the autumn rains of the Po valley in the east, blocked on the banks of the Serchio River in the west, struggling to the top of the peaks of the Apennines above Bologna in the centre, the Allies' midsummer optimism about a swift end to the war in Italy seemed to have been just that: optimistic. The Canadians, British, New Zealanders, and Greeks had swung west into the flatlands of Lombardy immediately after the fall of Rimini on 21 September. The British and Indians had taken the little Republic of San Marino on 20 September, and by the end of the month had joined the main body of the 8th Army on the edge of the plains of the river Po. For months, the dream of flat, rolling countryside had beckoned to the desert veterans of the 8th Army. When it materialized in October, when that 'one last ridge' at San Fortunato had been taken, the reality was a wet, waterlogged, and muddy anti-climax. Autumn rain swelled the rivers, the waters of the Po rose above it banks, and the Germans had dynamited many of the dikes and embankments that contained the irrigation channels of the valley. One British officer called it a 'green nightmare of rivers, dikes and soft water-meadows'. One hundred thousand men and tanks found themselves advancing through slurping mud. The 8th Army had taken enormous casualties on Operation *Olive*, both in men and vehicles, tanks particularly. They saw that a combination of geography and the weather blocked their advance westward towards Bologna, so they moved forward the only way they could, north along the coast towards Ravenna.

In the centre, the Indians had taken some of the Apennine peaks, but the Americans were stuck on the main mountain access road between Florence and Bologna. On the Mediterranean, the bad weather in the Serchio valley and the lack of experienced troops on the western flank had slowed the advance. By the end of October 1944, it was clear the Allies' chances of breaking through the Gothic Line before the following year were decreasing swiftly. But the planning officers of the Special Operations Executive and the Office of Strategic Services saw this as an even greater incentive to arm, finance, and train the partisans behind German lines, and to prepare for the moment the Allies occupied northern Italy.

————○·————

One of their main aims was to stop the Italian Fascists and Germans from destroying the economic infrastructure of northern Italy – its hydroelectric dams, factories, agricultural production, and banks. So they made an anti-scorch plan, code-named 'Rankin'. More SOE and OSS agents would be parachuted into the north, and partisan groups from the Ligurian coast in the west, via Turin and Milan to Venice and Trieste, would be kept strongly focused on the Allies' main strategic and tactical objectives. The SOE and OSS planners at Monopoli, Rome, and Siena called these operations 'anti-scorch'. They were determined to stop the Germans razing the economic powerhouse to the ground, making a post-liberation civil war all the more likely. While the Canadians, the Marathas, and the Buffalo Soldiers were drawing a breath after a month of combat, the Allied intelligence infrastructure was already making plans for the transition from war to some form of peace.

What they most needed was a united coalition of Italian partisan and political groups in the north with whom they could operate, and so far they had chosen the Council for the Liberation of Northern Italy, or CLNAI, headquartered in Milan. The partisan advisers working with the Allies in Rome and Siena, including Arrigo Paladini, told the Allies this coalition was their best chance. Keeping Communist political parties, and their attendant partisan acolytes, out of the operational mix was a priority. The Allies were also determined to stop Marshal Tito's Yugoslav partisans from encroaching onto Italian territory: to the east, the SOE was running a network of officers and agents who operated with these guerrillas. A British lieutenant colonel was constantly present at Tito's headquarters at Drvar, in northwestern Bosnia, keeping as firm a hold as possible on any westward territorial ambitions. The carrot they could wield with Tito was considerable: almost all of his weapons and medical and communications equipment was parachuted in from Italy by the Allies. But by the last week of October, the Russians were inside Hungary and had liberated the Yugoslav capital, Belgrade, on the 16th. The SOE mission in Yugoslavia was one of containment. For the Allies, keeping a tight hand on the troubled scruff of the northern Italian neck was vital. And the most important place in the north was Milan, and the most important people ex-General Raffaele Cadorna, the CLNAI and, by extension, Major Oliver Churchill.

The SOE agent had found that life in Milan was incredibly dangerous, complex, and fragile. He was operating under the assumed identity of a Slovenian immigrant employed by the state electrical company – Churchill's command of Italian was flawed, and Milan was the richest, most cosmopolitan and cultured city in the country outside of Rome. He felt that he stood out like a sore thumb. SS patrols were everywhere, Italian Fascist troops strode down Milan's elegant streets and swaggered through the piazzas, German regular army officers sat in cafés opposite the city's sixteenth-century Duomo, sipping coffee and grappa, watching the city flow past them. The six main political parties, and their accompanying partisan bands, knew very well that, by late spring of 1945, at the latest, the Allies would be across the entire country. They wanted power, they wanted to be in charge, and they wanted the money and control that would come with it. For every friend and ally Churchill had inside the CLNAI, he had another enemy. And this was before the Germans and the Italian Fascists were added to the potent list of threats.

He rarely stayed in the same place more than two nights running. In one particular week he moved six times.[1] He was kept alive by the training he had received at Arisaig and the 'spy school' at Beaulieu. He felt strange walking around the cosmopolitan streets of Milan in civilian clothes at a time when almost every single man, and many women of his generation, were in uniform. He also noted that in wartime Milan, most people were more smartly dressed than they were in peacetime England.

It was another element of his disguise he had to work on, along with his faltering language. It was classic intelligence work. Churchill had to meet regularly with General Cadorna, his liaison officer, and with representatives of another partisan network, code-named 'La Franchi', that the Allies were supporting. He had to evaluate the latest status reports on the CLNAI's interminable meetings, encode the results into ciphered messages, and place them in 'dead-letter drops' so they could be picked up by other partisan contacts. They would then take the messages up into the mountains, where they would be transmitted by radio back to Monopoli. Once a reply was received, Churchill had to pick it up, decode it, and pass the requisite instructions back to the partisans. It was lengthy, complicated, time-consuming, and nerve-wracking.

If the CLNAI decided at a meeting that they needed an airdrop of arms and explosives so they could protect a bridge or a hydroelectric dam, they would write out their list of requirements. These almost always exceeded their needs, sometimes by almost ludicrous levels. On two occasions, flamethrowers were requested. Churchill always told the partisans that their best source of heavier weapons – belt-fed machine guns, mortars – was from the Germans or Italian Fascist troops themselves. Using the enemy's weapons against it was a simple and extremely effective technique. In any firefight, it made it impossible for the Germans to tell who was who from the sound of the weaponry being used. MP-40s and MG-42s had significantly different muzzle reports from Sten guns, Carcano rifles, Bren guns, or .45 Thompsons. An experienced soldier or partisan fighter could tell where the enemy was by the sound of its weapons: if both sides were using the same equipment, this became impossible. It was also much easier to replenish ammunition by stealing or hijacking it from enormous existing enemy supplies on the ground than by going through the incredibly lengthy and complex process of organizing an Allied airdrop.

To pick up messages from partisan contacts, Churchill went through the dead-letter drop or pick-up routine. He always arranged to pick up or drop in a location like a café or a restaurant where people gathered; he'd enter, check the entrance and exit, order his aperitif or coffee, and then move to the bathroom. The message would be behind the lavatory cistern, under a tile on the floor, or tucked into the petals of a plastic flower in a vase in the corridor. Once picked up, he would settle back into the café – where he would inevitably be in sight of at least one German or Italian in uniform – and take his time with his Cinzano or grappa, his Scaloppini Milanese, his zabaglione, and his espresso, and then he'd leave. He was most vulnerable when the message was in his physical possession, but the forged SS *ausweis,* work identification document, he carried would get him safely past almost any checks. Once outside the café, he would use white chalk to 'stripe off' a nearby rubbish bin, or the back of a bench, indicating the message had been picked up or deposited.

La Franchi network took care of his accommodation: a partisan would be in charge of arranging for a bedroom or apartment where Churchill could stay, often with other partisans or agents. The *portinaia* (concierge) would be a man or woman who was sympathetic to the CLNAI 'cause'. When Churchill arrived at the front of the building, he was let in, told which floor and flat to occupy (only rich Italians lived in houses in cities) and the code word that would be used on the telephone if he and the other occupants needed to get out at three minutes' notice. He was always to assume that any meeting or place of accommodation was potentially compromised – he wrote that he found meeting Cadorna highly problematic as the general had absolutely no sense of security, and his behaviour in public verged on the theatrical, thinking he could disguise himself simply by wearing dark glasses.[2] Cadorna was very well known in Italy, and his outspokenly anti-fascist views made him a high-profile individual to meet in public. Churchill far preferred to liaise with Major Ferreo, the officer with whom they had parachuted in on the August drop above Bergamo.

## THE DIFFERENT PARTISAN GROUPS

The partisan groups in and around Milan were made up of the six strongest political–military protagonists, moving from left to right on the political spectrum: Communists, the Action Party, Liberals, Catholics, the Christian Democrats, and the numerous 'autonomous' partisan groups – like the Green Flame – operating in towns, mountains, and valleys across northern Italy. Churchill made two assessment trips outside the city. The first one was to Biella, a large industrial town northwest of Milan, famous for its textiles. There he met the Communist Party and the partisans attached to it, and reported back that they were effective and powerful but fundamentally untrustworthy. Churchill thought that La Franchi network and the autonomous, independent groupings like the Fiamme Verdi were the Allies' best and most reliable operational support.

After Biella, he moved south to the Langhe area south of Turin, north of the town of Cuneo. Turin is surrounded in a semi-circle by the Alps, and in the foothills and on the mountain slopes from the southwest to due north of the city partisan groups flourished and thrived. The region is made up of flat agricultural plains of corn, fruit orchards, and vineyards south of the city; to the west and southwest, steep foothills rise to 4,000 feet and lead up into the Alps, which march across the horizon. Three hours by train southeast lies the strategic port of Genoa, on the Gulf of Liguria. To the west, the railway line leads along the succession of pretty seaside towns – Imperia, Alassio, Bordighera – that make up the Italian Mediterranean Riviera. Across Liguria and Piemonte – the region around Turin – there was almost no fighting between the Germans and partisans on a sustained basis. The first were being held in reserve for the fighting that the Germans knew would come when the Allies broke through the Gothic Line. In western Liguria and up towards the Alps, the German lover of Scotland, Generalleutnant Ernst-Günther Baade, held his men in a calm, semi-operational check. The Highland claymore was firmly sheathed. The general knew that if he carried out violent and provocative *rastrellamente* actions across the mountains, he would be lucky to kill or capture ten or twenty partisans in an operation that could take a week and involve 3,000 of his men and the local Italian Fascists. He also believed that reprisal actions were completely counterproductive. His main priority was to protect his strip of frontier mountains from incursions from southern France, by either Free French troops or fighters from the resistance. And along the Italian Riviera? Churchill knew from information passed from other SOE missions that the partisans were simply waiting for the word from Siena or Monopoli that the Allies were approaching along the Mediterranean coast, and that it was time to blow up the coastal railway line and take control of the docks in Genoa.

Returning to Milan in early November, he was tipped off that his cover was blown and that he should leave immediately. Not wasting time to return to the safe house, he went straight to Milan's Centrale station and boarded a train to Como, crossing into Switzerland. He went to see Jock McCaffery, the head of SOE in Europe, at his headquarters in Berne, and made his report. The CLNAI, he said, was going to find it next to impossible to operate as a single, independent, and cohesive military force because it couldn't decide on a single, independent, and cohesive political plan. This was their main failing. General Cadorna should take charge of the entire group, by issuing a simple, clear order. But nobody had the confidence or drive to take charge. After Churchill had left Milan, he recommended that the Italian government in Rome issue a clear order to Cadorna: You're in charge. Take power. Act. So they did. And the CLNAI in Milan promptly staged a ten-hour meeting, the upshot of which was that they preferred their ineffectual, loosely democratic system. Nothing much functioned, and all sides essentially disliked and distrusted each other, but at least nobody rocked the boat. Churchill advised that each single Italian partisan group in control of a particular area should be assigned a British or American liaison officer: when the time came to put anti-scorch plans into effect, and confront the Germans and Fascists head-on, at least they could do it in a coordinated and planned way.

One reason the Italian partisans were afraid of taking autonomous direct action was what had happened in September and October in Domodossola. The town lies north of Biella towards the Italian–Swiss border and is a strategic road and railway link between both countries – it controls access to the Simplon Tunnel, which brings the main railway from Geneva to Milan. It lies in a glacial valley in the foothills of the Alps and is a centre of hydroelectric power. In May, a German *rastrellamento* had killed 200 partisans who wanted to establish their own independent republic on the Swiss border. McCaffery had urged caution, telling them that up against the better-armed and better-organized Germans and Italian Fascists, 'they should have patience and increase their hit-and-run routine, the only possible one against superior military forces far from being in disarray.'

The partisans of the glacial valley didn't listen. In September, they occupied the valley, declared an autonomous mini-republic, making and issuing its own laws and edicts, and shipped in their own exiled leader to take charge. One of their first demands was for enormous Allied support. Could this be the first spark in a chain of uprisings that would see the partisans try to establish control of behind-the-lines northern Italy, before the Allies had properly broken the Gothic Line? The SOE and OSS didn't think so. The 'Free Republic of Domodossola' stood in territory the Allies didn't really need – this wasn't Milan or Turin or Genoa. But in Milan, the CLNAI differed, and once the first partisan groups – Catholics and two independent ones – had done all the spade work and formed an autonomous administration, then the Socialists, Christian and Democrats, and Communists all gave the new 'Republic' their approval. They thought the Allies would come to help. They were mistaken. The only people to arrive were 12,000 SS and Italian Fascist soldiers in early October, who took precisely a week to force the 3,000 partisans back into the mountains or across the border into Switzerland. The CLNAI immediately blamed the Allies – who in turn riposted that they had never encouraged the formation of independent, partisan-run mini-republics. It was not the vision they had for post-war northern Italy, of small areas each controlled by a different armed group. They wanted uniform control by one political and military coalition over the entire area, with as little influence by the Communists as possible. Not surprisingly, the Domodossola incident quickly worsened relations between the SOE and the partisans, and made liaison with and influence over General Cadorna and the CLNAI in Milan much harder. Into the bargain, the Allies' advance into the north had slowed considerably, as the weather, the terrain, and the German opposition delayed them from the optimistic dash to liberate northern Italy that they had expected in the summer. The partisans suddenly started to feel isolated from the Allies' overall plan.

Despite this, Major Oliver Churchill ended his meeting with McCaffery by reiterating that each partisan group should have its own liaison officer. Not just for the anti-scorch operations that were part of the Rankin plan, but because it was only a matter of time before the first Allied infantry units were successfully across the Apennines, through the Gothic Line, and heading into northern Italy. Delayed by mud and weather they might be, but in the east the first British and Canadian units – the Westminster Regiment among them – were approaching the outskirts of Ravenna, where partisans, an OSS mission, and an Allied commando unit were waiting to greet them. The Marathas were over the Apennines and heading down towards the city of Forli. And in La Spezia and up to Genoa, the partisans were waiting desperately for the Buffalo Soldiers, the Brazilians, the South Africans, and their American armoured support to break through the Serchio valley. So as Churchill left by road for France, and thence for an aircraft back to Monopoli, the head of the SOE in Europe recommended that all SOE agents on the Rankin anti-scorch missions should be parachuted in immediately.

## KARL WOLFF AND THE SS INTELLIGENCE NETWORK IN NORTHERN ITALY

The head of the SS and Security Police in Italy in December 1944 was SS-Obergruppenführer Karl Wolff, nicknamed 'Karele'. His headquarters were in Milan, which was one of the reasons Oliver Churchill had noticed that the city was crawling with uniformed SS officers. Wolff had been Heinrich Himmler's personal adjutant, but after the death of fellow SS-Obergruppenführer Reinhard Heydrich in 1942, Himmler sent Wolff to Italy to work as a liaison officer and adjutant with Mussolini. Wolff had many priorities in Italy – the successful deportation of the Jews, looting of Jewish property and Italian artworks, commanding all SS combat troops and eventually Mussolini's Black Shirt Fascist units, running the Gestapo's operations against the partisans and Allied intelligence, and at one point reportedly devising a plot to kidnap the pope.[3] He had several assistants who helped run a vast intelligence network across Italy. One of these was an SS-Obersturmführer named Guido Zimmer.

Born in Westphalia, Zimmer was thirty-three in 1944, and an American intelligence file described him as 'a slim, athletic man of average height with dark brown hair and a high-pitched voice'.[4] He had joined the Nazi party in 1932 and the SS and Himmler's SD (*Sicherheitsdienst*, or Security Service) in 1936. And in 1940, as a member of Foreign Intelligence branch of the Reich Main Security Office, or RSHA, he was assigned to Rome. But Zimmer's cover was blown through a slip, and he was recalled to Berlin.

After the armistice, when the deportation of Jews from Italy began under the direction of Herbert Kappler, SS-Obersturmführer Zimmer was assigned to Genoa, where he hunted down Jews, appropriated their property and goods, and stole some of it for himself. He was responsible for SS intelligence gathering along the Ligurian coast from Genoa to the French border. He split his time between Liguria and Milan, where his immediate superior was based. SS-Standartenführer Walter Rauff was head of the Gestapo and SD for northwestern Italy and had been one of the original designers of mobile gassing vans designed to kill Jews and other concentration camp inmates. Zimmer's agents were not only in northwestern Italy and along the Ligurian coast but also in France, Switzerland, Austria, and all over central Italy.

Zimmer was self-protecting and pragmatic, and he looked to the future, which was why Wolff increasingly involved him with a burgeoning project that, by autumn 1944, had started to take a more concrete shape since the 20 July assassination plot against Hitler. The head of the RSHA Foreign Intelligence branch, Walter Schellenberg, wanted to begin tentative peace negotiations and discussions with the Allies, who would almost certainly demand the total and unconditional surrender of the German military and political hierarchy. But if a separate peace deal could be made among the Germans, Italians, Americans, and British – specifically excluding the Russians – Schellenberg was eager to pursue it. He, like others, was keen to keep the Red Army out of central and southwestern Europe, particularly Austria. So Wolff and his staff – which included Zimmer – were keen to build intelligence contacts with Italians on all levels, Fascist, partisan, businessman, politician or, even better, any combination of these four.

In the seaside town of Savona, just west of Genoa, Zimmer's main liaison officer with the Italian Guardia Nazionale Repubblicana, the Fascist security police, was a lieutenant colonel named Gastalde

Zofferino. He gathered information about partisan operations from wherever he could, and about SOE and OSS movements from captured Italian guerrillas, Allied POWs, and Italian civilians. One of Zofferino's main contacts in the regional town of Imperia, an olive-oil-producing port southwest of Savona, was a pro-Mussolini army officer named Vittorio Ordano. His wife, Ernesta, helped provide low-level intelligence and whatever information she could glean on partisan activities in and around Imperia, and in the mountains above it. It was, she was convinced, the best way to have some form of post-war security, when the Fascists would surely ultimately triumph. Their daughter, Paola, who was twenty, frequently disagreed and argued with her parents, and was often late arriving home in the evenings – or indeed absent. She explained to her mother that work kept her late, or she was staying with a girlfriend in neighbouring Bordighera, farther up the railway line. Ernesta could never understand why food and the olives from the grove in their garden so often went missing. She wondered what else was disappearing under her nose. But as autumn 1944 came around, and the summer sun started to fade over the dark cobalt Ligurian Sea, she never dreamed for a moment that her daughter was a full-fledged partisan, operating in the mountains above the city.[5]

## OPERATION *CHRYSLER*, THE OSS, AND THE COMMUNISTS

On the evening of 27 September 1944, four American soldiers from an Office of Strategic Services mission had stood on the edge of the runway at the Pisa airport. Since D-Day, the strategic situation in the European war had shifted fast, and suddenly the battles on the Gothic Line, overlooked for several weeks that autumn, were once more becoming a vital part of the conflict to shape southeastern Europe. Churchill and Eisenhower had foreseen this, and Stalin knew it. One of the places where the Allies and the Red Army risked meeting first was at the very bottom of southeastern Europe, at the Trieste Gap in southern Yugoslavia. To the north, the vastness of Germany, Poland,

and Hungary, and the huge German forces contained in those countries, separated the Allies in the west from the Red Army in the east. The enormous German Army Group Centre had been destroyed in mid-June in Belarus in Operation *Bagration* – the largest defeat in six years of Wehrmacht troops. The Russians now knew about the realities of the Holocaust after the Red Army liberated Majdanek concentration camp in late July.

While the SOE was hard at work trying to orchestrate a unified alliance in Milan, the OSS was planning to link up the partisans operating on the Adriatic coast, from Trieste down to Rimini. The next big Allied offensive on the Adriatic was going to be the attack on Ravenna in November. The British, Canadians, and Americans wanted the partisans to be united in tandem with their objectives. By mid-October, these firmly included the partisans in Yugoslavia. The SOE and the OSS were trying to prevent Marshal Tito's men from looking hungrily westward: it was only a matter of days before the Yugoslav capital, Belgrade, would be liberated by Red Army soldiers and Tito's partisans on the 16th. Both covert agencies knew that Tito would immediately begin looking towards Slovenia and northeastern Italy after they arrived. The Allies wanted the Ljubljana Gap – that led through Slovenia up to Austria – kept open at any cost so they could reach Vienna before the Red Army. The operational imperative to get to Ravenna – and afterward north up the Adriatic coast to Venice and Trieste – was thus increasing by the day. So there was a new front developing in the Gothic Line battles: the northeastern Adriatic front, the battle for the Trieste salient. And so, when on 16 October 1944, the Yugoslav and Bulgarian capitals of Belgrade and Sofia were liberated by the Russians, the Red Army was now only days away from the Adriatic coast, and possibly two weeks away from the crucial strategic junction of Yugoslavia, the Adriatic, and Italy. The Allies were very concerned. So the four-man mission waiting at Pisa's airport on the evening of 27 September had been just a small part of the Allied efforts to stall efforts by Italian Communist partisans to link up with their Yugoslav comrades.

The four American soldiers from an Office of Strategic Services operation code-named 'Chrysler' were parachuted into enemy territory. In keeping with official OSS orders, they were all wearing US military uniforms so that, if they were captured, they could not be executed as enemy spies. Unlike Major Oliver Churchill, operating in civilian suits and ties in a highly specific urban environment, the four men jumped fully armed into the area around Lake Como. Their assignment was to try to unite the partisan groups in this most northern section of Italy. Once they had made contact with the guerrilla leaders, their plan was to arrange a whole series of airdrops that would arm and equip several hundred men to fight on the Allies' side after the battle of Ravenna, as they pushed north to Venice and Trieste.

The team's commander was Major William Holahan, a forty-year-old lawyer who had a peacetime reserve commission in the cavalry. Accompanying him were three American Italians: 1st Lieutenant Victor Giannino, 2nd Lieutenant Aldo Icardi, and radio operator Sergeant Carl LoDolce, a Sicilian. The twenty-two-year-old Lieutenant Icardi was the only mission member able to speak the dialect of the region around Lake Como. Along with a submachine gun, pistol, hand grenades, medical equipment, ammunition, and other supplies, Holahan was carrying $16,000 worth of gold coins, US dollars, and Swiss and Italian money to finance their mission. They took off just before the sun set on 27 September.[6]

# 1 8

## REGULAR AND IRREGULAR FORCES

### *The Fall of Ravenna*

### November 1944

The weather in northern Italy had truly broken by November 1944. For the men who had fought in the south of the country, it was like being back in the valleys around Monte Cassino. Already-soaked boots got wetter every time they were put into a river or stream or water-logged field. Feet and boots never properly dried. Every day seemed to be a symphony of damp uniforms, rain, mud, physical effort, violence, cold food, and relentless discomfort. Jaundice hit the infantry particularly badly, and although the Allied troops were emerging out of the seemingly endless rows of Apennine ridges and mountains into the plains of Lombardy, conditions did not seem to improve. As one Canadian officer wrote, 'There always seemed to be one more battle we were being asked to fight.'[1] In October, the Canadians had fought a wet, arduous, morale-sapping battle for the Savio River west of Rimini; many of the officers believed it had been an unnecessary fight. That the river was or was not strategically and tactically important was not the main divisive issue. The river could have been outflanked, as it sat in empty countryside. What mattered to the Canadians was morale. The cold, the wet, the mud, the ceaseless slog of infantry attacks across rivers the Germans defended easily and with tactical élan made them feel that although they had advanced hundreds of miles geographically since the preceding year, here they were, still fighting, with no end in sight. The idiosyncratic and independent-minded Canadian generalship was arguing among itself again. Self-inflicted wounds, absence without leave, and desertion had become major problems, and the Canadians, normally stoic and resilient, were hit as hard as any Allied unit.

An officer from 1st Infantry Division noted that the attacks in October had been distinguished by the lack of time the Canadians had to prepare for them, the 'useless or impossible' nature of the objectives and plans, and not enough men. A company commander from Princess Patricia's Canadian Light Infantry said that the 'poor morale was due to the belief that the war would be over soon, the recollection of last winter's misery, the belief that the Gothic Line battles were supposed to be the last show for Canadian infantrymen in Italy and general war weariness, especially in Italy.' The major added that 'at the present time all brigades are busily occupied with Courts Martial, chiefly desertion and Absence Without Leave charges.'[2]

Available manpower was still being diverted in two directions where the strategic requirements had higher priority – northwest Europe and the Far East. In both theatres it was very obvious by November 1944 that the war was not, once again, going to be over by Christmas. In northwest Europe, the British, Americans, and Canadians were bogged down in eastern Holland and just inside the German border. For the Allied troops north of Rimini, this meant more battles and another wet, cold, snowy winter in Italy. Both Eisenhower, as supreme allied commander, and Field Marshal Alexander, as commander of troops in the Mediterranean, now had yet another priority in southeastern Europe.

First, they had to continue breaking through the Gothic Line, despite the onset of autumn and winter weather. Then they had to

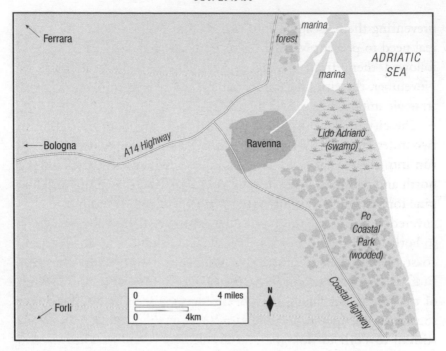

contain Generalfeldmarschall Kesselring's troops in Italy, and use the Italian partisans to their best strategic advantage, without letting them dissolve into internecine, strategically useless struggles with the Germans and each other as had happened over the self-declared Republic of Domodossola. In early November, Harold Alexander's orders made clear that they required 5th and 8th Armies to 'maintain maximum pressure . . . in early December' when Eisenhower was hoping to launch a major offensive in northwest Europe. This offensive was forever being delayed or postponed. Alexander and Churchill were frustrated at what they increasingly saw as a military 'housekeeping' role now that they had just begun to break the Gothic Line: they still insisted their strategic priorities in the Mediterranean remained Italy and the Balkans. Break the Gothic Line, they said, take Genoa, Milan, Turin, and Venice, advance on Trieste, and then head for Vienna, via the Brenner Pass and the Ljubljana Gap. It was no longer a matter of just containing Kesselring's forces in Italy and preventing them escaping into Austria and Yugoslavia; it was a very real need to prevent Marshal Tito's partisans and the Red Army that followed them from advancing beyond Trieste. So suddenly, by November, the cities on the Adriatic coast of Italy took on as much strategic importance as Milan and Genoa.

The city of Ravenna sits on the Adriatic coast north of Rimini, two miles inland. Two rivers flow through the town, and where they run into the sea there are large sandy beaches and salt flats. To the north and south are wide marshy areas of saltwater lagoons and low pine forests, where swampy water is crisscrossed by muddy stretches covered in reeds. The three main roads that trisect the city head west to Forli and Bologna, northwest to Ferrara, and due north along the coast towards Lake Comacchio and Venice. On 9 November the Indians took the town of Forli, the first major objective on the flank of the Apennines facing the Po. The mountains stretch in a direct southeast–northwest diagonal line across the top of Italy from Rimini to Forli to Bologna and eventually to Milan. They form a barrier in the west with the mountainous terrain of central Italy; in the east, they are the last border before the water-drenched plains of Lombardy, the Po valley. To avoid encirclement, the Germans had retreated in three directions: west to Bologna, north towards Ferrara and the Alps, and east to Ravenna. The 8th Army would be in charge of taking the last of these.

The main partisan group in and around the city was the 28th Garibaldi Brigade. Unlike some of the other advancing Allied troops, their morale was sky-high. It was simple: liberation from the Germans was imminent. Mino Farneti, the young partisan who had captured the German plans for the Gothic Line from the motorcycle dispatch rider outside Rimini, was part of this group. In mid-November, the Allies parachuted arms and equipment to him and his men. Their main commander was Arrigo Boldrini, nicknamed 'Bulow'.[3] He had devised a clever plan whereby the partisans, along with Allied armoured and infantry units supported by special forces, could capture the city. Ravenna was defended by three German divisions whose forces were deployed in a 360-degree defence. Bulow knew that the Allies desperately needed to take the city – but without destroying much of its art and architecture. He sent a radio message to the Allies, via the OSS, that his plan could help achieve this objective, but that he needed to meet with the Canadian and British commanders in person. He and his men were all Communist supporters, so Boldrini knew the importance of persuading the strongly anti-communist British that the 28th Garibaldi Brigade was a reliable asset.

The Canadians were based at Cervia, a town ten miles south of Ravenna on the coast. The Allies radioed back that they would send a submarine to pick up Arrigo Boldrini, but too impatient to wait for it and preferring to do things his own way, he set off by fishing boat. There were twelve Italian fishermen at the oars, and Bulow was also bringing with him two American air force pilots who had escaped from the Germans. Along with 'a few pistols and a large keg of wine', the group set off down the coast.[4] It was a moonlit night and the boat managed to reach Cervia without being spotted by the Germans. An OSS colonel was there to meet them. The American took the group straight to Allied headquarters, where Bulow explained to the new commanding officer of the 8th Army (Leese had by now been transferred to Burma), the English lieutenant general Richard McCreery, how he thought Ravenna could be taken.

The partisans from the Garibaldi Brigade would attack from the north and west; Allied infantry and tanks would come in from the south, up the main axis road from Cervia and Rimini; other partisan groups would ambush the Germans' escape route northwest to Ferrara; and an unorthodox formation of Allied commandos would storm into the city from the eastern seacoast. The Germans had opened the dykes on some of the waterways surrounding the city so that the main coastal road, Highway 16, was flooded in some places. Much of the land around Ravenna was underwater. But McCreery gave the plan the thumbs-up. Bulow went back to Ravenna with an 8th Army liaison officer.

McCreery's plan followed Bulow's. A composite force of tanks, infantry, engineers, artillery, and amphibious vehicle handlers would make up the main strike element. A British colonel named Andrew Horsbrugh-Porter from the 27th Lancers would command. His force, 2,000 men strong, was immediately dubbed 'Porterforce'. The cavalry colonel was an aristocratic Englishman who liked polo, had been wounded and decorated in the evacuation from Dunkirk in 1940, and had a keen understanding of irregular warfare. To aid his men and the partisans, he enlisted the help of one of the most unorthodox Allied fighting units of the war.

## POPSKI'S PRIVATE ARMY

'Popski's Private Army' was the unofficial name of Number 1 Demolition Squadron, a unit of British special forces set up in Cairo in 1942. It had operated with the Special Air Service and the Long Range Desert Group in North Africa, and had arrived in Italy in September 1943 at Taranto. They deployed in heavily armed Willys Jeeps, divided into 'fighting patrols' of six vehicles with three men in each. They had ample firepower, and the jeeps were mounted with .50 calibre and .30 calibre Browning belt-fed machine guns. Like the Special Air Service and the Long Range Desert Group, Number 1 Demolition Squadron recruited men from across the services, eschewed formalities of rank and parade-ground discipline, and operated as a cohesive small raiding squadron of special forces. By the winter of 1944, it included a wildly eclectic mixture of fighters – British, Europeans, Russians, and Italians who had been German POWs, as well as Italian partisans. The Canadian Westminster Regiment, no slouch itself in terms of individualistic soldiering, thought them the most glamorous unit operating in the 8th Army. If the Westminsters' snipers sported unorthodox uniforms and weapons, the men from Popski's Private Army carried everything they found that suited their purpose: not just .45 Thompsons and German Schmeissers, but also Italian MP-38 Berettas, American Garands, Lugers, and Colt .45 M1911 semi-automatic pistols. They had fought with Arrigo Boldrini's partisans before and knew the terrain around Ravenna. They were also experienced in landing an armed jeep from the amphibious vehicle known as DUKW (pronounced 'duck'), or from landing craft.

Their commanding officer was as unorthodox as his unit. Major Vladimir Peniakoff was a forty-seven-year-old Belgian Russian who had been educated at Cambridge and served in the First World War as an artillery gunner, where he spent a year in the hospital following a serious injury. Qualifying as an engineer after the war, he managed a sugar refinery in Egypt, learned Arabic, spent time climbing in the Italian Alps and exploring in the Middle East, and became a member of the Royal Geographical Society. He formed the Libyan Arab Force Commando (LAFC) in the Western Desert in 1941, and was awarded the Military Cross while raiding behind enemy lines with them and with the Long Range Desert Group. His nickname, and that of his guerilla force, was a sub-derivation of his name – nobody on the radio net could pronounce Peniakoff, so he and his guerrilla force were called 'Popski'. He formed his raiding squadron with two other officers who had all been in the LAFC with him – Captain Robert Park Yunnie and Major Jean Caneri.[5]

Porterforce was made up of the British 27th Lancers and King's Dragoon Guards, both based on Dingo, Ferret, and Scout armoured cars. The tanks of the Royal Canadian Dragoons and the Princess Louise Dragoon Guards backed them up. Popski's Private Army did the reconnaissance, while component parts of no fewer than five artillery regiments provided fire support, and three anti-tank regiments assured some protection against German tanks. Fourteen different British and Canadian units handled medical care, bridge building, engineering, military police, signalling, and vehicle maintenance. They had three infantry battalions attached to them, one from the British Essex Regiment, one from the Royal Air Force Regiment, and the Canadian Westminsters from British Columbia. 'In these improvised forces there was a return to the delightful informality and lack of spit-and-polish that characterized the Eighth Army's activities in its palmiest days in North Africa.'[6]

In no other single action in the Italian campaign had such a selection of units gathered on one target. In Ravenna itself was the

German 114th Jäger Division. The Westminsters had advanced slowly towards the city, across what seemed to them an endless variety of ditches, streams, rivulets, rivers, flooded fields, and canals. At every point behind them, the Germans had left mines and booby traps, each of which required personal clearance. 'Anyone who maintains that the Germans are an unimaginative race, tied to routine, obviously has never encountered those responsible for the mine-laying efforts on the Italian front,' noted the Westminsters' diary.

## THE ATTACK ON RAVENNA

Given the ironic and inappropriate name 'Operation *Chuckle*', the Allied and partisan assault on the city began on 29 November. On the evening of that day, Arrigo Boldrini split his 1,500 men into two groups of about 650 and 850. He then started to move them towards the outskirts of the city along paths and roads that the men knew by heart — most of them being from Ravenna. One partisan said that his mother had given him an extra helping of eels and polenta to keep him going throughout the night. An OSS document noted that along these routes the peasants had locked up their dogs and kept their doors unlocked in case the partisans needed to take cover quickly from the Germans. Bulow's smaller group of 650 partisans took position in a valley north of Ravenna, while the 850 deployed near one of the rivers that cut south of the town. A weapons drop from the OSS landed on 2 December, as the men waited for the Allies to get into position. On 3 December the OSS sent Bulow a simple message over the radio: 'Attack. Good luck!'

At three o'clock in the morning on 4 December, 823 partisans of the 28th Garibaldi Brigade armed with one 47mm anti-tank gun, four mortars, and a dozen heavy machine guns set off along sandy footpaths to their start-line positions to attack 2,500 Germans holed up in concrete bunkers, protected by tanks and artillery, guarding the seaward entry to the city.[7] The attack took two hours and the Germans surrendered with hardly a fight. Simultaneously, Bulow's partisans attacked pillboxes, roadblocks, machine-gun positions, and German unit headquarters set up in farmhouses and, in one case, a lockkeeper's cottage. Believing themselves surrounded, almost all the Germans surrendered, but not before they had transmitted the emergency radio signal burst to their colleagues that warned them they were being attacked. The fighting went on all night. At 5:30 a.m., Bulow's men took the enemy by surprise again. All across the area north of Ravenna, various partisan units went after different German strongholds, many of which surrendered after finding themselves surrounded.

Popski's Private Army had a four-mile-long section of the eastern flank, including the main Highway 16, which led from Ravenna to Rimini, and the seaboard approaches to the city. There were a sandy beach, dunes, low, stunted pine and oak trees hit by the maritime wind, while inland the Germans had flooded the marshland, salt flats, and fields: three straight canals flowed directly through them. The Germans had 75mm anti-tank, mortar, and machine-gun positions in all of their favourite locations, tried and trusted from one end of Italy to the other: in haystacks, on riverbanks, dug into embankments, in the upper and lower floors of farmhouses, and in stands of trees. The very open country gave them extremely clear fields of fire.

Popski's Private Army came ashore from small landing craft and from the amphibious, two-and-a-half-ton six-wheeled DUKWs. These carried Willys Jeeps up to the beaches, and they then drove off. The commandos spread out in their different fighting patrols to their different objectives. The first was the defended hamlet of Fossa di Ghiaia, which lay on the coast road into Ravenna, at the edge of one of the flooded areas of marshland bordering the coast. In the early-morning mist on 4 December ten jeeps drove up to the edge of the village and opened fire with their .30 and .50 cal Browning heavy machine guns. The defenders surrendered, as they did in five other positions.

The Germans had also established a strong position in one of the medieval watch towers that sat on the coast at the mouth of one of the rivers. Italian partisans from Arrigo Boldrini's brigade led the observation mission, and when they were sure of the movements of the Germans based inside, they sent a radio signal to the OSS in Cernia, which passed it to Popski's commandos. Fifteen of them landed on the beach and hid in a barn forty yards from the tower.[8]

At half past eight in the morning, the Germans called everybody for breakfast: five minutes later, three partisans and three commandos walked through the door, and the Germans surrendered. The captives were taken away. At midday, the same process happened again. And in the evening. By nightfall, the Germans were sufficiently worried by these mysterious disappearances that they pulled all of their forces south of the river back to the centre of the city. The Germans lost an estimated 40 killed and about 150 prisoners. The commandos: three dead and five wounded.

The German 114th Division tried to move its armoured cars and tanks out of the centre of Ravenna to confront the Canadians south of the city, but fast movement in the tight, enclosed streets – now suddenly full of partisans – was next to impossible. Popski's commandos held the bridges over the main river and two canals south of town, and when the Westminsters and Canadian 12th Royal Lancers arrived, with one of Bulow's partisan units leading them, the Germans realized they were trapped, and they decided to withdraw and retreat northwest towards Ferrara. But 650 partisans were waiting alongside the beginning of the road they took, and a Canadian tank regiment was accelerating fast around the city to cut them off. At four-thirty on the afternoon of 5 December, the OSS radio was able to send a succinct message: 'British in Ravenna. Regards to all.'

The Canadians took 171 prisoners, and lost 30 casualties. Arrigo Boldrini asked the 8th Army headquarters for formal permission to attach a unit of 800 of his men – and women – to the official British battle roster. Lieutenant General Richard McCreery, delighted at the success of the operation to liberate Ravenna, and the almost non-existent damage to the city, said yes immediately. The 8th Army now had an official Communist partisan unit in its ranks. And then McCreery went one better. He gave a victory parade in Ravenna's main square, in the shadow of the monumental statue of Garibaldi. Here Arrigo Boldrini was presented with Italy's Medaglio d'Oro for bravery in liberating his city. A large parade of his partisans observed the occasion. The British war artist Edward Bawden climbed to the top of a municipal building overlooking the piazza to draw the parade for the Imperial War Museum in London. He described the scene to his wife: 'Most of the square was clasped in shadow, only a few houses at one end and Garibaldi raised high on a pedestal caught the light, and his figure in white stone dominated the scene. For the occasion . . . a standard uniform was issued [to the partisans]: khaki pants, peagreen battledress blouse & cow pat cap. The red scarf around the neck links memories of Garibaldi to more recent ones of the hammer & sickle.'[9]

Lieutenant General McCreery was from the same generation, the same war, and the same background as Oliver Leese, but he was a different man and a completely different general. His father was an American Olympic polo champion, and his Scottish mother a descendant of John McAdam, who invented tarmac. McCreery inherited the dash of the former and the doughty persistence and reliability of the second. Like almost all of the senior generals in Italy, he had served in the First World War. Only seventeen when he joined up, he was awarded the Military Cross in 1918 and went on to higher command. He was a cavalryman from the 12th Royal Lancers, and loved horses and riding. Despite having lost several toes on the Western Front and having a hole in his right leg, he won prizes for equestrianism between the wars and by 1939 was a brigadier. He served at Dunkirk and as a chief of staff at El Alamein, taking over X Corps on its arrival in Italy in 1943. He was knighted in the same field in Italy by King George VI – travelling as 'General Collingwood' – that saw not only Oliver Leese knighted but also Major Jack Mahony receive the Victoria Cross. His style was completely different from Leese's: McCreery thought Montgomery too cautious and hesitant, and he knew that in the fast-moving battles in northern Italy that were going to follow the fall of Ravenna, the dash and buccaneering spirit of the polo field were going to be needed. Before Ravenna, the

Germans had either made sharp tactical withdrawals before battles were lost – as at Rimini, the Strait of Messina, and in Rome – or held the Allies on their own defensive terms, as in the Serchio valley and at Monte Cassino. Ravenna was the battle that broke the mould, where the Allies dictated both the tactical and strategic pace of the battle, and also crucially decided how the battlefield itself would look.

# 19

## CHRISTMAS IN THE SERCHIO VALLEY

### December 1944

In the first week of December 1944, American Marines in the northwestern Pacific watched as a small volcanic island ahead of them was bombarded by hundreds of naval guns and air strikes. The island they were about to storm was called Iwo Jima, and it was one of the last stopping-off points before the Japanese mainland. Eleven thousand miles and fourteen time zones to the west, the Germans were about to launch a massive counteroffensive in the Ardennes forest in Belgium. At the other end of Europe, in Greece, British and Indian troops had just arrived in Athens. The Germans had pulled out, and the partisans' Communist National Liberation Front was fighting against Greek nationalists who had sympathized and fought with the Germans. The Red Army was pushing towards eastern parts of Hungary. On the east coast of Italy, the Allies found themselves blocked – again – by the weather. The lightning strike of combined operations that liberated Ravenna at the beginning of December had turned into an impasse.

On the western flank of the Gothic Line, meanwhile, in the Serchio valley, the Buffalo Soldiers of the 92nd Division were confronting a new enemy none of them had ever seen before. Snow. On 6 December Private Ivan Houston received a message at headquarters of the 3rd Battalion of the 370th Regimental Combat Team. Effective immediately, all men in the 92nd Division were to stop stealing and killing chickens following persistent complaints from the local Italian population. It seemed a suitable message to accompany the men of his company into winter. The 370th was now under the command of a South African armoured brigade operating in western Tuscany in the Apennines between Bologna and the sea. It was an extraordinary racial mix: the white South African officers had black orderlies who would make their beds for them and do their ironing and bring them food. When the commanding officer of the 92nd asked a South African officer the size of the population of South Africa, he answered, 'We're three million white and ten million black.'

The one unifying factor between both units was that neither side had seen snow. Houston saw his friend Hiram MacBeth – who had slept through an artillery barrage in September – standing guard outside battalion headquarters wearing a white snowsuit and looking very cold. Houston thought it unreal that here were black troops from the American South wearing white snowsuits and fighting in ten-foot-deep snowdrifts. Houston was freezing. He wrote a letter to his grandmother asking for warmer clothing, and just before Christmas a newly knitted khaki wool sweater arrived for him, accompanied by one of his grandmother's fruitcakes. He put on the sweater, and on Christmas Day 1944 shared the fruitcake with a friend in battalion headquarters. The holiday was quiet.

Then just before dawn on Boxing Day, the radio net almost seemed to blow up with activity. The Germans had counterattacked along the Serchio River. Machine-gun, mortar, and artillery fire started coming into the positions held by the 1st and 2nd Battalions of the 92nd, trying to push them back down the Serchio valley towards Barga and eventually Lucca. It was the terrain they had fought so hard to take since September. The most advanced position held by the Buffalo Soldiers was in Sommocolonia, a small mountain village up in the valley. Two platoons of a sister unit of the 92nd were pinned down in an observation position in a stone house set on a steep slope facing the enemy. The squads from the 366th Infantry Regiment, entirely made up of African-American officers and men, were advised to withdraw.

One of the platoon commanders was a young 1st lieutenant from Cincinnati, twenty-nine-year-old John Fox. Knowing the Germans and Italians were attacking with several battalions, Fox volunteered to stay behind in Sommocolonia with his men to coordinate and observe artillery fire: without this, the Germans would simply break through unchecked straight down the strategically vital Serchio valley. During Christmas night, German and Italian soldiers had gradually infiltrated the town of Sommocolonia in civilian clothes, and in the early morning were joined by other uniformed units. The Germans stormed into the village under cover of an enormous artillery barrage that began at four o'clock in the morning of Boxing Day. Most of the American units in the town withdrew.

By eight o'clock, Fox and his party had been forced to pull out of the village and climb into the second-floor bedroom of the stone house – almost like a small tower – that overlooked Sommocolonia and the advancing Germans. Here he had set up his radio communications, while the men with him opened fire with their Garands and a .30 cal Browning machine gun. Battalion headquarters told Fox to withdraw. He stayed put. Six miles down the valley, 105mm and 150mm artillery pieces opened fire on Fox's defensive fire coordinates, the shells whistling and screaming over the snow-topped mountains to land exactly where the lieutenant wanted them: right in front of him. At 0800 hours, Lieutenant Fox reported that the Germans were in the streets and attacking in strength. So he called for more defensive artillery fire to slow the enemy' advance, but the Germans continued to attack towards the area behind the village and on the mountain slope that he occupied, so he issued a new set of fire orders, bringing the incoming shells much closer to his own position. The German soldiers were right in front of his platoon's position – he urgently needed time to allow other American units behind in the valley to reorganize for a counterattack. So now he radioed in to have the artillery fire adjusted closer to his position, then radioed again to have the shelling moved even closer. The soldier receiving the message was stunned, for that would bring the deadly fire right on top of Fox's position; there was no way he would survive. This shelling delayed the German advance until other units could reorganize to repel the attack. Finally Fox was warned that the next adjustment would bring the deadly artillery right on top of his position. Lieutenant Fox acknowledged the danger but insisted this was the only way to defeat the attacking soldiers. He said, 'Fire it.'[1]

Later that day, a counterattack retook the position from the Germans, and Fox's body was found, with some hundred dead bodies of German soldiers around it. The citation for his Distinguished Service Cross stated, 'His gallant and courageous actions, at the supreme sacrifice of his own life, contributed greatly to delaying the enemy advance until other infantry and artillery units could reorganize to repel the attack. His extraordinary valorous actions were in keeping with the most cherished traditions of military service, and reflect the utmost credit on him, his unit, and the United States Army.'[2]

As the Germans were attacking the Serchio valley, the Maratha Light Infantry and the 21st Indian Infantry Brigade were dug into positions on the top of the Apennines, facing German paratroopers, where the temperatures were considerably colder than down towards the coast. A Scottish officer fighting alongside the men from Bombay in the same brigade described the conditions in a letter:

> I know how my grandfather felt at Majuba Hill [a battle in the Boer War, 1881]. We had the high ground and it was of little use to us. Our positions were under constant observation. We had to sit tight all the time, just like old Bill in Flanders [cartoon character – an unhappy soldier in the First World War]. A bitter wind whistled up the valley and curled over the crests, adding one more misery to sitting in a slit trench all day and all night, with a drizzle gradually soaking clothing and blankets, and freezing the bones. A heavy mist would come down; if the paraboys could not see

us, neither could we see them. It was rather eerie this being hunted through the fog, and we grew very quick on the trigger.

The Indians knew the attack in the Serchio valley was important. The area around Lucca and the coastline was logistically vital to the American formations, which landed almost all of their supplies in Leghorn, or Livorno, a port less than forty miles behind the front. The tightly stretched supply route then ran to Pisa, towards Lucca and up into the Serchio valley itself. Intelligence reports reached General Dudley Russell's HQ on 22 December: almost all of his 8th Indian Division apart from one brigade had to move to Tuscany. For the Marathas, like the rest of the division, it was a logistical nightmare: their unit was scattered across different Apennine peaks. Captain Eustace D'Souza's company of the 1st Battalion was a whole mountain away from battalion headquarters. He ordered his men to climb out of their frozen slit trenches, shoulder all of their weapons and equipment, and just follow him down the mountain. The scene couldn't have been farther from the summer evening at the Castello di Montegufoni, guarding the Italian art, walking under the mandarin trees. In late December, the Marathas were dressed in a combination of issued snowsuits, makeshift white cloths tied around their helmets, heavy greatcoats that got wet very quickly and then froze each night, and their 38 Webbing equipment that was a non-compliant mass of hard, dirty, frozen canvas straps. Nevertheless, by Christmas Eve, the Marathas were ready and headed out. A day later they were in the Serchio valley, deploying into defensive positions. For four months, the riverbed had become a nightmare incarnate for the Buffalo Soldiers of mountain ridges, mud, rain, artillery fire, and well-dug-in Germans. For the Marathas, arriving from the very top of the frozen Apennines, things looked rather different. 'The Serchio valley is wide, easy and well cultivated. A railway and two highways follow the line of the river, a quiet stream which averages 100 feet in width. The area is heavily populated, with clusters of farmhouses and small hamlets scattered along the roads and in the glades among the beech woods.

The countryside exhibited no signs of devastation, and the gracious contours and pleasant expanses delighted the Indians, fresh from a nightmare existence in the gale-swept valleys of the winter Apennines.'[3]

The German 148th Division held the line advancing down the Serchio valley. It was accompanied by parts of three Italian Fascist divisions, and all the troops were of what the Allies called 'second-rate quality'. There were a lot of Polish troops in the German units, and the Italian divisions had a desertion rate of forty soldiers per day. One Italian sergeant from a mountain unit was stationed on the top of a mountain in a windy grove of elm and hazel. He had a German headquarters team attached. Unlike most of their fellow countrymen's military units after the armistice, the Italian Alpini units – their mountain troops – were extremely capable. The Italian Alpini sergeant was told by a German NCO that the troops opposite them in the line were the Buffalo Soldiers and Indians 'I knew then it was not going to be an easy or even fight.'[4]

It was not. The German offensive lasted a little under forty-eight hours. The advance positions of the 92nd and the 366th held the Germans long enough to allow the Marathas, the Argyll and Sutherland Highlanders, and the Punjabi Frontier Force Rifles to dig in and form blocking positions as far back as the outskirts of Lucca. General Russell took command of all the troops in the valley – including the Americans and South Africans – and went straight on the offensive. In a small skirmish that hardly made the divisional log, but that would stay with him all his life, Captain Eustace D'Souza was wounded and decorated leading a platoon of C Company of the Marathas as they forced a company of Germans back from a forward American position. An enemy soldier – D'Souza for some reason always thought he was Polish – got off a loose round from his Mauser rifle that went through the Bombay officer's side without touching any organs, arteries, or veins. Like many people who are shot, D'Souza at first didn't notice it, as he led his three sections straight at, and around, the Germans. It was only afterward that one of his corporals pointed out that he was bleeding all down his right side, the bloodstains spreading under his greatcoat, which he had opened because he was so hot. He was Mentioned in Despatches as a result of this small action. One battle diary described it thus: 'After the rigours and deadly encounters of the mountains, this excursion into the west had proved to be something of a frolic. It was a different enemy and a different sort of war.' [5]

It wasn't a frolic for the Marathas, and especially not for D'Souza. But by 30 January, the Frontier Force Rifles had relieved the Argyll and Sutherland Highlanders so they could go off and enjoy the feast of New Year's Eve, their traditional Hogmanay. And so 1944, under the shadow of the gentle snows of the Serchio valley, became 1945.

# 20

## EAST WIND

### *The Different Flavours of Communism*

When the Germans invaded Yugoslavia in 1941, the country was broken up into pieces. Mussolini took Slovenia – the region closest to Italy – Kosovo, and most of the Adriatic coast, including almost all of its islands. The Germans occupied Serbia and created the Independent State of Croatia, which covered much of modern-day Croatia and Bosnia. Bulgaria and Hungary occupied parts of the north and east. Josip Broz Tito's Communist Party of Yugoslavia, which had been banned since just after the First World War, set up a vast multi-ethnic partisan army. This was referred to as the National Liberation Army and Partisan Detachments of Yugoslavia. For ease of reference in a region used to lengthy acronyms, it was called the Narodno Oslobodilačka Vojska, or NOV, simply meaning the National Liberation Army. They fought against the Germans and the Croats, as well as the Serb nationalist Chetnik guerrillas, who wanted to bring back the Serbian monarchy. According to Tito, the national composition of the partisan army in May 1944 was 44 per cent Serb, 30 per cent Croat, 10 per cent Slovene, 5 per cent Montenegrin, 2.5 per cent Macedonian, and 2.5 per cent Bosnian Muslim.[1]

In partitioned Yugoslavia, partisan resistance as a multi-ethnic, popular front developed as a matter of physical necessity and survival.

The Slovenes in German-annexed Slovenia engaged mostly in small-scale sabotage. In Serbia, a nationalist Chetnik resistance organization developed under a former Yugoslav Army colonel, Draža Mihailović, intent on bringing back Yugoslavia's deposed monarchy; it initially received support from the British SOE and MI6, but in June 1941, the Germans killed dozens of them in an uprising that completely deflated any thoughts of confrontation. The Communist-dominated popular partisan organization under the leadership of Marshal Tito was a multi-ethnic resistance force – it included, as noted, Serbs, Croats, Bosniaks, Jews, and Slovenes.

By 1943, the Allies were supporting the National Liberation Army in two main ways – through direct parachute drops of arms and equipment, and by sending liaison and training officers from the Special Operations Executive. British support to the nationalist Chetniks evaporated after about 1942, when it became apparent that their approach to the Germans had become largely collaborationist. The Germans and the ultra-right-wing Croatian extremists, the Ustashe, were responsible for the deaths of up to 80,000 Serbs, Muslims, and gypsies in the concentration camp system set up at Jasenovac. The Germans frequently commented that the Ustashe were their most willing collaborators, even compared to the anti-Semitic nationalists in the Baltic states of Latvia and Lithuania, who had assisted the SS Einsatzkommando groups in 1941 and 1942 after Operation *Barbarossa*. Serb Chetniks killed tens of thousands of Bosnian Muslims in eastern Bosnia, and the Germans killed thousands of Serbs and gypsies in northern Serbia, on the banks of the Danube. For most Yugoslavs, belonging to the partisans was about living.

Based primarily in Bosnia and northwestern Serbia, Tito's partisans fought the Germans and Italian Fascists most consistently and played a major role in driving the German forces out of Yugoslavia in 1945. By April 1945, there were some 800,000 soldiers in the partisan army. Tito went to great lengths to portray the NOV as a multi-ethnic people's army – which it was – instead of a Communist militia. It had an air force and a small navy, fought in large, highly disciplined units, and was very much a force to be reckoned with.

The Yugoslav partisans could almost be called a mixture of Socialists and protonationalists, since they too were a multi-ethnic collective defending their homeland, their families, and their livelihoods against a wide range of threats from the Germans, Italian Fascists, Chetniks, and Ustashe. Without belonging to the NOV, most people in Yugoslavia could not have survived. They were as far as it was possible to be from the Marxist–Leninist doctrines of the Red Army and the Soviet Union, and this made Stalin extremely uncomfortable. The British and Americans understood that their 'communism' was in fact populist, people's socialism, in the same way that Italian 'communism' among the partisans was more of a direct anti-reaction to Mussolini.

Tito's partisans wanted to take the territory of Slovenia and the Adriatic islands back from the Italian Fascists, and as they watched the Germans and Fascists defeated by the Allies in 1945, they saw an opportunity to regain territory they saw as theirs. Tito was far too clever, too populist, and too wily a leader to let the Red Army and the Soviets occupy and control Yugoslavia, so he simply told Stalin that he would function as a Soviet-friendly buffer state between him and the Allies in Italy and Austria. He knew how to keep the simmering cauldron of volatile ethnic tensions that was Yugoslavia under control, off the boil. Stalin knew this too and was happy to let him govern the country. As an ethnic Georgian, Stalin was under no misapprehension as to how small, and probably bloody, a welcome the Red Army would receive from newly liberated Yugoslavs who had suffered so harshly under the Croats and Germans. Two-thirds of Stalin's army was not Russian, hailing from Mongolia or Tatarstan or Turkmenistan or Siberia; if the Yugoslavs were prepared to turn on each other, he thought, quite correctly, what would they do to outsiders who tried to impose their authority? Stalin understood the Balkans.

On 12 August 1944, in the Bay of Naples, Churchill had welcomed Marshal Tito to lunch. His guest wore a magnificent gold-and-blue uniform, which was very tight under the collar and singularly unsuited to the blazing heat, wrote Churchill. The Russians had given him the uniform, and the Americans the gold lace. Tito insisted on having two armed bodyguards in the dining room, for fear of assassination during the meal. Eight months later, in April 1945, after the death of Roosevelt, Churchill prioritized the imperatives of the United States as sevenfold: the first was that 'Soviet Russia had become a mortal danger to the free world.' The seventh was that 'Marshal Tito's aggressive pretensions against Italy must be curbed.'[2] So when it came to the actions of his partisans approaching Trieste, and their cross-border operations with Italian Communist partisans, the Allies were understandably nervous. Two particular operations showed how badly things could go wrong, how all sides could misunderstand each other, and how the actions of friends and allies, like Tito and the British and Americans, could fragment into perceived aggression when the common unifying factor of the enemy – the Germans – was removed, and a rogue other – the Soviets – introduced. Tito was also very dissatisfied with the Allies for not breaking through the Gothic Line in the winter of 1944, and then liberating Yugoslavia. He always said that this failure pushed him closer to the Red Army.

In northern Italy there were four major anti-fascist groups: Socialists, Action Party, Christian Democrats, and Communists, as well as the smaller autonomous groups. Operation *Chrysler* had parachuted into this volatile partisan mix to establish a show of authority and liaison in the area in anticipation of an early German surrender. The mission was then changed to help the partisan units with parachute drops of arms and supplies. The Germans knew that the OSS mission forces were operating in the area of Lake Orta, forty miles northwest of Milan in the foothills of the Alps. They used direction-finding technology to try to pinpoint the OSS radio transmitter and managed to do so one day to within 100 yards, but partisans intercepted three Germans and a Swiss interpreter with their own direction-finding gear and shot them. But in December, an independent partisan leader called Cinquanta betrayed the *Chrysler* men to the Germans. Cinquanta was later assassinated. The OSS team had no idea this had happened. On 2 December Major Holahan sent Lieutenant Icardi to meet with the local Communist commander, Vincenzo Moscatelli, a partisan leader who operated in the mountains above the lake. This was arranged by a middleman who also wanted the arms drops funnelled through him. The Communists, who made up about three-quarters of the partisans in the *Chrysler* area, were supposed to receive equal allocations of the two arms drops, but they frequently stole weapons and equipment intended for rival groups. Into this operating environment, Holahan's men thought he too was determinedly anti-communist.

On 6 December 1944, the OSS men were hiding in Villa Castelnuovo on Lake Orta when two friendly Catholic priests arrived and warned them they should leave the villa as quickly as possible. As the Americans ran out of the building in the darkness, automatic gunfire burst out. Holahan, Icardi, LoDolce, and two Italian agents fired back. The team had made a plan that, if attacked, they would split up and meet separately at the Communist Party headquarters. But when all the men finally reunited, Holahan was missing. Icardi radioed a message to headquarters about the incident. The American major did not reappear. Two weeks later, an OSS man from Milan visited Lake Orta and investigated Holahan's disappearance. At the villa, the officer found spent 9mm shell casings and, on the beach, one of Holahan's hand grenades. The surviving *Chrysler* men continued to arrange supply drops to the partisans, but of Holahan himself there was no sign. In February 1945, the *Chrysler* mission was ordered to Milan. Their commander was still missing.

The suspicious circumstances surrounding his disappearance were of huge concern to the OSS and SOE, but in terms of complicated relations with the Communists, they were overshadowed by an event in the small mountain village of Porzûs at the beginning of February. The hamlet sits above the city of Udine, the most northeastern in Italy before the port of Trieste and the Slovenian – then the Yugoslav – frontier. A British SOE operation code-named 'Coolant' was operating around Udine, on anti-scorch operations as well as trying to stop the

Germans from demolishing road and rail links that could prevent the Allies from advancing. The Germans had also established a defensive line near Tarvisio, and the Coolant mission spent as much time as possible trying to destroy parts of it. The leading partisan group they were operating with was an independent Catholic group called Osoppo. The Slovenian Communist partisans operating with the Patriotic Action Group, from across the border – which was only three miles away – were territorial, idealistic, and material rivals with Osoppo and their British SOE liaison officer. They made it clear they equated them with Italian Fascists, and that it was only a matter of time before a confrontation broke out between the two sides. They delighted in spreading pro-Tito and pro-Soviet propaganda in the Italian border area.

On 7 February a group of about a hundred Slovenes gathered outside the Osoppo headquarters in the village of Porzûs – they had already betrayed the location of the partisan headquarters to the local German-recruited forces, who were a company of Cossacks. Claiming that they were in danger of being attacked, the Slovenes tricked their way into the Osoppo compound, which had about twenty partisans. Once inside, their leader accused the Osoppo brigade of hindering the collaboration with the Yugoslav NOV, of hindering cooperation over the distribution of arms drops, and of being in contact with the Fascist government. Their final point was that the British-supported Catholic partisans were going to try to prevent the annexation of the Istria, Giulia, and Friuli border area once the Germans were defeated. Over the following week, the Slovenes proceeded to hang, and then shoot, all twenty of the partisans.

Once the SOE liaison officer discovered what happened, he and the OSS realized it could be a clear and terrifying precursor of what was to come in northern Italy. And what could happen once the unifying enemy – the Germans – were defeated, the Russians were advancing westward, and Tito's partisans were in the ascendancy across the border, only five miles away.

# PART FIVE

## AFTER THE LINE

# 21

## THE SECRET SURRENDER

*Operation* Sunrise

### February–March 1945

On 9 February the representative of the Office of Strategic Services in Berne, Switzerland, sent a telegram to the office of the president in Washington. The Yalta Conference was still ongoing – Churchill, Stalin, and Roosevelt were meeting in the Crimea to discuss the postwar situation in Europe. The OSS Berne office was receiving information from a high-level and well-connected informant who had intelligence links to the German Wehrmacht in Italy, the SS, Mussolini's supporters, and the German diplomatic service in Switzerland. The informant reported that the German consul in Lugano, Switzerland, had just returned from a meeting with Generalfeldmarschall Kesselring, SS-Obergruppenführer Karl Wolff, and Rudolf Rahn, the German ambassador to Mussolini's Salò Republic in northern Italy. The consul, Alexander Konstantin von Neurath, had told the informant that he felt that German units in northern Italy were being kept by Hitler and Himmler specifically for the protection of the Nazis' last-ditch 'inner fortress' based around Austria and Bavaria. Kesselring in Italy and Gerd von Rundstedt in the west did not appear ready to surrender yet. The OSS cables to Washington did not make it immediately clear who was providing the information to them in Switzerland. Neurath? Somebody in the SS? An Italian?[1]

While the 'Arguing Allies' were discussing the breakup and layout of post-war Europe, the Germans in Italy suddenly started to make overtures for a separate surrender of all their forces there. The Red Army had occupied Budapest, the capital of Hungary, on 13 February, and the last German forces, including SS-Sturrmbannführer Walter Reder and the 16th SS-Panzergrenadier Division Reichsführer-SS, were retreating towards Austria. They were hoping to be able to surrender to the British or Americans, not the Russians.

By 24 February the OSS in Berne received information that Kesselring and Ambassador Rahn were 'ready to surrender and even to fight against Hitler, if the Allies can make it worth their while'. Kesselring, said the secret informant, felt that he was destined to retire to the Alps as a last stand where, overseen by SS officials, he would die in the final battle against the Allies or instead be killed for not resisting them. The plot thickened. On the same day, the *London Daily Dispatch* ran a story from its Bern correspondent stating that 'Kesselring has offered secretly to the Allies to withdraw under pressure, leaving North Italian cities intact and preventing Fascist destruction, in return for which he has asked for assurances that he would not be considered a war criminal and would be allowed to retire his troops to Germany to maintain order.'

For another two weeks, the office of the OSS was silent on the matter. Both sides were preparing their ground. The German military, SS, and diplomatic community in northern Italy knew that a German military collapse was imminent in Europe and that a surrender deal should be discussed. But with whom? Where? With the Americans? The British? Heinrich Himmler had already made it clear to Karl Wolff that the Italian forces in northern Italy, particularly the SS, should pull back into Austria before the Allies' long-expected spring offensive could begin, rather than negotiate a surrender deal.

Walter Reder and his colleagues from the 16th SS-Panzergrenadiers had already gone to Hungary – a German offensive to try to save the capital, Budapest had just failed, and the city had fallen. Reder and his unit were somewhere near the Austrian border.

Then the SS played its hand in Switzerland. On the morning of 8 March, Obergruppenführer und General der Waffen-SS Karl Wolff, the Higher SS and Police Leader in Italy, and a German High Command representative from Kesselring's staff arrived in Lugano, on the Swiss–Italian border. Dressed in smart civilian clothes, they said they were prepared to make definite commitments in regard to 'terminating German resistance in North Italy'.

The OSS representative in Berne believed that Wolff was truthfully working with Kesselring, and that the two generals might actually effect an unconditional surrender. Absolute secrecy, they said, was essential for this to work, and the OSS representative was ready to arrange with complete secrecy for the entry into Switzerland in civilian clothes of fully authorized representatives of the Supreme Allied Mediterranean Command. The operation was given the code name 'Sunrise'; the intelligence intermediary, 'Crossword'. It was a major intelligence coup for the Americans, but it was simultaneously a success for a relatively low-level SS intelligence officer. For behind it was one of Wolff's intelligence deputies, the SS-Obersturmführer Guido Zimmer, who for three months had been guiding much of the German overture to the OSS.

In November 1944, there had been a meeting of RSHA foreign intelligence officials in Verona, which had been convened by their resident expert on Switzerland, Klaus Huegel. SS-Obersturmführer Zimmer was present at the meeting, as he had good intelligence contacts with both the Swiss and the Italian partisans. What none of the three sides – American, German, or Italian – then knew was that Zimmer was keeping a diary throughout the negotiation process. At the November meeting, he suggested contacting Allied intelligence in Switzerland through one Baron Luigi Parrilli, an aristocratic Fascist businessman from Genoa. Parrilli had worked with Zimmer in his intelligence work and was also well connected with the Italian partisans not just in his native Liguria but around Milan as well. It was in Parrilli's interests as a business owner in northern Italy that the SOE and OSS anti-scorch plans worked. He didn't want to lose hundreds of millions of lire of property and assets to either the Germans or the partisans. As a Fascist sympathizer, he could see the end coming and knew that he needed some powerful new allies, fast. Zimmer's boss, SS-Standartenführer Rauff, and other RSHA officials contacted Berlin, and the plan to contact the Americans was given the go-ahead in February 1945, reportedly by Himmler. Karl Wolff approved of it too. The operation to approach the Allies via Luigi Parrilli was code-named 'Operation *Wool*'.

At the beginning of February, Zimmer made the following entry in his notebook:

P[arrilli] was invited to my place for a meal today in order to discuss quietly once more the Swiss trip which he is to begin on the 20th of February. Apart from the tasks already laid down in writing, I went one step further today with reference to the conversation with Mr. Von F[ische] and SS. Col. R[auff], and am having P. make an official visit to the English and American ambassadors. There to set forth our common view on the Communist danger and in this connection to intimate that SS 1st Lt. Zi[mmer] has already tried more than once to make contact with influential Englishmen, since he is of the firm conviction that he has things to say which are most certainly of interest to England. He should further intimate that Zi, without the knowledge of his office belongs to some circles of influential people who are pursuing a definite political course that is of importance to Englishmen, provided that the decision has not already been settled to destroy Germany at any cost and leave the field open for Russia.[2]

Zimmer, Wolff, Parrilli, and three others then met with the OSS representative in Berne on 8 March, where the Americans duly reported back that Karl Wolff was willing to try to take the German forces out of the war in northern Italy, but that he had not yet 'won over' Kesselring to the plan. Wolff also claimed that Heinrich Himmler in Germany had no idea of what he was doing, although the Americans were not sure whether to believe this, given the close friendship and working methods Wolff and Himmler had developed since 1933. The Germans needed to persuade the Allies that they meant business. So they brought with them to Switzerland a well-known Italian partisan leader named Ferruccio Parri. He was a famous ex-soldier, journalist, anti-fascist activist, and partisan leader. He was the head of the Action Party partisan groups in northern Italy; the Germans had arrested him in January 1945 in Milan, and tortured him in prison. Parri had no idea what was happening when the SS came to his cell in March and took him away in a car. He thought he was going to be shot. At the meeting in Switzerland on 8 March Zimmer and two other officers, SS-Obersturmbannführers Eugen Dollmann and Eugen Wenner, accompanied Wolff along with Baron Parrilli. Following the meeting, Allen Dulles, the OSS station chief in Switzerland, made the following notes about Karl Wolff: 'He is a distinctive personality, and evidence indicates that he represents the more moderate elements in Waffen SS combined with a measure of romanticism. He is probably the most dynamic personality in North Italy and, next to Kesselring, the most powerful.'

Wolff stated that the time had come for some Germans with the power to act to lead Germany out of the war in order to end the useless human and material destruction. He said he was willing to act and felt he could persuade Kesselring to cooperate, and that between the two of them they controlled the situation in North Italy. As far as the SS was concerned, Wolff stated that he also controlled western Austria, since his authority included Vorarlberg, Tyrol, and the Brenner Pass with both its northern and southern approaches. Wolff said that joint action by Kesselring and himself would leave Hitler and Himmler powerless to take effective countermeasures like the ones employed after the 20 July assassination attempt. Wolff felt that all they needed was one German general to take the lead. The Americans reported that he 'made no request concerning his personal safety or privileged treatment from the war criminal viewpoint'. Nobody said or noted anything about what terms Zimmer might have put forward to protect himself from possible prosecution after the war.

By this point, the British could only assume that Moscow had seen the newspaper story from Berne and that, paranoid and suspicious to the core, Stalin would have believed it. They also knew that Stalin had a number of agents operating in northern Italy, some of them inserted by the SOE itself at the request of Pavel Fitin's NKVD (the Soviet secret police) in Moscow, on an operation code-named 'Pickaxe'. They had to assume the Russians knew about the German approach: if Zimmer had included the SS, a leading Fascist businessman, the Americans, the RSHA, and two separate groups of Italian partisans in his plan, who else knew about it? The British believed it was likely the Italian Communists knew, and that they had passed the information to the Russians.

So on 12 March Sir Archibald Clark-Kerr, the British ambassador in Moscow, told the Russian Foreign Ministry that, along with the Americans, they had received tentative approaches from the Germans in Italy who were interested in discussing a possible surrender. He told the foreign minister, Vyacheslav Molotov, that no further contact would be made with the Germans until the Russians had indicated how they wanted to proceed; Clark-Kerr made it very clear that a Russian presence at the meetings in Switzerland would be welcome. And that the British and Americans were prepared to help smuggle a plainclothes Russian representative into the country.

On 16 March Molotov in Moscow went to see the British ambassador. He was furious. He told Clark-Kerr that the Soviet government found the attitude of the British government 'entirely inexplicable and incomprehensible in denying facilities to the Russians to send a representative to Berne'.

Sir Archibald Clark-Kerr tried to reassure the furious Russian, a Bolshevik of the old school. He said that the British and Americans were trying, in the first instance, to see if the German approaches were genuine before they took them any farther, and before they set up a formal meeting to which they would of course invite the Russians. Molotov was completely unconvinced and left the British embassy in Moscow in a temper, shouting about Allied duplicity.

Whoever had devised and was running Operation *Sunrise* had achieved something unintended: engineering a split of confidence between the Allied leadership at precisely the moment when the three leaders thought they had negotiated a compromise about post-war Europe at Yalta.

In Switzerland, Wolff further tried to reassure the Americans. Not only had he brought the partisan leader, Ferruccio Parri, with him to Switzerland, he had also delivered back to the Americans a leading OSS intelligence asset, Major Antonio Usmiani, whom the Germans had arrested in Milan. Zimmer commented that Wolff 'had given up our two biggest hostages'. Further, the SS general went further: he said he would discontinue active warfare against the partisans, except that required to keep up a pretense of ongoing conflict while Operation *Sunrise* was finalized. He agreed to release several hundred Italian Jews who were in a detention centre at Bolzano near the Swiss border – he denied that he had taken any ransom money from the Jewish families to make this offer, but Rauff and Zimmer almost certainly had. Wolff also offered to free one of Major Oliver Churchill's two key partisan links, who had also been arrested. Edgardo Sogno ran La Franchi and had protected Churchill in Milan – Sogno himself was the Liberal Party representative at the CLNAI. He was also heavily involved in smuggling Jews out of Italy into Switzerland, so the fact that Wolff and Zimmer offered both him and the Bolzano Jews as part of the deal was no coincidence.

On 19 March Wolff, Zimmer, and Dollmann met with representatives of Field Marshal Harold Alexander near Lugano. Alexander's officers, theatrically, wore plain clothes and did not give their names or ranks but simply described themselves as 'advisers of the OSS representative'. Wolff said that Kesselring had been assigned to Marshal von Rundstedt's command in the west and had not even been allowed by Hitler's headquarters to return to Italy to pack up his effects. Thus Wolff had not been able to see Kesselring since the *generalfeldmarschall*'s first meeting with the OSS representative at the beginning of March. Generaloberst Vietinghoff, who acted as deputy commander in Italy for Kesselring, had gone to Germany on leave in mid-January, and subsequently had held a brief command in Kourland on the Baltic Eastern Front. After a short conference at Hitler's headquarters, he was ordered to return to Italy to assume command. It appeared that Hitler was none the wiser about Operation *Sunrise*.

If neither of these officers wanted to act with him, Wolff said that he could bring with him the assets he commanded in Italy at that point. These included some 15,000 Germans and 20,000 Soviets, mostly Don and Kuban Cossacks and Turkomans. He had 10,000 Serb monarchists, 10,000 Slovenes, 5,000 Czechs, parts of an Indian SS legion, and 100,000 Italians. He also had 65,000 subsidiary Wehrmacht supply and service troops, so some 225,000 men in all.

After this meeting, the Allies waited impatiently to learn what news Wolff bought of Kesselring. In Russia, meanwhile, Molotov had furiously assigned his NKVD network the specific task of finding out what the Americans, the Germans, and the British had been doing. It didn't take his men long to present their answer. He told Stalin – who sent a telegram to Churchill to the same effect – that 'negotiations have been going on for two weeks behind the Soviet Union's back'. Sir Archibald Clark-Kerr still tried to say it was simply a case of sounding things out. Molotov then laid down another card of diplomatic insult: 'In this instance the Soviet government sees not just a misunderstanding but something worse.' Operation *Sunrise* was splitting the Allied alliance.[3]

———————— ·O· ————————

By the evening of 26 March the OSS in Switzerland had heard nothing further from Wolff. The strategic situation in Europe was becoming more desperate for the Germans – Field Marshal Montgomery's troops had crossed the Rhine on 24 March at Wesel. Then SS-Obersturmführer Zimmer re-contacted the OSS: Hitler had recalled his senior officers from Italy to a conference in Berlin, where he was now running operations from his bunker under the Reich Chancellery. Wolff had not left to join the meeting. Zimmer reported simply that Hitler wanted to use the remainder of German forces in Italy to defend Austria and Bavaria.

The OSS may have heard nothing from Wolff, but the telegram traffic between Stalin and the dying President Roosevelt had been daily. Franklin Roosevelt's response to Stalin was simple: 'I cannot avoid a feeling of bitter resentment towards your informers, whoever they are, for such vile misrepresentations of my actions or those of my trusted subordinates.'

Churchill, insulted and stung by Molotov's remarks, had adopted a silent, sulking approach. Stalin, petulant, paranoid, feeling betrayed, realized this. And so he communicated with the Americans, and not Churchill, in an attempt to drive a wedge between the Western Allies. Over and above the question of whether the Germans had or hadn't sued for peace, and whether the Americans and British had or had not tried to exclude the Russians, Stalin felt bruised and deceived by Churchill, particularly over what should happen in Poland. Churchill had been convinced since the Warsaw Uprising in August 1944, when Stalin had refused to rescue the Poles, that the Soviet leader would occupy Poland and deny the Poles any remote form of autonomy and self-government. They would be a Communist satellite. Churchill and Roosevelt had argued strongly at Yalta that Poland should be divided between the inhabitants of that country and Russia. From 1940 onward, Churchill's diaries and telegrams to Roosevelt and his ministers reverberate with his concerns about Poland. Stalin, of course, was intending to simply occupy the country. And Operation *Sunrise* was the last straw – here, for Stalin, was finally consummate proof that Churchill in particular was deceiving him. Of what use were such allies? Stalin asked.

Churchill's telegrams to Roosevelt were being answered by his chief of staff, General George Marshall. The last time Churchill was to see the dying Roosevelt was post-Yalta, when the two Western leaders had a meeting on a naval ship in Alexandria harbour in Egypt. Churchill said that Roosevelt seemed 'to have a slender contact with life'. Churchill followed up this sad encounter with a lunch meeting at an Egyptian desert oasis at Fayoum with the crown prince of Saudi Arabia. The oasis's residents were simply removed for the day to the surrounding desert. The British prime minister was the host of the meeting. On being told that Prince Ibn Saud did not drink or smoke, Churchill took it upon himself to say that 'if it was the religion of His Majesty to deprive himself of smoking and alcohol, I must point out that my rule of life prescribed as an absolutely sacred rite smoking cigars and also the drinking of alcohol before, after and if need be during all meals and in the intervals between them.' The Saudi prince accepted this position. In return, Churchill gave him a Rolls-Royce.[4]

On 1 April the OSS office in Switzerland was suddenly in contact with Washington again. Wolff had sent Zimmer to see the Americans, to say that the SS general had tried to meet with Kesselring, but the latter had left Italy before he could get to him. By this time, Allied troops were only six miles away from Kesselring's headquarters. The Luftwaffe *generalfeldmarschall* told Wolff to go through with the plan, and he in turn had told Zimmer to go to Berne to tell the OSS that a full German delegation was ready to meet with the Allies. Zimmer also transmitted the message that Wolff had been in Germany and had told Himmler about the state of negotiations. Himmler ordered him not to go to Switzerland again, but then left in a furious hurry for Hungary, which had just fallen to the Red Army, which was preparing for an onward attack on Austria and Vienna. Zimmer finished his presentation of his superiors' deliberations with a flourish: Kesselring had told Wolff that Hitler was still determined to hold out to the last, trusting in secret weapons.

The meetings with Karl Wolff to discuss a German surrender never took place. So divided were the Americans, Russians, and British by

Stalin and Molotov's accusations of treachery that the matter was dropped, deemed far more damaging than beneficial to the Allies' joint position. On 20 April a telegram from Washington was forwarded to the OSS in Switzerland:

> The Joint Chiefs of Staff have today directed that all contact with the German emissaries mentioned in my memorandum to you of 18 April 1945 be terminated. This action came about as the result of dispatch by the Combined Chiefs of Staff of a message to the Supreme Allied Commander, Mediterranean Theater, stating that in view of (1) their belief that the German Commander in Chief, Italy did not at this time intend to surrender on acceptable terms and (2) complications which had arisen with the Russians on the matter it had been decided by the Governments of the United States and Great Britain that the contact should be broken off.

The entire affair had led to huge complications with the Russians. So who *did* benefit from Operation *Sunrise*? Karl Wolff? Or Guido Zimmer and his Italian and SS colleagues?

# 22

## THE LAST BATTLES
### *Colle Musatello and Chioggia*

### April 1945

By April 1945, the Red Army was closing in on Vienna and fighting on the Seelow Heights outside Berlin. They had occupied Danzig and Slovakia, and broken through into Austria. The Americans had meanwhile arrived in Frankfurt. General Eisenhower had already broadcast an appeal for the Germans to surrender. In the Pacific, the Americans had landed on Okinawa, the closest island to the Japanese mainland, which they would use as their springboard for a planned invasion. But on the Gothic Line, some of the German units appeared to be determined to hold out to the last. There were three reasons for this. First, regiments or battalions made up of soldiers who originated from eastern Germany, in territory now occupied by the Red Army, knew they had no homes to return to. Second, some units preferred to face the Allies in open battle rather than retreat through territory behind their own lines that was controlled by Italian partisans: they stood a much better chance of making it alive as prisoners of the Allies than as prisoners of the partisans. Third, until the fall of Bologna, Milan, Turin, and Venice in April, discipline among the majority of German units across northern Italy remained relatively high.

So in late March, when Daniel Inouye and the 442nd Regimental Combat Team arrived back from France at the Tuscan port of Livorno, there was still fighting to do. The unit had been involved in extremely heavy combat in the Vosges mountains of eastern France since before Christmas. They had taken very high casualties – at the end of one battle in November, no more than half the unit could physically walk, or stand up, to parade before their commanding officer. General Mark Clark had asked that the Nisei be returned to Italy, and on disembarking on the Tuscan coast, they jumped straight into trucks to join the new division to which they were now attached. It was the 92nd, the Buffalo Soldiers. They would be fighting together as the American advance pushed up the western flank of the Gothic Line.

Inouye was now a lieutenant, having been given a battlefield commission in France. On the day his commanding officer told him to report to regimental HQ, the young Japanese-American sergeant had weighed exactly 111 pounds. Eating K-rations and fighting in combat for months on end, he had lost nearly 30 pounds. Astounded to be told he was being promoted, Inouye was then told that an officer had to weigh a minimum of 135 pounds. There was no way he could put on 24 pounds instantly, so the paperwork was altered, and 1st Lieutenant Daniel K. Inouye took over command of his men. The officer's bars weighed heavily on his shoulders. On the naval transport from France back to Italy, he had eaten in the officers' mess while his non-commissioned colleagues and enlisted men in his company queued up with their mess tins in the chow line in the galley. Inouye found the wine, the cognac, and the cigars amusing. It seemed a million miles away from the war.[1]

The 442nd and the 370th Regimental Combat Teams were given the task of taking a mountain that overlooked the main coastal highway that led to the key port of La Spezia. At midnight on 5 April they moved through a gorge and climbed the cliffs on the enemy's right flank. It was completely quiet. Some men lost their footing on the climb and slipped and bounced to their deaths on the rocks below. Yet not one of his men made a sound, the lieutenant noted. The Germans were lining up for breakfast when the Nisei charged them; two hours later, they were surrendering. The Allies had been blocked on this section of the Gothic Line since the previous winter, when the Indians and the 92nd had driven off the German counterattack on the Serchio valley. Snow, mud, bad visibility, and roads washed to nothing had blocked any advance. The men of the 442nd were given a week to take the first position; they did it in one night. For the following week, they moved up and down hills and mountains, through freezing streams, and over scrub-covered mountains. The Germans were being pushed back towards La Spezia and up the western seaboard of Italy. Daniel Inouye said there was a cautious feeling throughout the 442nd 'that the end might be in sight. The Allies were nearing Berlin. If we could drive the Germans out of Italy, they would *have* to surrender.'

Later that week, headquarters gave his company the task of taking a village called Altanagna. It lay on the mountains overlooking the coast. It was dusk, and suddenly spring seemed to be coming. When the Germans opened fire with mortars and machine guns, Inouye's platoon, from long and instinctive practice, hit the ground. Shrapnel hit one of his men, who crawled away behind some rocks and bled to death; his friends found him only days later. It was the only soldier Lieutenant Inouye was to lose as an officer. The village of Altanagna was tiny, and a company of Germans was defending it, but overnight, as the Nisei waited to attack, the Germans suddenly pulled out. The Japanese Americans charged into the village and searched it. Clearing the basement of one house, ready to throw a hand grenade through a door that barred his way, Inouye found a group of terrified nuns hiding there. He left them, excusing himself in a few words of bad Italian, and rushed forward to take command of his platoon – a German counterattack could only be hours away. And when it arrived, he positioned himself in the church steeple, directing his men's fire. By daybreak, the Germans had fled.

His men started reloading their Garand, BAR, and Thompson magazines. The wounded were treated; the soldiers wolfed down cold K-rations, smoked, and slurped water from the village standpipe. Then, in the middle of the night, with oil lamps burning, a delegation of villagers came to talk to the young officer. Despite the war, despite the fighting, they had put on smart suits and dark dresses, 'shabby with age and streaked with the grey dust of war'.[2] They thanked Inouye and asked him, in recognition of what he had done, if he would do them the honour of becoming the mayor of their village. Inouye insisted that the villagers had nothing to thank him for. But they insisted. An Italian who spoke some English pointed to three of the younger girls of the village, who were doing their best to hide and vanish into the shadows. 'The villagers ask me to tell you that they have bought these three maidens for your comfort, Lieutenant. They wish you a pleasant evening.'[3]

Inouye realized what the Germans had made the Italians expect after a battle. He addressed the whole village and told them that he had not come to take their wine, their women, their food, or their land. They were different from the Germans. They bought peace. The three girls kissed him on the cheek. The next morning, as he led his men out of the village, the local people cheered the platoons passing ahead of his, but Inouye's platoon was bombarded with flowers.

Once again, he thought, he had survived another night and day of combat. He didn't know what to attribute it to. Was it the lucky charms he and his men carried? Some of the Nisei carried a *sen ninbari* in their pockets, given to them by old ladies in Honolulu before they shipped out. The piece of white cloth had a thousand stitches and was meant to protect the wearer against one thousand misfortunes. Other soldiers carried a St Christopher medal or a Buddhist charm. Inoue carried two silver dollars he had won gambling back in the States – he carried them in a breast pocket, and they were bent and disfigured after absorbing the impact of a German bullet in France. Ever since, he had not gone into battle without them.

## THE ATTACK ON COLLE MUSATELLO

When the 442nd RCT heard that Franklin Roosevelt had died of a cerebral haemorrhage on 12 April, they were in the middle of attacking an enemy position uphill. When word got to them, the men began jumping out of their foxholes and tore straight at the enemy. That day, said Inouye, 'we were moving up for FDR. Every Nisei who had been invested with first-class citizenship by virtue of the uniform he wore knew this.' The 2nd and 3rd Battalions of the 442nd were now just south of La Spezia: for two weeks they advanced up and down mountains 3,000 feet high, encircled, flanked, marched, crawled, and fought and fought and fought. They were up against MG-42 positions dug into the mountains that looked directly over at the Mediterranean and La Spezia – to the north they could almost see as the coast curved around and became the Gulf of Genoa. In the third week of April, the regimental commander – who had received some word of Operation *Sunrise*, of other peace overtures being made by the Germans – called his officers together. The war, he said, could end next year or next week, he didn't know. So nobody was to take any unnecessary chances. And on 20 April headquarters gave Inouye and Easy Company of his battalion a new objective: a high and heavily defended ridge called Colle Musatello. At dusk, the men went off to prepare for the following day's battle. As he opened cardboard boxes of .45 ammunition for his Thompson, and transferred the heavy golden rounds into his magazines, Inouye knew something was missing. He checked his equipment. Pistol, sidearm magazines, magazines and pouches for his Thompson, knife, canteen, six grenades, medical equipment, water . . . but he couldn't find his two lucky silver dollars. He looked everywhere, but without any luck. He had lost them. And 'from the message centre in my heart, I kept hearing forebodings of disaster'.[4]

The attack went in at first light. Inouye strode calmly up the hill, directing artillery on his radio. A mortar and machine-gun position were destroyed. Their platoon had outflanked the Germans and arrived abreast of them before the other two platoons had reached them. So Inouye led his men forward. Three machine guns opened up. The young lieutenant lay on the grass, devoid of cover, then pulled out a grenade, stood up, and threw it. There was a sudden wallop in his side as though somebody had punched him. He lobbed his grenade over the logs in front of the MG-42 position, and as it exploded, blowing showers of mud, metal, and wood out of the position, he machine-gunned the crew with his Thompson. He waved his men towards the other two gun positions as one of his GIs screamed at him that he was bleeding. The Germans had shot him in the stomach. The men were pinned down. Inouye knew it was up to him. When informed of the severity of his wound, he refused treatment and rallied his men for an attack on the second machine-gun position, which he successfully destroyed before collapsing from blood loss. As his squad distracted the third machine gunner, Inouye crawled towards the final bunker, coming within ten yards. As he raised himself up and cocked his arm to throw his last grenade, 'I saw him, that faceless German, like a strip of motion picture film running through a projector that's gone berserk. One instant he was standing waist-high in the bunker, the next he was aiming a rifle-grenade at my face from a range of ten yards. And even as I cocked my arm to throw, he fired and his rifle grenade smashed into my right elbow and exploded and all but tore my arm off.'

The primed grenade was reflexively clenched in a fist that suddenly didn't belong to him anymore. Inouye's horrified soldiers moved to his aid, but he shouted for them to keep back out of fear his severed fist would involuntarily relax and drop the grenade. While the German in the bunker reloaded his rifle, Inouye pried the live grenade from his useless right hand and transferred it to his left. As the enemy soldier aimed his rifle at him, Inouye tossed the grenade into the bunker and destroyed it. He stumbled to his feet and continued forward, silencing the last German resistance with a one-handed burst from his Thompson, 'the useless right arm slapping red and wet against my side'. Then, before being wounded in the leg and tumbling unconscious to the bottom of the ridge, he awoke to see the worried men of his platoon hovering over him. His only comment before being carried away was to order them back to their positions, saying, 'Nobody called off the war!'

## THE LIBERATION OF CHIOGGIA

On the same day, 21 April, a week before the end of the war in Italy, a former college football player, 1st Lieutenant George M. Hearn, was operating on the northeast coast of Italy. Originally from the United States Marine Corps Reserve, he was now attached to the Office of Strategic Services. He was on a boat off the Adriatic coast near the town of Chioggia, which lies on a sea lagoon south of Venice and north of Ravenna. George Hearn had entered the Marine Corps in 1943 following graduation from San Jose State College in California, and after being commissioned, he had immediately volunteered for duty with the OSS. As soon as he finished his Marine basic training, he was sent to the OSS operating base at Algiers, and afterward he joined one of their Maritime units operating in the Adriatic.

In the dying days of the war in Italy, he was operating with a group of partisans who had been detailed with finding a way to negotiate the fall or surrender of Chioggia, a medieval city that is surrounded by water on two sides. The Germans had 88mm maritime coastal batteries on the seawalls and moles protecting the lagoon, and anti-aircraft batteries that could be used against any attacking infantry. They also had three whole battalions of combat soldiers. Hearn had one American corporal with him, a company of Italian Marines, and the equivalent of two platoons of partisans. They were based on the Isola della Donzella, a large area of lagoons, reeds, swamps, and low-lying fields that lies at the mouth of the river Po, where it merges into the Adriatic south of Chioggia. They were forty miles ahead of the combined armies of the advancing Allies, who had just taken a three-pronged route of advance now that they were through the Apennines and across the Gothic Line. In the centre of the country, their main line of assault was towards Bologna, and four American and Indian divisions were heading for it. Two more were aiming for Ferrara, and another for Venice. The race was to get to Trieste – Marshal Tito's partisans had liberated the city of Zagreb, and were heading south towards the Adriatic. In the forefront of the Allied advance was a New Zealand division, but from Venice southward to the defences of Chioggia, there were only partisans, the OSS, and one SOE mission. Farther south still, the town of Argenta and the huge saltwater lagoon of Lake Comacchio had been the scene of incredibly heavy fighting in the first half of April as the Allies tried to dislodge two divisions of German defenders. By mid-April they had succeeded.

On the night of 22 April an Allied airdrop parachuted additional arms and ammunition to Hearn and the partisans on Donzella. Then familiar reinforcements arrived. At ten o'clock the next morning, several landing craft flying the White Ensign of Britain's Royal Navy growled into the Po's estuary. On board were sixty commandos from Popski's Private Army with twenty jeeps and half a dozen Italian Marines. Hearn was to help their operations by going back to the mainland himself and organizing guerrilla support for both the commandos and any advancing Allied ground troops so all sides could take Chioggia and move north.

That night, as Hearn and his men lay waiting, hundreds of refugees from the fortress town of Chioggia arrived at Hearn's perimeter and told them what was happening inside the city: the Germans were evacuating.

Hearn decided to enter the city immediately. With all his men he set off, expecting to find only a handful of Germans still clinging onto the old town. The six-foot-tall Californian had spoken to lots of his OSS colleagues and to other American, Canadian, and British officers who had been involved in the liberation of other towns and cities farther south. One moment, they had said, a town could be the most heavily defended of positions, impenetrable, a suicidal proposition to attack. An hour later, it could be deserted. It was always a matter of seizing the moment.

Within fifteen minutes, three Germans carrying a white flag appeared. Hearn stood there, hands on hips, his .30 cal M1 carbine held in one arm. He told the Germans he had been sent to accept the surrender of Chioggia. They seemed not to have any idea what to say. They looked at the dirty, tanned man with the filthy blonde hair and the small rifle cocked across his arm, and suggested he come meet their commander. Hearn took one Italian with him and moved off. 'In ten minutes we were in the town proper. One glance at the streets and I knew my worst fears were justified. For the first time a sharp sense of personal fear hit me. Hundreds of heavily armed German troops were milling around; every second one had an automatic weapon slung over his shoulder. Barbed wire and sand bagged buildings were everywhere. Surrender? If ever a place looked ready for a fight this was it.'5

Hearn and his Italian-American OSS colleague went to the main hotel, where they met twelve Germans, of whom the most senior was a German navy captain. Hearn laid out his hand. A huge American air strike on Chioggia was ready: the fighter-bombers were just waiting for the all-clear code word from Hearn. The whole town, and the German defenders, would be shot and rocketed to pieces. However, they had one chance. If they surrendered now, and Hearn called off the attack, all could be saved. He stood there and looked at the Germans. There was silence. Then the Germans gave in. Hearn said that he had to return to his unit to make radio contact, and then would come back to the Germans to take their surrender. And incidentally, asked the American officer, how many men would the Germans be surrendering?

Eleven hundred, was the answer. Hearn was stunned. He and his corporal walked outside, climbed into a horse-drawn cart, saluted, and clip-clopped off. How on earth was he going to arrange for the surrender of eleven hundred men? The Germans would discover pretty soon that Hearn had less than a platoon.

It was a couple of hours later when he found a jeep carrying Lieutenant Harold Wallbridge of Popski's Private Army roaring along the road. The officer listened to Hearn. Then he sent the jeeps of R Patrol off to find a way into the town. Hearn and Wallbridge found two bicycles and pedalled furiously back to Chioggia and told the German captain that the air strike had been called off. All Hearn had to do now was to keep up the bluff for another two days, until the advance guard of Allied troops arrived; in the interim, he and his thirty-five men, along with the six jeeps of R Patrol of Popski's Private Army, took the surrender of a whole regiment, along with eight batteries of coastal 88mm guns, the maps to the minefields outside the town, the personal weapons of 1,100 men, ammunition, shells for two artillery batteries, and all of their vehicles. Not a single shot was fired. It was an honourable surrender – and a triumphant bluff.

# 23

## THE LAST DAY OF BATTLE

*Surrender in Italy and Operation* Unthinkable

### Northern Italy, 26 April–2 May 1945

When Private Ivan Houston went to see Pope Pius XII on 25 April 1945, there were only about a hundred other Allied soldiers in the audience. They represented a cross-section of the multi-national armies that had fought in Italy. There were Poles, French, Brazilians, South Africans, British, and others. The Pope was carried in on a litter by the Swiss Guards and spoke to the men in Polish, Italian, and English. Afterward, Houston walked across Rome with another soldier from the 92nd, went to see the spot where Julius Caesar's funeral pyre had been erected, and then a Roman street artist drew his picture for a few lire and some cigarettes. Halfway through drawing, the artist looked up at Houston and said, 'I'm sorry for your president.' (Franklin Roosevelt had died two weeks earlier of a cerebral haemorrhage, and now Harry Truman had been sworn in.)

The following day, Houston and his friend returned north to Barga to find their unit – and discovered that it had disappeared. It took them three days to find their battalion, and they linked up with them only on 30 April. During Houston's leave, the Buffalo Soldiers of the 370th had decided to break the line northward. Accompanied by the Brazilian Expeditionary Force and around 1,000 partisans, they had stormed north in one of the most aggressive and tactically successful advances of the whole war in Tuscany. They cleared out the Serchio valley, fought the Germans off the mountains overlooking it, and suddenly, like a hole appearing in a dam, the flood began. The Germans started retreating all the way up towards Genoa. The 370th arrived in the town of Pontremoli, sixty-five miles north of their start line, five days later, thousands of retreating Germans in front of them. Houston joined them on the last day of the month. Partisans were shooting into the air. There was a lot of celebrating. Houston asked what was going on. The answer stunned him. 'Ah, Benito Mussolini and his mistress were caught trying to go to Switzerland. They were shot – their bodies are in front of a gas station in Milan!' one partisan told him.

The 92nd Division stormed north. A British SOE officer, working as official liaison, and a stream of partisans accompanied them. He arrived in Genoa ahead of the unit, just after the Ligurian partisans had liberated it. Men jumped on his jeep as he arrived in Piazza Verdi. Flowers poured down. There was shooting into the air, and women embraced him. There was, he said, something theatrical about the scene, 'the half-light of approaching night, the sea of upturned faces, the flowers, the noise . . . it only lacked Verdi's music to complete the opera.'

This scene was repeated all over northern Italy as it was liberated. The following morning, the SOE officer was awakened by the sound of running feet, shouting, and the noise of a very angry crowd. They surrounded a man they recognized as a member of the Fascist Black Shirts. He was completely enveloped by the mob in the middle of Piazza Verdi; they closed in on him, he disappeared beneath their feet, and that was it. 'A gory mess of human flesh lay in the square, bathed in the bright sunshine, and I turned away from the square duly sobered by my first taste of mob violence. By the time the American advance guard arrived that evening, the Piazza Verdi was clean again.'

To the west of Genoa, partisans liberated Imperia, running down from the mountains that crowd above the port, and driving in commandeered German trucks and civilian cars along the seafront that stretches and winds for two miles. The oleanders were starting to bloom, and the city was warm under the platoons of huge palm trees that march in stately fashion along the sea. Revenge for German and Fascist atrocities, and the occupation, was not slow in coming. Behind a makeshift partisan police station, a terrified and screaming middle-aged woman was being dragged, hands tied behind her back. Imperia rises out of the sea and holds tight to the hills and mountains behind it; there are plenty of walls that back into the slope. Partisans pushed the woman up against one of them, a line of six men noisily cocked shells into the breeches of their Carcano rifles, and opened fire, blowing her backward, dead, against the blood-splashed wall. The woman was Ernesta Ordano, the wife of the Fascist officer Vittorio, and mother of the partisan, Paola. The execution warrant was simple, taut, and precise: 'On the 28th April 1945, the Fascist spy Ordano Ernesta was shot. The execution took place at 22.30.' It was signed by the commander of the 6th Partisan Assault Division, Garibaldi Liguria. Her husband was shot as well. As her fellow partisans were executing her mother, Paola was with her colleagues from her guerrilla brigade, driving in open-topped cars along the seafront, shooting weapons in the air, waving flags, drinking wine. Later, she, like every other partisan who was demobilized, would receive a certificate from Field Marshal Alexander congratulating her on her exemplary performance and bravery. She would also receive a notice from the partisan social welfare committee that she would be allowed to go to Milan to continue her studies once hostilities had finally ceased. And as an orphan, she would learn, she was allowed an extra ration of seven ounces of marmalade per month.[1]

The partisans from Piemonte attacked Turin two days before on 27 April at dawn, and by the middle of the day, full-scale fighting between them and German and Fascist Italian units raged throughout the city. A British sergeant radio operator from the SOE was with the rebel units advancing into the city. Trying to control their efforts to liberate the town, he said, had been like King Canute's efforts against the tide. The German commanders in the whole region of Piemonte of northwestern Italy surrendered to the British SOE station chief in Biella, a town near the Alps. He had been just about to enjoy his first safe, post-liberation hot bath in five months. The Germans didn't want to surrender to the partisans, so under a white flag, a German oberst surrendered to the SOE officer and to an American colonel from an armoured unit whose first tanks and armoured cars had just driven into the streets of the town. When the shooting died down, and the American tank and armoured car hatches opened, the Italian crowd was ecstatic, dancing, throwing flowers, offering wine to their liberators. Then they were completely and momentarily taken aback. Emerging from the vehicles' turrets were 'unmistakably Japanese heads'. The Nisei had arrived.[2]

The efforts by the partisans and the SOE and OSS to carry out anti-scorch operations were largely successful. Partisans had captured twelve Germans in civilian clothing trying to sneak into a power station. They were shot on the spot. In Milan, the news of the liberation came on a fast transmission of Morse code from the SOE: 'Free Milan here, Free Milan here . . .' The CLNAI, now united after its sombrous December declaration to Field Marshal Alexander and the heads of the SOE and OSS in Europe, appeared on the streets, some in ad hoc uniform. One of the first actions they had taken on 27 April was to sign a document establishing war crimes tribunals and commissions of justice. They sentenced members of the Fascist government to death. That evening, Mussolini and his mistress fled the city, with 2,000 Fascist and German soldiers accompanying them. But when stopped at a roadblock and confronted by a heavily armed and determined group of partisans, the number of men who actually voted to fight for Mussolini was just six; the rest surrendered or fled. The partisans took Il Duce away, and a message was passed back to General Cadorna in Milan: What should we do with him? The CLNAI, including Cadorna, said he should be shot. The following morning, a huge crowd was coursing through the piazzas and boulevards of Milan: the bodies of Benito Mussolini and his mistress,

Clara Petacci, were hanging bloody and bruised upside-down outside a gas station in the centre of the city.

On the afternoon of 29 April the first American units appeared in the centre of Milan: a large group of SS men had barricaded themselves into the Hotel Regina and refused to surrender to the partisans. They threatened to open fire on the huge crowd outside unless American or British officers appeared. The first Allied officer to arrive outside the hotel in a commandeered staff car was a British captain, Alan Whicker, who operated as a war reporter with one of the 8th Army's Film and Television units. Whicker knew that the first American units were not far behind him, but before they arrived, the SS men in the hotel wanted him to sign for, and take safe delivery of, their entire vault of cash. They wanted it to be given to the Allies, not to the partisans. A stunned Whicker, holstered revolver on his hip, stood at the bottom of the staircase inside the hotel Regina. SS-Obergruppenführer Karl Wolff's men dragged a huge cabin trunk towards him and told him it was his to take away. In it, said Whicker, were millions upon millions of dollars, Swiss francs, Italian lire, and British pounds. He signed a piece of paper as a receipt, saluted, took the trunk out to his car and, feeling desperately lucky not to have been shot, drove around the corner, wondering what to do next. The Americans arrived and took the Germans' surrender an hour later. The following day they, and representatives of the new Allied Military Government, took over the administration of Milan and the province of Lombardy.

In the town of Piacenza, forty miles southeast of Milan, three American Sherman tanks attached to the American 135th Infantry Regiment joined the partisans fighting against 500 die-hard SS men: after a night of combat, the Germans pulled out, heading north as fast as they could. The partisans took over the town. It was a scene repeated dozens of times across northern Italy as Allied divisions advanced furiously, and the German and Italian defence crumbled. A British SOE captain found himself in the middle of newly liberated Piacenza with some partisans, CLNAI officials, and an American major who represented the fledgling Allied Military Government. The major turned to the SOE captain and said clearly that what they most needed there and then was a local election. 'I vetoed the election . . . this was no time for a sudden outbreak of democracy,' wrote the SOE captain afterward.[3]

Far northeast of Piacenza, SS, Wehrmacht, and Italian Fascist units were streaming north. The Allies were about to issue an order commanding every unit from all sides to freeze in a line exactly where they were, but before this happened, the Germans and Italians were fleeing, chased, ambushed, blown up, killed, harassed, looted, shot at, robbed, imprisoned, and ignored by thousands and thousands of partisans. On the lagoon off Venice, several small Allied landing craft chugged across the sea, each one flying the flag of the British Royal Navy. Two days before, on 29 April, a British Royal Navy and Engineers unit had met up with Lieutenant Colonel Vladimir Peniakoff – 'Popski' – in the newly liberated Chioggia. He was waving a large, shiny chromium-plated hook that had replaced his left hand, which he'd lost in action near Ravenna, where he had also won a Distinguished Service Order. Canadian troops were going to go into Venice from the north, but Peniakoff wanted to take part too, so he turned to the British engineer officer and said to him, 'We'll go in from the south – by water! Nobody is going to stop us now, boys!'

The landing ships thundered right up to the edge of the medieval jetty beside St Mark's Square and put down their ramps. For the first time ever in the history of Venice, wheeled vehicles went into the beautiful historic piazza. Six armed jeeps from Popski's Private Army, cheered on by Italian civilians, drove around and around St Mark's Square in celebration. The British Royal Engineers officer who had captained the landing craft that brought them in to Venice summed up the moment in his diary: 'The thrill of that moment can never be told properly. There were a few snipers to sort out and then we were going to experience something that no man had ever done. We were going to drive a vehicle around St Mark's Square. The whole of the population of Venice seemed to be in the square cheering us as we went round. This was a marvellous moment – perhaps the most marvellous one experienced by any of our Allies in the war.'[4]

Then on the other side of Italy at twenty past seven on the evening of 2 May, in the town of Pontremoli, the headquarters of the 1st Battalion, 370th Regimental Combat Team of the 92nd Infantry Division – the Buffalo Soldiers – received word the war was over. Ivan Houston saw in the battalion log the words '*Finito le Guerra in Italy*'.

## OPERATION *UNTHINKABLE*

The Yugoslav partisans beat the Allies to Trieste by a day. The city was no stranger to German or Italian Fascist atrocities – the only concentration camp in Italy that had a crematorium was in a suburb of Trieste called San Sabba. Built in April 1944, about 3,000 Jews, Yugoslavs, and Italian anti-fascists were killed there, and thousands of others were imprisoned before being transferred to other concentration camps in the Reich. The Allies had bombed Trieste, as it was an important port and naval base. On 30 April 1945, the National Liberation Committee – a sub-branch of the CLNAI – started a riot in the city. Thousands of Yugoslav partisans arrived shortly afterward – the Germans finally surrendered to a New Zealand Division that arrived the next day. The Germans were handed over to the Yugoslav partisans, who controlled the city until 12 June. An Indian and an American division arrived to reinforce the New Zealanders. Thousands of Germans and Fascist Italian troops and sympathizers just disappeared – the caves and ravines and chasms of the rocky Dalmatian coast, and the mountain plateau above it, were littered with their bodies.[5] Tito and Harold Alexander eventually oversaw the withdrawal of partisan forces from Trieste, after which it came under joint British, Yugoslav, and American military administration until 1947, when the Paris Peace Treaty established the Free Territory of Trieste. And after two years of non-stop combat, the Indian 4th Division found its time in Trieste in May 1945 a very welcome diversion:

> Fortunately force was not necessary. The Yugo-Slavs stood their ground but sedulously avoided incidents. There were many opportunities for

friction in this double occupation: the common use of crowded roads; different curfews (Yugo-Slav time being two hours ahead), contiguous billeting areas, incessant propaganda in which the Italians participated, an abundance of pretty girls and harsh wines. British commanders refused to allow villages to be searched for Fascists and alleged enemies of the state. British medical officers insisted upon a standard of field hygiene with which the Yugo-Slavs were unfamiliar. At times these irritations prickled, and hot-headed local commanders bluffed. Mortars were mounted to command British airfields. An 88 millimetre gun was trained at point blank range on a park of British tanks in a village piazza. But always good sense prevailed and the spectacle was witnessed of men deployed to thwart each other mounting double guards, chatting over handfuls of cherries, kicking a football together in the village streets, and side by side examining with horse-lovers' eyes animals lately 'requisitioned' from White Cossack prisoners. This forbearance in the first days of impact bore bountiful fruit. Second thoughts succeeded first impulses, and the two forces settled down in amity to the joint occupation. [6]

Unfortunately, this respite was temporary. Winston Churchill, meanwhile, found the moment of liberation and triumph very hard to reconcile with his increasing fears about Soviet belligerence. He was surrounded on every side by congratulation, decoration, salutation, and admiration from politicians, generals, admirals, presidents, and millions upon millions of average civilians and soldiers, airmen, and sailors. But fears about a salient Russia, more powerful now that the Germans had surrendered, wilfully disregarding obligations and promises made at Yalta about Poland, frightened him in his moment of victory. When news came at the beginning of June from Bulgaria of the alleged torture of one of the prime minister's secretaries, a man who had been a British agent, Churchill noted furiously in his diary: 'Wherever these Bolsheviks think you are afraid of them they will do whatever suits their lust and cruelty. But the Soviet Government has no wish to come out into the world smeared with such tales. Let them behave, and obey the ordinary decencies of civilisation.'[7]

In his mind, the situation was getting worse. And he feared that the Americans, exhausted by five years of war, of coming to the assistance of Europe, might pull out and depart the continent after a year or two. So, not taking any chances, and assuming that the Russians would break promises and renege on deals, he instructed his chiefs of staff to come up with a plan. He decided to code-name it 'Operation *Unthinkable*'.

'RUSSIA – THREAT TO WESTERN CIVILISATION', said the clumsy, pencil-written capital letters on the outside of the resultant War Cabinet File.[8] It was a plan to attack the Red Army in Poland, Germany, and across central Europe if the Russians didn't stand by their agreements about Poland. And if the Americans decided to pull out of Europe, leaving the British exposed and vulnerable, it was the plan for the definitive pre-emptive strike against the Red Army. In this, Britain and her Allies would co-opt up to 100,000 remaining German forces onto their side in the attack.

> Great Britain and the United States have full assistance from the Polish Armed Forces and can count upon the use of German manpower and what remains of German industrial capacity. The date for the opening of hostilities in 1st July 1945. The overall or political object is to impose upon Russia the will of the United States and the British Empire. 'The will' of these two countries may be defined as no more than a square deal for Poland, that does not necessarily limit the military commitment. A quick success might induce the Russians to submit to our will at least for the time being – but it might not. If they want total war they are in a position to have it.

The British envisioned a first strike of enormous strength, designed to cripple the Red Armies. They were stronger in physical numbers of men, aircraft, and tanks, but the quality of the Allies' men, training, and air power was so superior that the British estimated that, in real terms, the Russians outnumbered them only three to one. This really was to be the first battle of the Cold War, of the Third World War.

Churchill was going to impose his way on the Soviet Union in the only language they understood – by force. 'The only way in which we can achieve our object with certainty and lasting results is by victory in a total war . . . Apart from the chances of revolution in the USSR and the collapse of the present regime, the elimination of Russia could only be achieved as a result of . . . the occupation of such areas of metropolitan Russia that the war-making capacity of the country would be reduced to a point at which further resistance became impossible.'

British equipment and morale were much better, the report estimated. It was written by a very small group of generals, admirals, and experts in the Cabinet War Office. The number of people, including Churchill, who were allowed to see the draft plan was only about twenty. Britain was just finishing the largest conflict known to mankind, and the military and civilian governing complex in the country was huge. Here, though, was a plan so secret that its title was drafted in pencil, its distribution list limited to almost nobody. On 8 June the British chiefs of staff said to Churchill that 'the less put on paper on this subject the better'. To get around the problem of Russia's vast manpower, the Allies would need the resources of the United States and the re-organization and re-equipping of the German armed forces, some 100,000 of them. 'The defeat of Russia in a total war would be necessary . . . To win it would take us a very long time. We must envisage a world-wide struggle.'

The Red Army was going to be the most formidable foe for the Allies. Its submarines and bombers could not inflict damage on Britain like the Germans did. But the Russians could occupy Norway up to Trondheim, down to Turkey, close the Black Sea, with southeastern Europe the worst hit in terms of a major disruption of Britain's influence and commerce. There was a possibility that they would also lose the Iraqi and Persian oil fields, a major supplier of fuel oil. The Russians had eleven divisions in the region, opposite three different Indian brigade groups deployed by the Allies. But the British didn't think the Russians would go as far as India or Egypt. Instead they would ally with Japan, which would attack China again, and there would be stalemate in the Far East.

The principal theatre of war would be central Europe with probable confrontation in Iran. The Royal Navy and Royal Air Force would have a distinct superiority over Russia in the air and at sea, which would allow them to control the Baltic. The launching of an offensive against the Russians is described in characteristically understated terms – 'a hazardous undertaking'. The Allies would deploy forty-seven infantry divisions, of which fourteen were armoured, against 170 Russian ones, of which thirty were tank units. The war would mainly be fought in central Europe. There would be an aggressive reaction from Yugoslavia, the Russians would attack Austria, and the Allies would defend this from Italy. Only ten German divisions would be re-equipped at an early stage, with more following later. The Russians had in total 540 brigades of varying strengths in Europe – the Poles would be mostly anti-Russian. The documentation of the plan continued, covering almost every single contingency, but with one overarching aim – 'total war' against the Soviet Union, designed to cripple the country militarily once and for all.

The Czechs would support the Russians, sabotage in Europe was to be expected by Communists, and above all, the Allies wanted 'one great engagement'. But they realized that up against estimates of 6 million Russian troops and 600,000 NKVD personnel in Europe, this would be difficult, and a longer-lasting 'total war' would be the result. But with the Russians, lack of discipline and drunkenness were huge problems, and they would worsen with a new war. The British and Americans would cut off all supplies to Russia, including the estimated 50 per cent of aviation fuel the Soviet Union got from the Allies: this would cripple their air capacity unless they could occupy Persian and Iraqi oil fields. 'We should be committed to a protracted war against heavy odds – the odds would become fanciful if the Americans withdrew, distracted by the Pacific.' The document was signed by Admiral Sir Andrew Cunningham, who was first sea lord; General Sir Alan Brooke, chief of the Imperial General Staff; and Air Chief Marshal Sir Douglas Evill.

Churchill's reply to the three on 9 June, after having looked at their assessment and draft of Operation *Unthinkable*, was that he had had a study made about 'how we could defend our islands if the Americans move to the Pacific and US, this remains a precautionary study of what, I hope, is still a purely hypothetical contingency'.

General Alan Brooke, chief of the Imperial General Staff, had one reaction when he looked at the planned attack on the Soviet Union: 'Oh dear, Winston already wants another war.'

Provisions were made in case of a Russian invasion – it would take them several years, and most of Europe would have to be abandoned by the British. The Russians could not achieve their ends with airborne forces alone, and the greatest threat was from rocket attack. On 30 August 1945, the chief of the British Joint Staff Mission in Washington, Sir Henry Maitland Wilson – nicknamed 'Jumbo' – who had previously commanded Allied forces in the Mediterranean, had lunch with his American counterparts. By this point, Winston Churchill had just lost a general election to the Labour Party in July 1945 and was now an outgoing leader. The Americans, in their telegrams in response to the plans for Operation *Unthinkable*, immediately identified the area around Trieste and Friuli–Venezia Giulia as the most dangerous flashpoint in Europe. In that area, they said, there was a very real possibility of new general conflict in Europe with Russia as the main aggressor. Italy, the battles for the Gothic Line, and the strategic developments since 1944 had led to the first confrontation and nearly the first battle of the Cold War. Down on the Adriatic coast, near Trieste, as early summer 1945 arrived, it felt as though the thunderclouds of new conflict were approaching. Europe was shifting its allegiances like a suddenly changing chessboard where black and white pieces have suddenly been swapped over. The Second World War was finished, and now it was time for the liberation, and the complex internecine conflicts that were to accompany the peace, and the first days of the Cold War.

# 24

## Justice for the Germans

The story of what happened to the main German characters in this book is the story of post-war justice for Nazi Germany. While the Nuremberg trials were dealing with the higher echelons of the National Socialist apparatus, the middle- and lower-ranking Nazis escaped, were spared trial, changed sides, were imprisoned or, in many cases, just disappeared. In late February and early March 1945, the 16th SS-Panzergrenadier Division, the Reichsführer-SS, moved from northern Italy into Hungary. Together with the rest of the unit, **SS-Sturmbannführer Walter Reder** surrendered to British forces near Klagenfurt. As a senior SS officer, he was arrested but was released soon after because of his wartime wounds. However, he was rearrested by the Americans in Salzburg and held in an internment camp. He was then handed over again to the British. In May 1948, he was extradited to Italy. An Italian military court in Bologna sentenced him to life imprisonment in 1951 for the massacre at Marzabotto, and he was sent to the fortress prison of Gaeta, on the coast north of Naples. One of his former colleagues, an SS officer named Ernst-Günther Krätschmer, launched what he called Gaeta-Hilfe 'Gaeta Help' in 1957. He and five other SS men championed Reder's cause, and 285,000 letters by soldiers from 35 countries were sent to the Italian government urging Reder's release. Reder expressed 'profound repentance' in a December 1984 letter to the citizens of Marzabotto. The current citizens and survivors of the massacre voted 237 to 1 against freeing Reder. (The one person was never identified.) But Reder was released from prison on 24 January 1985, and promptly flew back to Vienna. He was received at Schwechat airport by the minister of defence of Austria and immediately retracted his apology. He stated explicitly that he had pronounced 'such words of apology solely to exploit a political opportunity'. He died in Vienna in 1991, at age seventy-six, and is buried in Gmünden.

**SS-Obergruppenführer Karl Wolff** was arrested on 13 May 1945, in Schöneberg, and put on trial at Nuremberg. He gave evidence against former colleagues and then spent time in a British prison in Minden: he was released in 1947, but the German government had earlier sentenced him to a prison term. He served this under house arrest, and then received five years for his membership in the SS: this was cut to four, and he was duly released. He then lived with his family in Starnberg and worked in public relations. There were repeated allegations that as a result of Operation *Sunrise*, he had been recruited to work for the OSS and then the CIA. In 1962, new evidence appeared in the trial of Adolf Eichmann in Israel showing that Wolff had organized the deportation of Italian Jews in 1944. He was arrested again in Germany. Convicted in 1964, he was sentenced to fifteen years on three main charges: the deportation of 300,000 Jews to Treblinka, the deportation of Italian Jews to Auschwitz, and the killings of Italian partisans. He was released in 1969 due to poor health, and the Germans restored his full civil rights in 1971. He died in 1984, age eighty-four, in Rosenheim.

**SS-Gruppenführer Max Simon**, commanding the 16th SS-Panzergrenadier Division, surrendered to the Americans in May 1945. He was sentenced to death by the British for the massacre at Marzabotto, and this was later commuted to life imprisonment. He was pardoned in 1954, released from prison, and died in 1961, at age sixty-two.

**SS-Obersturmbannführer Herbert Kappler** tried to take refuge in the Vatican as the Allies closed in on Rome but was arrested by the British in 1945. In 1947, he was sentenced to life imprisonment at

Gaeta. He married his nurse in a prison wedding in 1972, and in 1975 was moved to a military hospital in Rome. He had cancer. In 1978, his wife smuggled him out of prison in a suitcase, and he escaped to Germany, where he died in 1978, age seventy.

**SS-Obersturmführer Guido Zimmer** escaped arrest, and the OSS hired him to investigate post-war Nazi resistance movements. He then became the secretary for former Fascist Luigi Parrilli and applied for Italian citizenship. He was never arrested or prosecuted.

In June 2005, an Italian military court in La Spezia sentenced, in absentia, ten SS men involved in the massacres at Sant'Anna di Stazzema to life imprisonment and ordered them to pay compensation of €100 million to the survivors and relatives of the victims. A further seven accused were acquitted. All of the accused live in Germany and almost certainly will not be extradited to Italy. In April 2004, as the trial of those responsible for the massacre in Sant'Anna opened in La Spezia, the *Frankfurter Rundschau* wrote, 'It is not only in Germany that the wheels of justice grind slowly, in Italy also the prosecution of countless massacres of the civilian population by German troops in the final phase of the Second World War has largely petered out. In the early 1950s, when memories were still fresh and many of the culprits – German soldiers and Italian Fascists – could still be apprehended, many of the files were closed.' In August 2006, *Kontrast* magazine reported on eighty-two-year-old **Karl Gropler**, who was involved in the massacre in Sant'Anna di Stazzema and had lived undisturbed for decades in Wollin, a village in Brandenburg. Since early 2005, **SS-Untersturmführer Gerhard Sommer**, also sentenced by the court in La Spezia for his participation in the Sant'Anna di Stazzema massacre, has reportedly lived in an old people's home in Hamburg. The public prosecutor's office refuses to continue to level charges against the war criminals in this case as well, despite contradictory accounts of a German regional prosecutor's office opening a new investigation into Sommer's case in 2015. In 2002, Gerhard Sommer appeared on German television and stated, 'I have an absolutely clear conscience'. At the time of writing, in December 2014, Sommer was reportedly still alive.

# EPILOGUE

## *What Became of the Characters in the Book*

**Captain Daniel Inouye, 442nd US Army Regimental Combat Team DSC**

After leaving the army as a captain, he returned to Hawaii, studied law, and in 1959 was elected to the US Senate, being re-elected eight times. He died in 2012. President Clinton upgraded his Distinguished Service Cross, won at Colle Musatello, to the Congressional Medal of Honor.

**Lieutenant George M. Hearn, Office of Strategic Services**

He returned to North Carolina, left the Marines, and worked for a car dealership.

**1st Lieutenant John Fox, US 92nd Division**

In 1997, President Clinton upgraded Fox's Distinguished Service Cross to a Congressional Medal of Honor. He is buried in Whitman, Massachusetts.

**General Mark Clark, US 5th Army**

He fought in Korea, then served as president of the Citadel military college in South Carolina, dying in 1984.

**Peter Tompkins, Office of Strategic Services**

He wrote four books – an account of his time in wartime Rome and three books about ancient civilizations. He died in 2007 in Athens, Georgia.

**General Eustace D'Souza, Maratha Light Infantry**

He became one of India's longest-serving – fifty-nine years – and highest-ranking generals, leaving the army in 2002. He died in 2012.

**Major Oliver Churchill, Special Operations Executive, DSO MC**

After leaving the SOE, he married one of the senior code-breaking officials from Bletchley Park in England. They moved to Cambridge, where he worked as an architect until his death in 1997.

**Lieutenant General Sir Oliver Leese, British 8th Army, KCB CBE DSO**

He retired from the army in 1947 and became a horticulturalist, known for his collection of rare cacti. He died in 1978.

**Lieutenant General Sir Richard McCreery, British 8th Army, GCB KBE DSO MC**

After the war, he became commander-in-chief of the British Forces of Occupation in Austria. He left the army in 1949 and spent the post-war years as a gardener and horseman. He died in 1967.

**Lieutenant Colonel Andrew Horsbrugh-Porter, 27th Lancers, DSO and bar**

He retired to Oxfordshire in England as a landowner, and spent time writing for *The Times* as a polo correspondent.

**Major Vladimir Peniakoff, Popski's Private Army, DSO MC**

After the war, he became the liaison officer between the British troops and the Russians in Vienna. He later moved to England, where he became well-known for his radio broadcasts and newspaper articles. He died of cancer in 1951 at age fifty-four, and is buried next to his wife at Wixoe in Suffolk.

**Major Jack Mahony, Westminster Regiment, VC**

He retired from the army in 1962. He returned to Canada and became a lawyer. He died in 1990. His family donated his Victoria Cross to the Canadian War Museum.

**Sergeant Len Bailey, Westminster Regiment, MM**

He moved back to British Columbia as a farmer and died in 2005.

**Paola Ordano**

The partisan from Imperia lived all her life on the Ligurian coast after studying in Milan. She married, and died in 2011.

**Arrigo Paladini**

He was the first director of the Via Tasso Museum and Archives after the war, then became a professor of philosophy and literature. He died in Rome in 1991.

**Operation *Chrysler* Team**

Vincenzo Moscatelli, an Italian Communist partisan commander who after the war became an Italian senator, admitted to the murder of Major William Holahan in 1944, but only after two other members of the *Chrysler* team had been indicted, tried, and acquitted on a variety of charges, including murder. The case became a cause célèbre between Italy and the United States in the early '50s.

**Arrigo Boldrini**

After being the first director of the National Association of Italian Partisans, he was a senator for many years in Emilia-Romagna and the author of six books of military history. He died in 2008.

**Helmut Bücher, 1st Fallschirmjäger Regiment**

He is buried in the Futa Pass war cemetery, which is built on the Gothic Line outside Bologna.

**Generalfeldmarschall Albert Kesselring, Luftwaffe**

He was sentenced to death for war crimes by a British military court in Venice, but his sentence was commuted to life imprisonment because Italy had abolished the death penalty, and he was released in 1952. Several Allied figures, including Oliver Churchill, Harold Alexander, and Oliver Leese, had lobbied for the commutation of his execution. He died in 1960.

**Generalleutnant Ernst-Günther Baade, 90th Panzergrenadier Division**

He was wounded in the last days of the war in Europe after an Allied fighter-bomber strafed his car in Germany. He died of his wounds on 8 May 1945, the last day of the war in Europe.

**Ivan Houston, US 92nd Division, 'Buffalo Soldiers'**

On 4 September 2014, eighty-nine-year-old Ivan Houston sat with his son and daughter-in-law on the terrace of Villa Orsini outside Lucca. Now called Villa la Dogana, the beautiful rambling Tuscan house had been the headquarters of K Company of the 1st Battalion of the 370th Regimental Combat Team in early September 1944, as they advanced on Lucca. Since the war ended seventy years before, Houston had revisited Italy often. The weather in late summer was warm and balmy and his welcome was assured; the Italians were delighted to see him. This year, there was going to be a launch of his book,

*Black Warriors: The Buffalo Soldiers of World War II,* at an art gallery in Lucca, as well as speeches by the mayor, a civic welcome, a large commemoration for the seventieth anniversary of the liberation of Lucca.

On the terrace of the house, overlooking the gardens filled with magnolia, palm, and olive trees, lunch was being served. Grilled fish, green salad and, in tribute to the Americans' place of origin, Southern grits. Their hostess was Mattea Piazzesi who, along with her husband, ran the villa as a classy old-style *pensione.* Things were done at a measured, stylish pace. The warm summer air trembled lightly in the afternoon heat. Cats basked on the lichen-covered greystone of the terrace. The occasional train clicked across the level crossing outside, en route from the seaside at Viareggio to Lucca itself, two miles away.

Piazzesi was, curiously, dressed in full 1945 American military uniform, as were two dozen men in her large garden, military re-enactors from a local society celebrating the liberation. Houston himself was a celebrity. Italian men dressed as GIs and paratroopers, in full original uniforms, posed with him for photographs, A convoy of original American military vehicles was parked in the garden, ready to drive out to Lucca for a celebratory parade. Garands and .45 Thompsons were clipped across the bonnets of Willys Jeeps; re-enactors sported M1 carbines. Somebody even had a flamethrower. Some of the re-enactment society were dressed not in American military uniforms, or as US nurses, or as partisans, but as German soldiers. In the shade of a pine tree, a man dressed in the full summer uniform of the Wehrmacht lugged a deactivated MG-42 across the garden. The atmosphere was easygoing and relaxed. At dusk, leading the way, spearheading the crowd, Ivan Houston climbed into a Willys Jeep and rolled into Lucca for the 70th anniversary of its liberation.

Arriving back in the United States shortly afterward, he received a letter from an old colleague from the 92nd, Emmett Chappelle, whom he had last seen seventy years before. They had sat on together the train to basic training, and after that, Houston had never seen him again. Now here he was, back in touch. In the intervening seventy years, Chappelle had become a well-known engineer at NASA, designing ways to keep astronauts alive in space. But as he said to Houston on the telephone that evening, 'So much of who I became – and who I am now – was determined by my years as a Buffalo Soldier.'

# NOTES

## Preface

1    The 15th/19th first operated with the 2nd Battalion, 506th Infantry Regiment of the 101st Airborne on 18–21 September, 1944, around the town of Son, on the Eindhoven–Veghel highway. Their enemy was the 107th Panzer Brigade, led by Major Berndt-Joachim Freiherr von Maltzahn, itself part of General Kurt Student's 1st Paratroop Division. The 101st also operated with British armour from the 44th Royal Tank Regiment.

## 1. Beware of the Rabbit

1    The information on Arrigo Paladini comes from the extensive archives of the Via Tasso Museum in Rome. His messages are still preserved on the walls of the old cells. After the war, he was the first director of the museum set up in the old Gestapo HQ.

2    Taken from the citation for the *Medaglia d'Oro al Valore Militare* for Paladini, signed by General Angelo Odone, which is in Via Tasso.

3    Gavin Mortimer, *Stirling's Men: The Inside History of the SAS in World War II* (London: Cassell, 2005).

4    Online archives of the ANPI, the Associazione Nazionale di Partigiani d'Italia (National Association of Italian Partisans). The ANPI is linked to the sizeable network of the ISSMLI, the Istituto Nazionale per la Storia del Movimento di Liberazione in Italia (National Institute for the History of the Liberation Movement in Italy). In seventy-five different towns and cities in Italy there is a museum of the activities of the Italian partisans, the liberation, the resistance, and the history of the German occupation. Each museum contains the personal wartime files of many members of partisan units that fought in that area; the museums also contain huge archives of original German and Italian Fascist materials, documents from the Allied forces, along with books, CDs, hard copy files, photographs, and film footage. (Hereafter cited either as ANPI, or as a specific museum and archive. The archives at the former Gestapo headquarters at Via Tasso in Rome will be cited as Via Tasso Archives.

5    Charles Foley, *Commando Extraordinary: Otto Skorzeny* (New York: Putnam, 1955).

6    Personal experience. The author suffered twice from malaria in 1998, transmitted by *Anopheles gambiae* mosquitoes in southern Sudan. He is the author of *The Deadly Air: Genetically Modified Mosquitoes and the Fight Against Malaria* (London: Guardian Books, 2013).

7    Alan Axelrod, *Patton: A Biography* (New York: Palgrave Macmillan, 2006).

8    Mark W. Clark Collection, Citadel Archives and Museum, the Military

College of South Carolina, Charleston.

9    Rudyard Kipling, *The Irish Guards in the Great War* (Garden City, NY: Doubleday, 1923), vol. 2.

10   David Hunt, *A Don at War* (London: Frank Cass, 1990).

## 2. The Torturers of Via Tasso

1    Museums of the Liberation and Resistance in Rimini and Florence. Paladani edited a book after the war about the Via Tasso prison, simply called *Via Tasso*, about OSS and partisan activities, drawing on a number of sources, some of them contradictory. His own account of his arrest, torture, and escape was published in *Il Messagero* newspaper on 11 July 1984, and then included in this book.

2    Peter Tompkins wrote a memoir of his time in the OSS: *A Spy in Rome* (New York: Simon & Schuster, 1962).

3    Winston S. Churchill, *The Second World War,* Volume VI: *Triumph and Tragedy* (Boston: Houghton Mifflin, 1953), p. 64.

4    Another, slightly conflicting account has Paladini arrested at a checkpoint outside Rome, where he was travelling in a car accompanied by two partisan colleagues. In this account, partisan women on bicycles riding ahead of them as lookouts had failed to alert them to a German roadblock. This account is questionable, not just because Paladini himself says he was arrested inside Rome. For one thing, as the Germans knew that partisans often used bicycles as a swift and simple means of escape, they had, on 29 December 1943, issued orders to the German and Italian military, and Italian Fascist police, to shoot anybody seen on bicycles at any time of day anywhere. So it seems unlikely that six months later, in broad daylight, Paladini's partisan colleagues would be riding bicycles as lookouts.

5    SS Service record of Herbert Kappler, US National Archives, trial transcripts of his post-war court hearings, captured SS documents, Via Tasso Archives.

6    An original copy of Kesselring's declaration is in the Via Tasso Archives.

7    The original of her letter is in the Via Tasso Archives.

8    Via Tasso Archives.

9    ANPI; Via Tasso Archives.

10   Tompkins, *A Spy in Rome.*

## 3. Italy: A Country Made for Defensive Warfare

1    See image section.

2    Interview with the author.

3    Churchill, *Triumph and Tragedy,* p. 64

## 4. Nisei Soldiers and the Battle for Belvedere

1    The information on Daniel Inouye's life and military career is taken from several sources: media interviews conducted since the late 1960s; his

autobiography, *Journey to Washington* (Englewood Cliffs, NJ: Prentice-Hall 1967); Daniel K. Inouye Institute, Honolulu, Hawaii; the official history of the 442nd RCT, published by its veterans; online interviews with 442nd RCT veterans; and ANPI records in the Resistance Museums of La Spezia, Biella, and Carrara.

2    *A Pocket Guide to China* (Washington, DC: Government Printing Office, 1942).

3    0Speech by President Roosevelt announcing the formation of the 442nd RCT, 1 February 1943.

## 5. Indians on the Road to Florence

1    This is drawn from Eustace D'Souza's *A Saga of Service: A History of 1st Battalion: The Maratha Light Infantry.* Also *The Tiger Triumphs: The Story of Three Great Divisions in Italy* (London: Her Majesty's Stationery Office, India, 1946), and a history of Castello di Montegufoni. The story of the statues, paintings, and the Indian soldiers is also recorded by Eric Linklater in *The Art of Adventure* (London: Macmillan, 1947). The BBC correspondent Wynford Vaughan-Thomas also wrote about it, in an article in the British magazine *Everybody's Weekly,* 4 March 1950. An alternative account is provided in Robert M. Edsel, *Saving Italy: The Race to Rescue a Nation's Treasures from the Nazis* (New York: W. W. Norton, 2013).

2    *The Tiger Triumphs.*

3    Lieutenant General Vijay Obcroi (ret.), former vice chief of the Indian Defence Staff, quoted in the *Times of India,* 9 March, 2014.

4    John Masters, *Bugles and a Tiger: My Life in the Gurkhas* (London: Cassell, 1956).

5    *The Tiger Triumphs.*

6    Mark W. Clark diaries, Citadel Archives.

7    The US Army's World War II Medical Research Center documents the wartime activities, illustrated with personal testimonies, of almost every medical unit, evacuation, and general hospital that served in every war theatre.

## 6. Blood and Honour

1    Museum of the Liberation and Resistance, Turin.

2    Museum of the Liberation and Resistance, Florence, La Spezia, Lucca.

3    War Diary of the 1st Derbyshire Yeomanry, 16 and 17 July, 1944; War Diary of the 1st British Guards Brigade, 17 July, 1944.

4    Documentation of Walter Reder's actions at Marzabotto can be found in several main locations: the International Documentation Centre for the Gothic Line at Rimini (hereafter cited as CIDLG); the records of his post-war trial in Bologna in 1948, by an Italian military court; the Report of the British War Crimes Section of Allied Forces Headquarters on German Reprisals for Partisan Activities in Italy (Washington, DC, 1946); and the Museums of the Liberation and Resistance in Florence, Lucca, and Bologna. Reder also gave an interview

to a German magazine in 1956 from his prison cell in Naples. The Austrian journalist Christian Ortner published a biography of Reder: *Marzabotto: The Crimes of Walter Reder, SS-Sturmbannführer* (Vienna: Dokumentationsarchiv des österreichschen Widerstandes, 1986*)*. Ten members of the 16th SS- Panzergrenadier Division were tried *in absentia* by a court in July 2005 in La Spezia in connection with other war crimes committed in Tuscany, notably the killings at Sant' Anna di Stazzema in August 1944. The court passed sentence on 22 June, 2005. The documentation of the trials is held by the Italian Ministry of Interior in Rome. The events that took place at Marzabotto were documented by an Italian government white paper in 1961. Janet Kinrade Dethick's *The Arezzo Massacres: A Tuscan Tragedy, April–September 1944* (Lulu.com, 2013) provides a good overview of the climate of reprisals in the summer of 1944 in central Italy. Subsequent footnotes on Walter Reder will be referenced to one of the above sources.

5    Ortner, *Marzabotto*.
6    The word means guerrilla or partisan or bandit, and was at the centre of Himmler's 'Anti-Bandit' dictats.
7    The court proceedings that took place at La Spezia, in Tuscany, in 2004 and 2005 against ten members of the 16th SS-Panzergrenadiers provide some of the most accurate testimony of the killings above Lucca in those four days. As does the US National Archives and Records Administration, RG 238, Office of the Chief of Counsel for War Crimes, Location: 190/10/34/25, Entry 2, Box 10, Case 16–62 (Santa Anna). Also the Italian writer Carlo Gentile, 'Le SS di Sant'Anna di Stazzema: azioni, motivazioni e profilo di una unità nazista', in Marco Palla, ed., *Tra Storia e memoria* (Rome, 2003).
8    Resistance Museum, La Spezia.
9    Photographs exist in Italian archives of that day.

## 7. Best-laid Plans: The SOE and OSS in Northern Italy

1    The letter is in the Via Tasso museum in Rome.
2    Quoted in *Mission Accomplished* by David Stafford, p. 190.
3    David Stafford, *Mission Accomplished: SOE and Italy 1943–1945* (New York: Vintage, 2012), pp. 190–191.
4    The information on Oliver Churchill, Operation *Fairway*, the SOE in Italy, and the CLNAI in Milan comes from the following main sources: the War Office and Foreign Office records of SOE operations and wartime activities, including personal files, on Operation *Fairway* and Major Churchill held by the National Archives at Kew, in London; from similar and in many cases identical documents held by the Churchill family; from the Resistance Museums in Milan and Turin; from the Imperial War Museum in London; and from numerous books on SOE's wartime activities, the most detailed and authoritative of which is David Stafford's *Mission Accomplished*, (Vintage, 2012). Some of Professor Stafford's information also draws on similar or identical documentation, so in some cases the narrative of Operation *Fairway*, and the operations with the CLNAI in Milan are similar, if not the same. The

information is also drawn from documents and personal testimony of partisans who fought with the Fiamme Verdi group, including Tani Bonettini, whose wartime diary *La Neve Cade Sui Monti – del Diario di un Ribelle* was republished in 2014. And from personal research carried out by Andrea Cominini, an amateur historian from outside Milan who has traced the progress of Operation *Fairway* on the ground in Italy.

## 8. Dug-in Defence

1    Archives from the CIDLG Rimini; Tompkins, *A Spy in Rome.*
2    Online documents originating from the Historical Museum of the Resistance in Lucca.
3    Diary of 1st Parachute Division chief of staff.
4    Among other sources, including archives and Wehrmacht and British documents, mention of this is made in Carlo D'Este's *Fatal Decision: Anzio and the Battle for Rome* (New York: H0arper, 1991).
5    The documentation about the battle for San Lorenzo in Strada is best found in the CIDLG. Records of the Royal Canadian Regiment's operations around Rimini include details, as do the enormous German archives at bundesarchiv.de.

## 9. The Complexities of Command

1    *London Gazette,* 14 November 1916.
2    Richard Mead, *Churchill's Lions: A Biographical Guide to the Key British Generals of World War II* (Stroud, Gloucestershire: Spellmount, 2007).
3    Chester Wilmot, *The Struggle for Europe* (New York: Harper, 1952).
4    Paul Douglas Dickson, *A Thoroughly Canadian General: A Biography of General H.D.G. Crerar* (Toronto: University of Toronto Press 2007).
5    The author's family home as a child, Avisford Park, in Sussex in the south of England, became a temporary billet for Canadian units in 1943 and 1944.
6    Major J. E. Oldfield, *The Westminsters' War Diary: An Unofficial History of the Westminster Regiment (Motor) in World War II* (New Westminster, BC: Mitchell Press, 1964), chaps. 4–7.
7    Victoria Cross citation for Major Jack Mahony.
8    Field Marshal Viscount Slim, *Defeat into Victory: Battling Japan in Burma and India, 1942–1945* (London: Cassell, 1956), pp. 377–78.

## 10. A Multi-national Assault

1    Inouye, *Journey to Washington.*

## 11. With Infantry and Tanks

1    Oldfield, *Westminsters' War Diary.*
2    In 2012, *Shooting Times* magazine listed the weapon in a series called 'History's Greatest Sniper Rifles'.
3    *Shooting Times*, David Fortier, July 2012.

4    Quoted in *The Tiger Triumphs*, Chapter 10.
5    Ibid., chaps. 5–7.
6    War diary of Canadian Artillery Lieutenant Stan Fowler, Veterans of Canada organization.
7    The International Documentation Centre of the Gothic Line, or CIDLG, was run by the exceptional Italian historian Amedeo Montemaggi, who made it part of his life's work to document the battles for the Gothic Line, in particular the battle for Rimini, until his death in 2011. Drawing on the huge archives in the centre – that he created – he wrote and published thirteen books about the battles for the Gothic Line, Rimini, San Marino, and Gemmano, and about partisan operations in Rimini. These include *Gemmano: La Cassino dell'Adriatico/The Cassino of the Adriatic* (bilingual) (Rimini, 1998); *La Linea Gotica* (Rome: Edizioni Civitas, 1985–1990); and *Linea Gotica 1944: La battaglia di Rimini e lo sbarco in Grecia decisivi per l'Europa sud-orientale e il Mediterraneo* (The Battle for Rimini and the Landing in Greece were Decisive for Southeastern Europe and the Mediterranean) (Rimini: Museo dell'Aviazione di Rimini, 2002).
8    The CIDLG in Rimini has the world's largest collection of German, British, Canadian, American, Italian, and Polish documents, CDs, archives, maps, diaries, and books on the battles for Coriano and San Fortunato ridges.

## 12. Green Devils on the Adriatic

1    CIDLG.
2    Duhaime was one of thirteen children, from Espanola in Northern Ontario; he married the widow of one of his best friends, who had been killed in the war.
3    Douglas Orgill, *The Gothic Line: The Italian Campaign, Autumn, 1944* (New York: W. W. Norton, 1967).

## 13. Mules, Bulldozers, and Bailey Bridges

1    *The Tiger Triumphs.*
2    Quoted ibid.
3    D'Souza, *A Saga of Service.*
4    CIDLG, Rimini.

## 14. Alienating the Italian Population

1    Speech by Mussolini, comments made to an aide after his first meeting with Hitler, 1934, quoted in Winston S. Churchill, *The Second World War*, Volume I: *The Gathering Storm* (Boston: Houghton Mifflin, 1948).
2    Interview with Walter Reder, 1956. An English approximation would be 'Bloody hell, dammit, a whisky!'
3    Ibid.
4    See chapter 24, 'Justice for the Germans', and the Italian Interior Ministry's white paper in 1951 on the judgment of the Bologna military tribunal of Major Walter Reder.

5    Ibid.; see Ortner, *Marzabotto*.

6    Albert Kesselring, *Kesselring: A Soldier's Record* (New York: William Morrow, 1954).

## 15. Fighting German Artillery and Jim Crow

1    The story of the 92nd Division in Italy is from Ivan J. Houston, *Black Warriors: The Buffalo Soldiers of World War II* (Bloomington, IN: iUniverse, 2011); a lengthy personal interview between Mr Houston and the author carried out in Tuscany in September 2014; records from the Resistance Museum in Lucca; the US National Archives; Hondon B. Hargrove, *Buffalo Soldiers in Italy: Black Americans in World War II* (Jefferson, NC: McFarland, 1985); Mark Clark's diaries; and the war record of the 442nd RCT.

2    Ivan Houston was a perfect recorder of information about the wartime training and operations of the 370th. He was the battalion and company clerk of his unit in Italy in 1944 and '45, and kept the unit's war diary. The author conducted a lengthy interview with Houston in September 2014 at the Villa Orsini, the old wartime headquarters of one of the 92nd's companies, outside Lucca. Houston described his time in Italy in 1944 from the moment he arrived to when he left.

## 17. Behind Enemy Lines

1    The details of Churchill's time in Milan are drawn from his report on Operation *Fairway* in the British National Archives (previously the Public Records Office) listed as SOE Documents WO 204/7296, and, as noted above, from the extensive collection held privately by the Churchill family. David Stafford's account in *Mission Accomplished* (pp. 171–208) draws on the same sources, although it has a broader range in terms of the wide variety of SOE wartime papers and reports available. The Museum of the Resistance and the Institute for the History of Lombardy in Milan at Via Garibaldi contain documentation from General Cadorna and the CLNAI, from Edgardo Sogni, La Franchi network, and others.

2    Quoted with permission from Stafford, *Mission Accomplished*.

3    Reports that Hitler ordered Wolff to lead an SS unit to occupy the Vatican and kidnap Pope Pius XII surfaced in interviews Wolff gave before his death in 1984. The American journalist Dan Kurzman, who had served in the US Army, wrote *A Special Mission: Hitler's Plot to Seize the Vatican and Kidnap Pope Pius XII* (Cambridge, MA: Da Capo, 2007). In 2005, the Italian newspaper *Avvenire*, owned by the Catholic Church, published documents that it said were based on an interview with Wolff in 1974, in which he claimed he 'tipped off' Pius XII to the possibility of a kidnap plot in May 1944.

4    US National Archives and Records Administration, Interagency Working Group/Record Group 263: Records of the Central Intelligence Agency – Records of the Directorate of Operations/Analysis of the Name File of Guido Zimmer.

5   Complete records of the operations and personnel of the Ligurian partisan brigades are in the Liberation and Resistance Museum in Imperia, including the complete personal file of Paola Ordano and her father and mother, including photographs.

6   US National Archives and Records Administration, Record Group RG226: Office of Strategic Services (OSS), Entry 124, Box 30, Folder 235, declassified archival documents, CHRYSLER. The story of the *Chrysler* mission was heavily reported on after the war, particularly by the *New York Times* from 1951 to 1956.

## 18. Regular and Irregular Forces

1   *Westminsters' War Diary.*
2   CIDLG; Imperial War Museum, London.
3   CIDLG; Imperial War Museum, London.
4   Peter Tompkins from the OSS detailed the partisans' liaison mission in his wartime diaries.
5   Vladimir Peniakoff, *Private Army* (London: Jonathan Cape, 1950)
6   Oldfield, *Westminsters' War Diary*, p. 136.
7   OSS Report.
8   ANPI, No.1 Demolition Squadron official operational account as written at the request of King George VI.
9   Imperial War Museum, London, caption to Edward Bawden's painting based on sketches in Ravenna on 5 December 1944.

## 19. Christmas in the Serchio Valley

1   The 366th Battalion's unit war diary, and the citation for the Distinguished Service Cross for Lieutenant John R. Fox.
2   Ibid.
3   The official war record of the 4th, 8th, and 10th Indian Divisions; *The Tiger Triumphs.*
4   Documentary interview on Italian television with Alpini Sergeant Gian Ugo Taggiasco from the Monterosa Division, 2010.
5.  *The Tiger Triumphs*

## 20. East Wind

1   Holocaust Encyclopedia, United States Holocaust Memorial Museum, www.ushmm.org/learn/holocaust-encyclopedia.
2   Churchill, *Triumph and Tragedy*, p. 371.

## 21. Secret Surrender

1   Aside from OSS, British, and Russian governmental records – and Churchill's diaries – the most thorough book on the subject is Bradley F. Smith and Elena Agarossi, *Operation Sunrise: The Secret Surrender* (New York: Basic Books,

1979). Also Wolff's colleague Eugen Dollmann, *Call Me Coward* (London: William Kimber, 1956), and Allen Dulles, *The Secret Surrende* (New York: Harper, 1966).

2    Quoted and cross-referenced in the CIA IWG report on Guido Zimmer, US National Archives and Records Administration, Interagency Working Group, Record Group 263: Records of the Central Intelligence Agency, Records of the Directorate of Operations – Analysis of the Name File of Guido Zimmer. The OSS records of communications with Washington in 1945 are also filed under the IWG bracket heading.

3    Churchill, *Triumph and Tragedy*, p. 361.

4    Ibid., p. 326.

## 22. The Last Battles

1    Inouye, *Journey to Washington*.

2    Ibid., p. 145.

3    Ibid.

4    Ibid., p. 149.

5    OSS records; Diary of George M. Hearn; Peter Tompkins' account of OSS operations in the Po Delta, April 1945.

## 23. The Last Day of Battle

1    The original documentation of all the partisans who fought in Liguria, including all personal and partisan papers of Paola Ordano, are held by the Museum of the Liberation and Resistance in Imperia.

2    SOE Cherokee Mission records of the liberation of Biella, quoted in *Mission Accomplished* by David Stafford, pp. 313–14.

3    Alan Whicker, *Whicker's War*, (London: Harper Collins UK, 2006).

4    *Daily Telegraph* obituary of Captain Brian Thomas, 28 July 2014.

5    Thousands of them are still there today – the author worked between 2008 and 2010 with the International Commission on Missing Persons, an international organization that handles all aspects of missing persons cases in the former Yugoslavia. During exhumations of burial sites of victims of the 1992–1995 wars across the former Yugoslavia, extensive sets of German skeletal remains from the Second World War are still unearthed, particularly in Croatia, Bosnia and Slovenia.

6    *The Tiger Triumphs*, epilogue.

7    Churchill, *Triumph and Tragedy*, p. 593.

8    Russia – Threat to Western Civilisation, War Cabinet File, National Archives, London. Number CAB 120/691/109040, from British War Cabinet Joint Planning Staff, May 22, 8 June, and 11 July 1945.

# INDEX

Cromwell, Oliver 142
Cromwell tanks 16, 17

# D

*Daily Telegraph* (newspaper) 147
Daugette, Col. Clarence W., Jr. 219
deception operations 28–30, 39, 165,
  165-166, 167–168
decoding procedures 44–46
delay in Allied advance across northwest
  Europe 211–212
deportations of Jews and Communists 50,
  97, 98, 245, 246, 310
Dieppe raid, the 146–147
disagreements among the Allies 92, 96,
  126, 130, 144–145, 153–154, 251,
  252
disinformation schemes 28–30, 40
division among the Allies 281–283, 284,
  286, 304
Dollmann, SS-Obersturmbannführer
  Eugen 280, 282
Domodossola 243
DSC (Distinguished Service Cross), the
  142, 265
DSO (Distinguished Service Order), the
  86, 116, 142, 152, 166, 170, 302
D'Souza, Gen. Eustace 80, 82, 84–86, 87,
  89, 100, 165, 193–195, 196, 200,
  266, 267–268, 312
DUKW amphibious vehicle (US) 256,
  258
DZ (parachute drop zones) 120–121

# E

Eden, Anthony 34
E&E (escape and evasion) 118–119
Eichmann, Adolf 310
Eisenhower, Gen. Dwight 35, 38, 39, 91,
  117, 247, 252, 287
El Alamein, battle of 27, 40
Emmanuel, King Victor 34

engineering logistics in the Appenines
  196–198, 199
English Civil War, the 142
Enigma encryption machines 44, 147
equipment in backpacks 88–89
escape of SOE operatives from Corfu
  118–119

# F

Fairbairn–Sykes commando knife (UK)
  116
Farneti, Mino 126–127, 128–129, 253
Fascist troops, the 42, 43, 47, 49, 82, 94,
  97, 108, 113, 166, 204, 245, 298,
  299, 300
Fiamme Verdi (Green Flame) brigade, the
  120, 122, 123, 124, 241
firepower of infantry squads 62–64
FlaK range of anti-aircraft weapons 62
Fleming, Lt-Cmdr. Ian 147
Florence, liberation of 80, 90, 93–94
Florence and Bologna, map of **101**
formation of independent partisan mini-
  republics 243–244
'four-by-two' rifle cleaning cloth 193
Fox, 1st Lt. John 264–265, 312
'Free Republic of Domodossola' 243–244
Free Territory of Trieste 303
friendly fire incident 231–232

# G

Gaeta-Hilfe 'Gaeta Help' 309
Galler, SS-Hauptsturmführer Anton 108,
  110
Gari River attack, the 154
Garibaldi Brigade, the 127
Garibaldi monument, Ravenna 260
Gemmano, capture of 188–189, 232
George VI, King 18, 152, 260
German anticipation of Allied attack on
  the Gothic Line 100–101, 126, 130,
  138–140, 165–166, 169

# Z